Xavier

# Our Holy Faith

## A RELIGION SERIES
## for
## THE ELEMENTARY SCHOOLS

**UNDER THE DIRECTION OF**

### Rt. Rev. Msgr. Clarence E. Elwell, Ph.D.
Superintendent of Schools, Diocese of Cleveland

**WITH THE ASSISTANCE OF**

### Rt. Rev. Msgr. A. N. Fuerst, S.T.D.
Professor of Theology and Catechetics, St. Mary's Seminary
Cleveland, Ohio

### Rev. Bernard T. Rattigan, Ph.D.
Department of Education, Graduate School of Arts and Sciences
Catholic University of America
Washington, D. C.

# Our Faith: God's Great Gift

Based on the first half of the Revised
Baltimore Catechism Number Two

Sister Mary Eligia, H.H.M., M.A.
Sister Marie Corona, H.H.M., M.A.
Sister Mary Carolyn, S.N.D., M.A.
Sister Mary De Xavier, S.N.D., M.A.

### with the help of

Sister Mary Milburge, S.S.J., M.A.  Sister Mary Adele, I.H.M., B.A.
Sister Ann Michael, S.C., A.B.  Sister Mary Rosalia, V.S.C., B.S.E.
Sister Marie Jose, H.H.M., B.S.E.  Sister Mary Josette, O.S.U., B.S.E.
Sister Mary Francelia, S.N.D., M.A.  Sister Mary Adeline, S.S.J., B.S.E.

2017

ST. AUGUSTINE ACADEMY PRESS
HOMER GLEN, ILLINOIS

Nihil obstat:

Joannes A. Schulien, S.T.D.
Censor librorum

Imprimatur:

✠ Albertus G. Meyer
Archiepiscopus Milwauchiensis
April 18, 1959

# Acknowledgments

The zeal and devotion of many teachers have gone into the creation of this series. Their names will be revealed on Judgment Day when they will receive their reward.

The parts of the text of the Catechism No. 2 contained in this book are reproduced by the license of the Confraternity of Christian Doctrine, Washington, D. C., the only owner of the copyright of *A Catechism of Christian Doctrine — Revised Edition of the Baltimore Catechism No. 2*. Used with its permission. All rights revised.

We are also in debt to Benziger Bros. for the short prayers which have been reprinted from the *Raccolta*.

This book was originally published in 1959 by The Bruce Publishing Company.

This edition reprinted in 2017 by St. Augustine Academy Press.

Softcover ISBN: 978-1-64051-006-7
Hardcover ISBN: 978-1-64051-007-4

# Contents

# SECTION II

## God the Son, Our Redeemer

# SECTION III

## The Holy Ghost and the Church

Catechism

Catechism

# Prayers

### The Sign of the Cross

In the name of the Father, and of the Son, and of the Holy Ghost. Amen. (*An indulgence of three years; with holy water, seven years,* No. 678.)*

### The Lord's Prayer

Our Father who art in heaven, hallowed be Thy name; Thy kingdom come; Thy will be done on earth as it is in heaven. Give us this day our daily bread; and forgive us our trespasses as we forgive those who trespass against us; and lead us not into temptation, but deliver us from evil. Amen.

### The Hail Mary

Hail Mary, full of grace! the Lord is with thee; blessed art thou among women, and blessed is the fruit of thy womb, Jesus. Holy Mary, Mother of God, pray for us sinners, now and at the hour of our death. Amen.

### Glory Be to the Father

Glory be to the Father, and to the Son, and to the Holy Ghost. As it was in the beginning, is now, and ever shall be, world without end. Amen.

### The Apostles' Creed

I believe in God, the Father Almighty, Creator of heaven and earth; and in Jesus Christ, His only Son, our Lord; who was conceived by the Holy Ghost, born of the Virgin Mary,

---

* The number after the indulgences is the number under which the prayer or pious practice appears in the Church's official book of indulgences.

suffered under Pontius Pilate, was crucified, died and was buried. He descended into hell; the third day He arose again from the dead; He ascended into heaven, sitteth at the right hand of God, the Father Almighty; from thence He shall come to judge the living and the dead. I believe in the Holy Ghost, the Holy Catholic Church, the communion of saints, the forgiveness of sins, the resurrection of the body, and life everlasting. Amen.

## The Confiteor

I confess to Almighty God, to blessed Mary ever Virgin, to blessed Michael the Archangel, to blessed John the Baptist, to the holy Apostles Peter and Paul, and to all the saints, that I have sinned exceedingly in thought, word, and deed, through my fault, through my fault, through my most grievous fault. Therefore, I beseech blessed Mary ever Virgin, blessed Michael the Archangel, blessed John the Baptist, the holy Apostles Peter and Paul, and all the saints, to pray to the Lord our God for me.

May Almighty God have mercy on me, forgive me my sins, and bring me to everlasting life. Amen.

May the Almighty and merciful Lord grant me pardon, absolution, and remission of all my sins. Amen.

## Morning Offering

O Jesus, through the Immaculate Heart of Mary, I offer Thee my prayers, works, joys, and sufferings of this day for all the intentions of Thy Sacred Heart, in union with the Holy Sacrifice of the Mass throughout the world, in reparation for my sins, for the intentions of all our Associates, and in particular for . . . I wish to gain all the indulgences attached to the prayers I shall say and to the good works I shall perform this day.

## The Angelus

℣. The angel of the Lord declared unto Mary.

℟. And she conceived of the Holy Ghost.

Hail Mary, full of grace! the Lord is with thee; blessed art thou among women, and blessed is the fruit of thy womb, Jesus. Holy Mary, Mother of God, pray for us sinners, now and at the hour of our death. Amen.

℣. Behold the handmaid of the Lord.

℟. Be it done unto me according to thy word.

Hail Mary, etc.

℣. And the Word was made flesh.

℟. And dwelt among us.

Hail Mary, etc.

℣. Pray for us, O Holy Mother of God.

℟. That we may be made worthy of the promises of Christ.

### Let us Pray

Pour forth, we beseech Thee, O Lord, Thy grace into our hearts, that we to whom the Incarnation of Christ, Thy Son, was made known by the message of an angel, may by His passion and cross be brought to the glory of His resurrection, through the same Christ our Lord. Amen.

## Regina Coeli

(*Said during Eastertide, instead of the Angelus*)

Queen of heaven, rejoice, Alleluia.

For He whom thou didst deserve to bear, Alleluia.

Hath risen as He said, Alleluia.

Pray for us to God, Alleluia.

℣. Rejoice and be glad, O Virgin Mary! Alleluia.

℞. Because our Lord is truly risen, Alleluia.

**Let us Pray**

O God, who by the resurrection of Thy Son, our Lord Jesus Christ, has vouchsafed to make glad the whole world, grant, we beseech Thee, that, through the intercession of the Virgin Mary, His Mother, we may attain the joys of eternal life. Through the same Christ our Lord. Amen.

## Hail, Holy Queen

Hail, Holy Queen, Mother of Mercy, hail, our life, our sweetness, and our hope! To thee do we cry, poor banished children of Eve! To thee do we send up our sighs, mourning and weeping in this vale of tears! Turn, then, most gracious advocate, thine eyes of mercy toward us; and after this our exile, show unto us the blessed fruit of thy womb, Jesus! O clement, O loving, O sweet Virgin Mary! (*5 years*, No. 332)

## An Act of Faith

O my God, I firmly believe that Thou art one God in three divine Persons, Father, Son, and Holy Ghost; I believe that Thy divine Son became man, and died for our sins, and that He will come to judge the living and the dead. I believe these and all the truths which the Holy Catholic Church teaches, because Thou hast revealed them, who canst neither deceive nor be deceived. (*3 years*, No. 36)

## An Act of Hope

O my God, relying on Thy almighty power and infinite mercy and promises, I hope to obtain pardon of my sins, the help of Thy grace, and life everlasting, through the merits of Jesus Christ, my Lord and Redeemer.

(*3 years*, No. 36)

## An Act of Love

O my God, I love Thee above all things, with my whole heart and soul, because Thou art all-good and worthy of all love. I love my neighbor as myself for the love of Thee. I forgive all who have injured me, and ask pardon of all whom I have injured. (*3 years*, No. 36)

## An Act of Contrition

O my God, I am heartily sorry for having offended Thee, and I detest all my sins, because of Thy just punishments, but most of all because they offend Thee, my God, who art all-good and deserving of all my love. I firmly resolve, with the help of Thy grace, to sin no more and to avoid the near occasions of sin. (*3 years*, No. 36)

## The Blessing Before Meals

Bless us, O Lord, and these Thy gifts, which we are about to receive from Thy bounty, through Christ our Lord. Amen.

## Grace After Meals

We give Thee thanks for all Thy benefits, O almighty God, who livest and reignest forever. Amen. (*300 days*, No. 683)

May the souls of the faithful departed, through the mercy of God, rest in peace. Amen.

## The Mysteries of the Rosary

### The Five Joyful Mysteries

1. The Annunciation
2. The Visitation
3. The Birth of Our Lord
4. The Presentation of Our Lord in the Temple
5. The Finding of Our Lord in the Temple

## The Five Sorrowful Mysteries

1. The Agony of Our Lord in the Garden
2. The Scourging at the Pillar
3. The Crowning with Thorns
4. The Carrying of the Cross
5. The Crucifixion and Death of Our Lord

## The Five Glorious Mysteries

1. The Resurrection of Our Lord
2. The Ascension of Our Lord into Heaven
3. The Descent of the Holy Ghost upon the Apostles
4. The Assumption of Our Blessed Mother into Heaven
5. The Coronation of Our Blessed Mother in Heaven

## The Commandments of God

1. I am the Lord thy God; thou shalt not have strange gods before Me.
2. Thou shalt not take the name of the Lord thy God in vain.
3. Remember thou keep holy the Lord's day.
4. Honor thy father and thy mother.
5. Thou shalt not kill.
6. Thou shalt not commit adultery.
7. Thou shalt not steal.
8. Thou shalt not bear false witness against thy neighbor.
9. Thou shalt not covet thy neighbor's wife.
10. Thou shalt not covet thy neighbor's goods.

## The Commandments of the Church

1. To assist at Mass on all Sundays and holydays of obligation.
2. To fast and to abstain on the days appointed.
3. To confess our sins at least once a year.
4. To receive Holy Communion during the Easter time.
5. To contribute to the support of the Church.
6. To observe the laws of the Church concerning marriage.

### The holydays of obligation in the United States

The Immaculate Conception (December 8)
Christmas Day (December 25)
The Circumcision (January 1)
Ascension Thursday (40 days after Easter)
The Assumption (August 15)
All Saints' Day (November 1)

### The Seven Sacraments

Baptism, Confirmation, Holy Eucharist, Penance, Extreme Unction, Holy Orders, and Matrimony.

### The Manner in Which a Lay Person Is to Baptize in Case of Necessity

Pour ordinary water on the forehead of the person to be baptized, and say while pouring it:

"I baptize thee in the name of the Father, and of the Son, and of the Holy Ghost."

*N. B.*   Any person of either sex who has reached the use of reason can baptize in case of necessity, but the same person must say the words while pouring the water.

### Receiving the Sacrament of Penance

To receive the Sacrament of Penance worthily, we must:
first, examine our conscience;
second, be sorry for our sins;
third, have the firm purpose of not sinning again;
fourth, confess our sins to the priest;
fifth, be willing to perform the penance the priest gives us.

## INTRODUCTION

# Why Study the Truths of Our Faith?

This year we begin for the last time in our elementary school course, a complete study of *Our Faith: God's Great Gift*. It will be based on the revised Confraternity Edition of the Baltimore Catechism, No. 2. That means it will be a much more expanded study of our religion than we have had before.

This book will cover the first half of the No. 2 Catechism. After this there will be a year devoted to the Holy Bible; and a third year will end our course with a complete review, paying special attention to the second half of No. 2 Catechism.

Our holy faith is one of God's most important gifts. If we have faith, it can lead us to everything we need to insure eternal happiness. But if we lose our faith, we will have lost everything.

We can lose our faith if we do not appreciate its value and neglect it. We can protect our faith if we learn about it so that we will realize what it tells us and what it means to us. Let us resolve here at the beginning of the year to study our religion better than any other subject. And let us stop here for a moment to ask the Holy Spirit to help us.

## 1. Faith — God's Great Gift

Faith is often called the beacon light on our journey to eternity. We know that beacon lights guide planes on their course. We know too that the shining beam from a lighthouse leads ships safely to harbor. In much the same way, faith sheds a light over our path through life, showing us the errors we must avoid and the truths we are to believe.

God gave us this great gift of faith freely without any merit whatever on our part. Let us see if we can increase our appreciation for this great gift, calling to mind the words of St. Paul: "For by grace you have been saved through faith, and that not of yourselves, for it is the gift of God" (Eph. 2:8). Did you ever thank God for your faith?

## 2. Faith Is Necessary for Salvation

Our Lord preached and worked miracles just to strengthen the faith of the people. If He did not consider faith necessary, would He have done so many things to increase their faith?

St. Paul, in his Epistle to the Hebrews, explained the necessity of faith. He said, "Without faith it is impossible to please God." We know that only those who are pleasing to God can enter heaven.

## 3. Man Must Use the Gift of Faith

Everyone knows that athletes strengthen their muscles by using them in vigorous exercise. Champion runners and ball players spend many hours a day during their training period exercising, so that their muscles will become stronger and help them to victory. So it is, in a spiritual way, with faith. In order to make our faith stronger we must exercise it throughout the training period of this life.

Having a football and knowing the rules of the game does not make a football player. Can you explain why? Knowing and believing what the right thing is, is quite different from doing what is right. Just as we prove our love for our parents by obeying them, so we prove our faith by doing the things faith teaches us to do. What are some of the teachings of faith? What are some of the things we will do if we really believe them? You surely know.

You believe Christ's words, "Unless you eat the flesh of the Son of Man, and drink His blood, you shall not have life in you" (Jn. 6:54–57). To live up to this belief must you not receive Holy Communion often and devoutly?

Again, it is important to be able to list the Ten Commandments, and to know all the ways in which we can keep or break the Ten Commandments. But knowing the Ten Commandments is valuable to us only if it leads us to action. We must live according to our faith. We must observe the commandments in our lives. In other words we must do that which we believe. The great missionary, St. Francis Xavier, after instructing his boys in the truths of their religion, often said, "Now let us say a Hail Mary that we may believe these truths, and live according to them." Should we do the same thing this year? During our whole life?

## 4. Man Must Protect the Gift of Faith

Anything precious must be protected. The Declaration of Independence is carefully guarded. The nation's supply of gold is kept under close watch. Valuable gems are stored in safe places. Children are shielded by their parents. So also our faith, a gift of great value to us, must be protected.

One good way to protect our faith is to know it. We can learn to know our faith by studying the catechism, reading the Bible reverently and carefully, and reading other good books. The Church is so anxious for us to know the value of the precious treasure of our faith that she grants an indulgence of three years when we study Christian Doctrine for at least a half-hour (No. 693), or when we read the Bible for fifteen minutes as spiritual reading (No. 694). Imagine getting an indulgence for studying and for reading the Bible!

## Prayer as a Safeguard

We can guard our faith by making frequent acts of faith, including the Apostles' Creed. In our morning and night prayers, in our preparation for confession, and before receiving Holy Communion we can say, "Sacred Heart of Jesus, I believe in Thy love for me." We should pray for a strong faith. In little troubles and trials we can pray, "Lord, increase our faith.

## Other Safeguards of Faith

Do you know how the life of St. Ignatius became charged with a strong living faith? This great man was inspired by good reading. Other saints, like Francis Xavier, were influenced by good companionship.

We Catholics must do certain things and avoid others in order to safeguard our faith. What are the things we should do? *A Catholic can best safeguard his faith by making frequent acts of faith, by praying for a strong faith, by studying his religion very earnestly, by living a good life, by good reading, by refusing to associate with the enemies of the Church, and by not reading books and papers opposed to the Church and her teaching.* Let us do all these things. But this year especially let us study, on a higher level, the chief truths of our holy religion as found in the Apostles' Creed. Let us resolve to work hard, studying our holy religion so that we may appreciate how much it means to us and how good God has been to give us the great gift of faith.

# REVIEW

## WORD LIST

strengthen    accordance    associate    opposed

## THINGS TO REMEMBER

1. God gives us the gift of faith.
2. Faith is necessary for salvation.
3. We must use the gift of faith.
4. We must protect our faith.
5. We prove our faith by actually doing the things we say we believe in the Apostles' Creed.

## THINGS TO DISCUSS AND DO

1. Prepare a two-minute talk on "What My Faith Means to Me," or "What Life Would Be Like Without Faith," or "Pitch Dark and No Flashlight!"
2. Discuss whether knowing and believing the truths of our faith is sufficient to save us.
3. Tell how the Apostles' Creed is important to you as a Catholic.
4. In your own words tell what you need to do to keep your faith strong.

## SECTION I

# God, The Father Almighty, One in Three

*I believe in God, the Father Almighty, Creator of heaven and of earth . . .*

## Overview of Year's Work

This year in three successive sections we shall study about God: Father, Son, and Holy Ghost, as the Apostles' Creed and the Revised Baltimore Catechism No. 2 present the doctrines to us. Then in the fourth and final section we shall study about some of the most important duties we owe to God, as they are contained in the first three commandments.

## Overview of Section I

In this first section we shall learn about God and especially about those works of God which are usually connected with the first person, God the Father.

In Unit I, we shall study God and God's perfections. In Unit II we shall turn to God the Father as the Creator of all things, especially man. And in Unit III we shall learn many more important details about the Fall and its effects on us.

14

# Unit I. God and God's Perfections

## Part 1.  God Is Our Father and Creator

Let us now turn to the Apostles' Creed and study our Faith.

### 1. God Made Us

The first thing that our holy faith teaches us is that there is a God who made us.

Most men at some time or other have watched the countless creatures of the earth and have asked this question, "Where did they all come from?" A beautiful bird on the limb of a tree might have aroused their curiosity; an odd-looking giraffe at the zoo might have brought the question to mind; or again, it could have been a strange bug or pesky mosquito that caused them to wonder.

Some of them may have puzzled over the question, but as for you, you surely recalled your catechism answer that all creatures come from God: minerals, plants, animals, men, and angels. Man, the chief creature of God's visible world, came from God. What we learned as little children is true, God made all things. *God made us.* In gratitude then, we should learn as much as we can about the great and good God.

## 2. God Is the Supreme Being

God revealed to Adam and Eve who He is. As the number of people on the earth increased, they began to spread out. The truths which God had made known to Adam and Eve were confused or forgotten in the new settlements. The people, however, reasoning from the wonderful objects and order in the world, from the way in which day followed night, and season followed season, and from their own understanding of good and bad, knew — even if in a confused manner — that there is a Supreme Being. They tried to find Him in the universe in order to worship Him. Some thought that the Supreme Being was water; others identified Him with animals or other creatures of the earth.

To keep the idea of the true God alive in men's minds God revealed to the Hebrews who He was. He helped them to remember that *God is the Supreme Being, infinitely perfect, who made all things and keeps them in existence.*

We can recall the story of creation and remember that God created other things before He made man. What are some of these creatures? Heavenly bodies? Plants? What else? All these creatures provided for man's needs. The sun, moon, and stars give him light; plants and animals furnish him food, clothing, shelter, medicine, and service. Deep in the ground as in a basement, are stores of coal, oil, and gas for fuel; of gold, silver, and other minerals and elements for man to use. Because God took care to provide for all our needs we say He is our loving Father.

When Christ came on earth He wanted to make us realize this important truth that God is our Father. The Gospels give us many examples of this teaching. Let us read over and discuss some of these references from the New Testament.

". . . your Father knows what you need before you ask Him. In this manner therefore shall you pray: 'Our Father who art in heaven'" (Mt. 6:8–9).

"But when thou prayest, go into thy room, and closing thy door, pray to thy Father in secret; and thy Father, who sees in secret, will reward thee" (Mt. 6:6).

"Therefore I say to you, do not be anxious for your life, what you shall eat; nor yet for your body, what you shall put on. Is not the life a greater thing than the food, and the body than the clothing? Look at the birds of the air; they do not sow, or reap, or gather into barns; yet your heavenly Father feeds them. Are not you of much more value than they?" (Mt. 6:25–27.)

## 3. God Made Us to Share His Happiness

Since God has taken such care of us, we must realize that we are here on this earth because of His goodness and love. God is goodness itself. He did not need us to make Him happier. He made us so that we might share his everlasting happiness in heaven. Each one of us shows the goodness of God by the very fact of being alive. Each one of us then, should always remember that God made us so that we could be happy with Him in heaven forever.

This thought seemed to be uppermost in the minds of the American Indians. To them the biggest thing in life was preparing for "The Happy Hunting Ground."

Why do some people forget about the next life? Perhaps they have forgotten what they learned from their study of the catechism: *God made us to show forth His goodness and to share with us His everlasting happiness in heaven.*

## 4. God Gave Us the Means to Serve Him

God gave to man two great powers or faculties: intellect and will. No other creature on earth possesses these two precious gifts. The intellect helps man to understand, or know; the will gives man the power to do what he knows is right. When we use these two faculties or powers, in the right way, we are giving honor and glory to God.

God wants us to keep Him foremost in our minds so that we can become holy as He is holy. This does not mean that we may never think of anything else. It does mean that we should see and reverence God in everything. God allows us to take pleasure in the good things He has created. In fact He has given us many opportunities for enjoyment here on earth. Still, God wants us to realize that no earthly joy can equal the eternal happiness of heaven for which we are striving.

Above all, God gave us His divine Son, who became man to show us the way to serve His almighty Father and, by His death on the cross, to win for us supernatural life. God's Son, our Lord Jesus Christ, established a Church and the seven sacraments, so that men for all ages would be able to share in this supernatural life and grow "strong in grace and in truth." By becoming man, He gave us the example of His own life, showing us what we should be and do in order to be pleasing to God. He is with us daily in the Blessed Sacrament, inviting us to come and tell Him our problems and gain from Him wisdom to know what we must do and courage to do it. By making our lives like Christ's life, we will surely serve God in the right way.

## 5. Our Purpose: To Gain Heaven by Serving God

Since getting to heaven is the purpose of our life on earth, the Catholic Church maps out our course through life. The Church also supplies us with all the graces necessary for us in order to reach our heavenly home. Our lives here on earth must be governed by God's will if we hope to be happy with Him in heaven. In short, *to gain the happiness of heaven we must know, love, and serve God in this world.*

Can you see now that your life is a journey to the complete knowledge of God? The Church, through the articles of the Apostles' Creed points out the chief truths that are to be known about Him. By prayer and by receiving the sacraments we gain the grace to know and serve Him, and to increase our love for Him; and the commandments are the guides which show the way.

## 6. The Church Shows Us How

We can say it briefly and clearly in these words: *We learn to know, love, and serve God from Jesus Christ, the Son of God, who teaches us through the Catholic Church.*

From the earliest days of the Church, the teachings of Christ have been handed down by the Apostles and their successors. The chief of these teachings have been gathered together in a prayer known as the Apostles' Creed.

As the Church grew and spread, men studied the doctrines which Christ taught. The teaching of the Church developed. In all this the Catholic Church was not adding new truths, but unfolding, or explaining the truths which God has revealed so that men might understand them more easily and more fully.

*We find the chief truths taught by Jesus Christ through the Catholic Church in the Apostles' Creed.* Do you know the Apostles' Creed so well that you can write it without making a single mistake? You must know and be able to explain each of the twelve parts. They are listed here for you.

I believe in God, the Father Almighty, Creator of heaven and earth;
and in Jesus Christ, His only Son, our Lord;
who was conceived by the Holy Ghost, born of the Virgin Mary,
suffered under Pontius Pilate, was crucified, died and was buried.
He descended into hell; the third day He arose again from the dead;
He ascended into heaven, sitteth at the right hand of God, the Father Almighty;
from thence He shall come to judge the living and the dead.
I believe in the Holy Ghost,
the Holy Catholic Church, the communion of saints,
the forgiveness of sins,
the resurrection of the body,
and life everlasting. Amen.

## REVIEW, I–1

### WORD LIST

| | | | | |
|---|---|---|---|---|
| creature | gratitude | infinitely | existence | creed |
| visible | identified | supreme | intellect | doctrines |

### THINGS TO REMEMBER

1. God made us.
2. God is the Supreme Being.

3. God made us to show us His goodness and to share with us His happiness.
4. We will share God's happiness if we love and serve Him.
5. The Church teaches us how to serve God.

## THINGS TO DISCUSS AND DO

1. Discuss what we have studied in this part and tell how it should influence how we live.
2. Try to make the Sign of the Cross more fervently, as a profession of faith.
3. Visit our Lord in the Blessed Sacrament. Ask Him to help you to believe the truths of your religion which you have studied.
4. How can you help all men to know, love, and serve God?
5. What part of the answer to catechism question number two (p. 42) might you think of when you sit down to an excellent meal prepared by your mother?
6. Make up a prayer to God, praising Him for His greatness.
7. Make a visit to the church and ask God to help you grow each day in the grace He gave at baptism.
8. Each time you obey someone in authority, try to remember that you are really obeying God, your Father and Creator.
9. List the truths you find in the Apostles' Creed — put them in your own words.

Study Catechism Lesson 1, *The Purpose of Man's Existence*, pp. 42–43.

I am Who am

## Part 2. God Has Many Perfections

God's perfections help us know Him better. They show us how great and how good He is.

As we have already learned, God is the Supreme Being, above all creatures. This means that He is the highest power, the greatest authority that can exist. It also means that all creatures come under His power, that He has the right to rule them. Here is a definition of Supreme Being which should help us understand this better: *When we say that God is the Supreme Being we mean that He is above all creatures, the self-existing and infinitely perfect Spirit.*

**23**

## 1. God Is a Spirit

One of the most important things we know about God is that He is a spirit. *A spirit is a being that has understanding and free will, but no body, and will never die.* Because a spirit has no body, it has no parts and will live forever.

Angels also are spirits. So are our souls spirits. They also have an intellect for knowing and understanding, and a will for choosing. But these spirits do not exist from themselves. God made them. They are not perfect. But God is a spirit who is self-existing and who is also infinitely perfect. Let us examine these two ideas.

## 2. God Is Self-Existing

The idea of anything being self-existing is hard for us to understand. When we look around our room and see the things in it we realize they were all made from something. Some other being brought them into existence. So too we know there must have been some other person who first gave life to human beings. Indeed every created thing can be traced to some beginning from some other being. God alone had no beginning. He did not need help from any other being to exist. He is self-existing. *When we say that God is self-existing we mean that He does not owe His existence to any other being.*

## 3. God Is Infinitely Perfect

The word *infinite* means "cannot be measured" or "having no end." Nothing could make God any greater or more wonderful than He is, for there is no end to His perfections.

Sometimes we use the word *perfect* to describe the things we do or see. When we see a rainbow in the sky we marvel at its beauty. We say it is a perfect rainbow, and yet we know it is never quite perfect. At least when the rain stops the rainbow will vanish. We look forward to each birthday, and when the day comes, and we are having a happy time we say, "This is a perfect day." But even the best day has a few clouds, and just as the candles on the birthday cake burn down, so too must the day come to an end.

No matter how good the happenings of our lives may seem to be, they are not absolutely perfect, for they must all come to an end. We say they are finite, that is, limited, or having an end. But the perfections of God are infinite, without limit. *When we say that God is infinitely perfect we mean that He has all perfections without limit.*

God is so wonderful that on earth we do not fully appreciate Him. Only in heaven will we know how truly great God is. God has all perfections, that is, all good qualities found in persons or things. *Some of the perfections of God are: God is eternal, all-good, all-knowing, all-present, and almighty.* Let us examine more carefully the meaning of these perfections.

### 4. God Is Eternal

Have you ever stopped to wonder where you will be fifty years from now? Certainly you will not be here a hundred years from now. Life on earth comes to an end. It was correct in 1910 to say, "Pius X *is* our present pope." Now he is spoken of in the past tense; "Pius X *was* the Holy Father." Only God can be spoken of in the present at all times. Only He is eternal. *When we say that God is eternal we mean that He always was and always will be, and that He always remains the same.* He is older than the centuries but younger than tomorrow.

## 5. God Is All-Good

Sometimes we say we have read a good book, meaning that the book satisfied our need for recreation and gave us the information or entertainment we desired. Again we say we had a good dinner because it consisted of food we like, prepared in a way we enjoy. We often speak of someone as a good friend of ours, one who shares our pleasures and is interested in everything we are doing. Occasionally we describe a person as good, because he is kind and thoughtful, obedient and prayerful, and willing to make sacrifices for others. We say the saints led good lives.

These examples give us some idea of what goodness is. How can we apply this same quality of goodness to God? His goodness is limitless. He is Goodness itself. Everything about Him is absolutely lovable. He gives good things to everyone. He inspires us to keep trying, each in our own way, to become like Him in goodness. God loves all His creatures and bestows many blessings on them. *When we say that God is all-good we mean that He is infinitely lovable in Himself, and that from His fatherly love every good comes to us.*

God has loved every single one of His human creatures from the time of our first parents down to the present day, despite all the sins that they have committed through the years. He wants us to imitate His goodness. He wants us to work and sacrifice and pray so that others may know and love Him. He wants all men to belong to His kingdom. He is good. Completely good. All-good. He wants us to be good. He wants us to be good to others, as He is good to us and to them.

## 6. God Is All-Knowing

How many stars are there in the sky? A million? How many grains of sand are there in a handful? Is there anyone on earth who knows the answers to these questions? Hardly. The human mind is able to learn many things, but no human being will ever be able to know all the mysteries of life.

Try to imagine, if you can, a being capable of knowing, not only the exact answer to the mysteries of life around us now, but also the events and mysteries of life thousands of years ago, and all the happenings of the future. To our little minds this seems impossible, but nothing is impossible with God. God is all-knowing. *When we say that God is all-knowing we mean that He knows all things, past, present, and future, even our most secret thoughts, words, and actions.*

## 7. God Is All-Present

Did you ever stop to think that you are never all alone? Even when you are completely by yourself God is with you, because God is all-present. *When we say that God is all-present we mean that He is everywhere.*

When we are in the state of grace God is present in us in another and a special way. Then He is in our souls, reigning there as a king on a throne. St. Paul, wishing to teach the people of Corinth this fact, said: "Do you not know that you are the temple of God, and that the spirit of God dwells within you?" (1 Cor. 3:16.)

Did you ever see a thought? or a desire? No, because they are acts of our soul, which is a spirit. What is spiritual cannot be seen with bodily eyes. So, *although God is everywhere, we do not see Him because He is a spirit and cannot be seen with our eyes.*

**27**

Our eyes usually let us know who is in the room or in the house with us. There are times, however, when we know our father is upstairs although we do not see him for several hours. We have a feeling of security just knowing that he is near. We should always have this same feeling about God. We cannot see Him, and yet we know He is present in all things wherever we go.

We cannot ever run away from God. He sees us at work; at play. He sees our honesty in our games, and our helpfulness at home. God sees and loves and rewards each thing we do for Him. He sees and will punish everything we do against Him.

"Keep me, O Lord, as the apple of thine eye; beneath the shadow of Thy wings protect me."

## 8. God Watches Over Us — Divine Providence

When Abraham was a very old man God chose him to be the Father of the Hebrews. God spoke to him, telling Abraham to leave his own country and relatives and settle

in the land of Chanaan. Abraham set out obediently in search of the Promised Land. He reached Chanaan and settled there, and became the Father of the Hebrew nation. During the following years God's protecting care guided the Hebrews. They realized then, as we do now, that *God sees us and watches over us with loving care.*

From the history of the Hebrews we can learn much about God's loving care for His children. For a time they would be faithful to God, and then they would begin to worship strange gods. Over and over again God sent prophets to bring the Hebrews back to Him. Just as God watched over the Hebrews and protected them, so also He watches over every action of our lives. *God's loving care for us is called Divine Providence.*

Sometimes things happen to us which cause us great sorrow or trouble and make us wonder whether God is really watching over us. God often lets things happen to test our faith and love. It is not what happens to us that counts; it is what these joys and sorrows do to us that matters, and what we do with them. If we use all the happenings of everyday life, whether glad or sad, to make us love God more, then we are His true children, deserving of His care. Do you remember the story of Job?

## 9. Other Perfections of God

### God Is Almighty

As we said, God has all perfections. In addition to the perfections we have just studied, we could mention many others. An important one is that God is almighty. Do you understand what is meant by "almighty"? *When we say that God is almighty we mean that He can do all things.*

If a non-Catholic friend were to question whether there are other perfections of God, could you answer, *Yes, God is all-wise, all-holy, all-merciful, and all-just?*

## God Is All-Wise

We cannot always understand why things happen as they do, but we must believe that God knows best. His wisdom will guide us through life, for He sees and knows all things, whereas we see and know only in part.

Do you remember the story of the Samaritan woman at the well? In order to convert her, Christ showed this unfortunate woman His power of seeing her secret thoughts. He told her the sins of her life. Another time Christ scolded a group of the Jews for complaining against a woman who had been discovered as a sinner. They wanted to stone her. Our Lord said that the one among them who was without sin should cast the first stone. You may recall how they slipped away one by one. God knows all our secret thoughts, words, and deeds. This sounds frightening but it should give us courage rather than fear.

## God Is All-Holy

God is infinitely and absolutely holy. God's holiness is so much greater than the holiness of any creature that we cannot even make a comparison. Whenever we think of the Blessed Virgin Mary a happy feeling enters our hearts. We realize how holy she was, since she was chosen by God to be the Mother of His Son. We respect and love her because of this great holiness. But her holiness is as nothing compared to the infinite holiness of God. She is a creature.

## God Is All-Merciful

The great mercy of God is seen throughout the Gospels. Do you remember the story of Mary Magdalen, the sinful woman who lived during the time of Christ? Do you know the story of St. Peter? This beloved saint, whom Christ chose as the head of His Church, was a blustery man who loved to brag about his courage and loyalty. When Christ foretold that one of His Apostles would betray Him, Peter shook his head and declared boldly that he at least was ready to give his life for Christ. In spite of his proud boasting Peter denied our Lord; yet, his sins were forgiven.

It is the same with us. No matter how badly or how often we sin, God forgives us and receives us back into His love if we are sorry and ask His forgiveness. Every time we receive the sacrament of penance worthily, that is, with the intention of showing God we are sorry for our sins and of leading better lives, God shows His mercy to us, as He did to Mary Magdalen and Peter.

## God Is All-Just

Some people do not believe in hell because they think God is too forgiving and kind to punish anyone with such great suffering. We know, however, that if God's justice or fairness demands a reward for our good deeds, so also does it require punishment for evil. God is just. He would not be perfect if He were not infinitely just.

## REVIEW, I-2

**WORD LIST**

| | | | |
|---|---|---|---|
| eternal | limitless | Divine Providence | merciful |
| self-existing | security | existence | just |

## THINGS TO REMEMBER

1. God has all perfections in fullest measure.
2. God loves all His creatures.
3. God cares for all men throughout their entire lives.

## THINGS TO DISCUSS AND DO

1. When we think of God's goodness to us, we surely want to do something in return. What should we do?
2. God is all-merciful. How can we practice this virtue?
3. God knows all things. With this in mind, how should we live?
4. Prove from what you know about the universe that God is almighty.
5. How do trees, flowers, and animals give glory to God?
6. Can you tell how the human eye shows the wisdom of God?
7. Make a minute meditation on the Providence of God. Think of:

   What it means.
   How it is shown to us.
   What it should teach us to do.

8. When you eat your dinner, think of God's gifts of food and water. Thank and praise God for having given them to us.
9. Prepare an explanation you could give a non-Catholic friend who does not believe that God knows all things.
10. Give some instances of how Divine Providence is seen in the Old Testament, the New Testament, and in the world today.
11. Write a paragraph explaining why it is possible for God to guide the whole world.
12. In a drawing try to illustrate God's perfections.

Study Catechism Lesson 2, *God and His Perfections*, Questions 8 to 21, pp. 44–46.

## Part 3. Reason and Revelation Prove the Existence of God

### 1. Reason Can Prove There Is a God

God has given to men's minds the power to know Him. All men can know there is a God just by using their reason. We Catholics know it by faith. Yet we too should *know by our natural reason that there is a God, for natural reason tells us that the world we see about us could have been made only by a self-existing Being, all-wise and almighty.*

We can prove that there is such a Supreme Being to persons who do not have faith. We will learn many formal proofs in high school or college. Here we will examine just two of those that depend on reason. The first one comes from consideration of the great wide world in which we live; the second, from a consideration of the heart of man.

This wonderful world of ours could not have come into existence by itself; nor could it continue except by the power of a self-existing being. The sun must have been given its power by someone very mighty. The stars and the planets must be held in place by a master power and intellect. To think that such marvelous order could be kept up without the ceaseless watchfulness of an almighty Being is foolish indeed. The first spark of life, of beauty, or of power present in the world must have had its beginning in some first form of life.

Man himself gives proof that there is a God. In fact, man is the best proof. His body proves it. But his spiritual mind and will prove it better. Deep in the heart of every human person is a sense of right and wrong. An inner voice tells us that we cannot do evil without being punished by someone. Likewise we hope for a reward for our good deeds. Therefore, there must be someone greater than man, who rewards and punishes human behavior.

## 2. Revelation Also Proves There Is a God

Our natural reason is not the only means we have of knowing God, nor the best. As we learned in the introduction on Faith, God has revealed, or made known, many things about Himself. These truths, which God has revealed to us in Holy Scripture and Tradition, are called supernatural revelation.

God drew aside the curtain that hid Him from the eyes of men by speaking directly to the prophets of the Old Testament. As if this were not proof enough, God sent His Son, Jesus Christ, who established a Church to teach us about the nature of God. Consequently, *besides knowing God by our natural reason, we can also know Him from*

34

*supernatural revelation, that is, from the truths found in Sacred Scripture and in Tradition, which God Himself has revealed to us.*

We have learned much about God. It is good to know these things. But it is far better to appreciate what they mean. For then we will love and serve our great God as we should. Often those who are not so bright appreciate God far better than those who are much brighter. They think about God often and praise Him for His greatness. God loves such persons and often does marvelous things through them.

Think about God's many perfections when you pray. And praise Him for being so great, so holy, and so good. Sing "Holy God" to express your sentiments.

## REVIEW, I–3

### WORD LIST

ceaseless        revelation        natural reason

### THINGS TO REMEMBER

1. We can know by reason that there is a God.
2. Revelation is a better way to know God.
3. Revelation means the truths which God has made known to us.

### THINGS TO DISCUSS AND DO

1. Explain why it ought to be impossible for an intelligent person to deny the existence of God.
2. Write a letter to a non-Catholic friend explaining how man himself proves there is a God.
3. Explain what is meant by supernatural revelation.

Study Catechism Lesson 2 (Cont.), Questions 22–23, pp. 46–47.

# Part 4. The Unity and Trinity of God

## 1. There Is But One God in Three Divine Persons

What does God tell us about Himself? From the very beginning God made it clear that there is only one Creator, only one Lawgiver, and only one Judge. "I am the first, and I am the last, and besides me there is no God" (Isa. 44:6). In the New Testament the same truth is revealed to us: "That they may know Thee, the only true God" (Jn. 17:3). Reason also tells us there is only one Supreme Being. *Yes, there is only one God.*

Since God is supreme, He cannot have an equal. Our natural reason confirms or strengthens some of the truths God has revealed to us. It can prove there is but one God. However, *in God there are three divine Persons — the Father, the Son, and the Holy Ghost.* To the ancient Hebrews God said nothing directly about the three divine Persons in one God. There are hints of this truth in the Old Testament, however, showing that God was preparing the people for it.

After He had made the beasts of the earth, God said, "Let us make man to our image and likeness" (Gen. 1:26). Scripture used the word "us" and "our." Was it to hint that, while there is but one God, there are three Persons in God? Other references in the Old Testament lead our minds toward the Trinity, but they are not too clear.

It was God the Son who revealed fully the idea of one God in three divine Persons.

On many occasions during His public life our Lord claimed to be true God, equal to His heavenly Father. We shall discuss those claims of our Lord later on, when we consider His divine nature. The New Testament also has a number of passages which show that there are three divine persons in one God. Since the New Testament is God's inspired word, those passages are true and must be believed.

At the very beginning of his gospel account, St. Luke tells us about the Angel Gabriel's visit to Mary to tell her that she was to be the mother of the Redeemer. The greeting of the angel to Mary mentioned three separate Persons. The angel told her: "The Holy Spirit shall come upon thee and the power of the Most High shall overshadow thee; and therefore the Holy One to be born shall be called the Son of God" (Lk. 1:35). So we see that the angel names:

"The Holy Spirit," who is the third Person of the Trinity;* the "most High," who is God the Father and the first Person of the Trinity; and "the Holy One," who is God the Son and second Person of the Trinity.

At our Lord's baptism by St. John the Baptist in the Jordan three Persons are also mentioned. When Jesus had been baptized, He immediately came up from the water. The heavens were opened and He saw the spirit of God descending as a dove and coming upon Him. "And behold, a voice from the heaven said, 'This is my beloved Son, in whom I am well pleased' " (Mt. 3:17). It is not hard to point out the three Persons in this incident. While God the Son, Jesus Christ, is being baptized, God the Father speaks from heaven, and God the Holy Spirit appears in the form of a dove.

Just before His Ascension into heaven, our Lord emphatically mentions the three Persons in one God. Our Lord told His Apostles to baptize in the name of the three divine Persons, saying: "Go, therefore, and make disciples of all nations, baptizing them in the name of the Father, and of the Son, and of the Holy Spirit" (Mt. 28:19–20).

Jesus commanded the Apostles to baptize "in the name of." He did not say "in the names of." St. Augustine said that where you hear one name, there is one God. The Apostles were to baptize by the power and authority of the Father, the Son, and the Holy Spirit. They were to baptize in the name of one and the same God in whom there are three Persons, the Father, the Son, and the Holy Spirit.

The Church has always taught that there are three Persons

---

* The term Holy Spirit is used in the revised translation of the New Testament. It helps us understand more clearly the nature of the Third Person of the Blessed Trinity. For centuries, however, the term Holy Ghost was used by the Church, and is still used in the catechism. We shall, on occasion, use the term Holy Spirit to accustom you to the newer expression.

in one God. This is a mystery of faith. We cannot understand it, but we believe that it is true because God Himself has told us that it is true. We should be happy to say again and again: *The Father is God and the first Person of the Blessed Trinity. The Son is God and the second Person of the Blessed Trinity. The Holy Ghost is God and the third Person of the Blessed Trinity.*

## 2. The Three Divine Persons Are One and the Same God

In the previous lesson we mentioned the Blessed Trinity. We spoke of the Father, the Son, and the Holy Ghost, as Persons of the Blessed Trinity, who are one God. *By the Blessed Trinity we mean one and the same God in three divine Persons.* We should often call on the Blessed Trinity to help us, saying: "Holy Trinity, one God, have mercy on us."

## 3. The Three Divine Persons Are Equal But Distinct

Though they are but one God, *the three divine Persons are really distinct from one another.* The Father is not the Son, the Son is not the Holy Ghost, the Holy Ghost is not the Father or the Son. We can pray to one divine Person at one time, and to another divine Person at another time. When we address our prayers to one divine Person we are addressing them to God.

Now, although we speak of the Blessed Trinity as Father, Son, and Holy Ghost this does not mean that the Father is greater than the Son, or the Son greater than the Holy Ghost. *The three divine Persons are perfectly equal to one another, because all are one and the same God.*

Holy Scripture speaks of creation as the work of the Father. To the Son we owe the reopening of the gates of heaven, that is our redemption. And the Holy Ghost shows Himself within us by keeping us holy. Even though we ordinarily say that the Father created us, the Son redeemed us, and the Holy Spirit sanctifies us, these works are common to all three Persons. The three divine Persons cannot be separated, for they are one and the same God. And so, when the Father created us, the Son and the Holy Spirit were also present and shared in that wonderful work. When the Son redeemed us, the Father and the Holy Spirit also had a part in that work, although only the divine Son became man. When the Holy Spirit made us children of God at Baptism, the Father and Son also sanctified us. So we see that all three divine Persons together, create, redeem, and sanctify. The nature, the perfections, the works of God belong equally to the three divine Persons because they are one God. *The three divine Persons, though really distinct from one another, are one and the same God because all have one and the same divine nature.*

## 4. This Supernatural Mystery Cannot Be Understood

There are many things in nature that we do not understand. How much less should we expect to understand what belongs to God. Above all *we cannot fully understand how the three divine Persons, though really distinct from one another, are one and the same God because this is a supernatural mystery.* We are unable to understand how there can be three Persons, but only one God.

If we look at the noonday sun, our eyes would be blinded by its brightness. So it is with the Blessed Trinity. If we inquire into it, we are blinded with wonder. Yet if we refuse to believe in this mystery simply because we do not understand it, we are like a blind man who will not believe that there is a sun because he cannot see it.

## This Supernatural Mystery Must Be Believed on the Word of God

No one fully understands the Trinity except God Himself. We can, however, get some idea of the nature of the Blessed Trinity by comparing it with certain facts of nature. The flames of three candles placed together form but one flame; a white light can be divided into red, yellow, and blue rays, but together these colors form but one light. No matter how we try, our reason, which is human, can never of itself understand the mystery of the Blessed Trinity, because this truth is above our power to reason.

God has made the Trinity known to us, but our little minds cannot understand it. It is a supernatural mystery. *A supernatural mystery is a truth which we cannot fully understand, but which we firmly believe because we have God's word for it.* God asks only that we believe in this mystery; He asks only that we believe in this mystery because it has been revealed to us by Him who can neither deceive or be deceived. God will reward our faith.

Whenever we make the Sign of the Cross, let us make it slowly and reverently, as an act of faith, in honor of the Blessed Trinity.

*Glory be to the Father, and to the Son, and to the Holy Ghost. As it was in the beginning, is now, and ever shall be, world without end. Amen.*

## REVIEW, 1—4

### WORD LIST

| | | | | |
|---|---|---|---|---|
| divine | person | mystery | confirms | existence |
| attribute | spirit | idolatry | Trinity | advocate |
| enlighten | nature | unity | | |

## THINGS TO REMEMBER

1. There is only one God.
2. In God there are three Persons; the Father, our Creator; the Son, our Redeemer; the Holy Ghost, our Sanctifier.
3. The word trinity means three in one.
4. The Blessed Trinity is a supernatural mystery; that is, it is beyond natural human understanding.
5. Although God the Father is usually mentioned first, the three divine Persons are equal.

## THINGS TO DISCUSS AND DO

1. Write the Act of Faith. Underline the words that express ideas about the Blessed Trinity.
2. Draw as many symbols as you can that might express the mystery of the Blessed Trinity. Be able to explain them.
3. List the time throughout the day when you think of or express your belief in the Blessed Trinity.
4. Find some places in the Bible revealing the mystery of the Blessed Trinity.

Study Catechism Lesson 3, *The Unity and Trinity of God*, pp. 47–48.

## End-of-Unit Review — Unit I

**PART 1**

## CATECHISM

### LESSON 1

#### The Purpose of Man's Existence

1. Who made us?

   God made us.

2. Who is God?

   God is the Supreme Being, infinitely perfect, who made all things and keeps them in existence.

3. **Why did God make us?**

God made us to show forth His goodness and to share with us His everlasting happiness in heaven.

4. **What must we do to gain the happiness of heaven?**

To gain the happiness of heaven we must know, love, and serve God in this world.

5. **From whom do we learn to know, love, and serve God?**

We learn to know, love, and serve God from Jesus Christ, the Son of God, who teaches us through the Catholic Church.

6. **Where do we find the chief truths taught by Jesus Christ through the Catholic Church?**

We find the chief truths taught by Jesus Christ through the Catholic Church in the Apostles' Creed.

7. **Say the Apostles' Creed**

I believe in God, the Father Almighty, Creator of heaven and earth; and in Jesus Christ, His only Son, our Lord; who was conceived by the Holy Ghost, born of the Virgin Mary, suffered under Pontius Pilate, was crucified, died, and was buried. He descended into hell; the third day He arose again from the dead; He ascended into heaven, sitteth at the right hand of God, the Father Almighty; from thence He shall come to judge the living and the dead. I believe in the Holy Ghost, the Holy Catholic Church, the communion of saints, the forgiveness of sins, the resurrection of the body, and life everlasting. Amen.

## OTHER QUESTIONS AND EXERCISES

### (Do not write in this book.)

1. How can you increase the glory of God by giving good example?
2. What will our home in heaven be like?
3. How does the Church map out our way through life?
4. Why is the Apostles' Creed an important prayer?
5. Can we prove there is a God?
6. What is revelation?
7. How can you make your faith stronger?

8. How can you use the gift of faith in everyday life?

9. Must the honor we give to God be greater than that given to any creature?

10. How can you learn to know God?

11. What can you do to prove your love for God?

12. What is the best way to serve God?

13. Name some things that God keeps in existence and explain how He does it.

14. What can you do today to prove to God that you realize how truly great He is?

15. What could you say in prayer to God as you use one of His gifts today?

16. What did Jesus Christ do to help us learn to know, love, and serve God?

17. How does sharing God's gifts with others prove our love for God?

18. Why should we love the Catholic Church?

19. How can boys and girls your age prove they believe in God?

20. What does the word *Creed* mean?

## PART 2

## CATECHISM

### LESSON 2

#### God and His Perfections

8. **What do we mean when we say that God is the Supreme Being?**

When we say that God is the Supreme Being we mean that He is above all creatures, the self-existing and infinitely perfect Spirit.

9. **What is a spirit?**

A spirit is a being that has understanding and free will, but no body, and will never die.

10. **What do we mean when we say that God is self-existing?**

When we say that God is self-existing we mean that He does not owe His existence to any other being.

11. **What do we mean when we say that God is infinitely perfect?**

When we say that God is infinitely perfect we mean that He has all perfections without limit.

12. **What are some of the perfections of God?**

Some of the perfections of God are: God is eternal, all-good, all-knowing, all-present, and almighty.

13. **What do we mean when we say that God is eternal?**

When we say that God is eternal we mean that He always was and always will be, and that He always remains the same.

14. **What do we mean when we say that God is all-good?**

When we say that God is all-good we mean that He is infinitely lovable in Himself, and that from His fatherly love every good comes to us.

15. **What do we mean when we say that God is all-knowing?**

When we say that God is all-knowing we mean that He knows all things, past, present, and future, even our most secret thoughts, words, and actions.

16. **What do we mean when we say that God is all-present?**

When we say that God is all-present we mean that He is everywhere.

17. **If God is everywhere, why do we not see Him?**

Although God is everywhere, we do not see Him because He is a spirit and cannot be seen with our eyes.

18. **Does God see us?**

God sees us and watches over us with loving care.

19. **What is God's loving care for us called?**

God's loving care for us is called Divine Providence.

20. **What do we mean when we say that God is almighty?**

When we say that God is almighty we mean that He can do all things.

21. Is God all-wise, all-holy, all-merciful, and all-just?

Yes, God is all-wise, all-holy, all-merciful, and all-just.

## OTHER QUESTIONS AND EXERCISES

1. Tell in your own words what infinitely perfect means.
2. What is meant by "being in the state of grace"?
3. How can we thank God for watching over us?
4. How does God show His mercy to us?
5. Write 1 to 10 on a paper. Then match the following:

A. God is all-knowing.
B. God is all-merciful.
C. God is eternal.
D. God is all-present.
E. God is almighty.

F. God is infinitely perfect.
G. God is all-good.
H. Divine Providence.
I. God is all-holy.
J. God is all-just.

1. God watches over us with loving care.
2. God knows our most secret thoughts, words, actions.
3. God rewards good and punishes evil.
4. God is infinitely lovable in Himself, and from His fatherly care every good comes to us.
5. God hates what is evil and loves only what is good.
6. God can do all things.
7. God is the same, yesterday, today, forever.
8. God's perfections are without limit.
9. God forgives our sins when we are sorry for them.
10. God is everywhere.

**PART 3**

## CATECHISM

### LESSON 2

#### God and His Perfections (cont.)

22. Can we know by our natural reason that there is a God?

We can know by our natural reason that there is a God,

for natural reason tells us that the world we see about us could have been made only by a self-existing Being, all-wise and almighty.

**23. Can we know God in any other way than by our natural reason?**

Besides knowing God by our natural reason, we can also know Him from supernatural revelation, that is, from the truths found in Sacred Scripture and in Tradition, which God Himself has revealed to us.

## OTHER QUESTIONS AND EXERCISES

1. Tell two ways in which reason proves there is a God.
2. Where do we find the clearest proof that there is a God?
3. Why must we believe all that God has revealed to us?
4. How did God make known His truths in the Old Testament?
5. How does the voice of conscience tell us there is a God?
6. What reason could you give for some people not believing there is a God?
7. Is faith in God's revealed truth necessary?
8. Is reason a greater proof of the existence of God than revelation?
9. What is supernatural revelation?
10. Should our daily conduct prove to our friends that we believe in God?

**PART 4**

## CATECHISM

### LESSON 3

#### The Unity and Trinity of God

**24. Is there only one God?**

Yes, there is only one God.

**25. How many Persons are there in God?**

In God there are three divine Persons — the Father, the Son, and the Holy Ghost.

26. **Is the Father God?**

The Father is God and the first Person of the Blessed Trinity.

27. **Is the Son God?**

The Son is God and the second Person of the Blessed Trinity.

28. **Is the Holy Ghost God?**

The Holy Ghost is God and the third Person of the Blessed Trinity.

29. **What do we mean by the Blessed Trinity?**

By the Blessed Trinity we mean one and the same God in three divine Persons.

30. **Are the three divine Persons really distinct from one another?**

The three divine Persons are really distinct from one another.

31. **Are the three divine Persons perfectly equal to one another?**

The three divine Persons are perfectly equal to one another, because all are one and the same God.

32. **How are the three divine Persons, though really distinct from one another, one and the same God?**

The three divine Persons, though really distinct from one another, are one and the same God because all have one and the same divine nature.

33. **Can we fully understand how the three divine Persons, though really distinct from one another, are one and the same God?**

We cannot fully understand how the three divine Persons, though really distinct from one another, are one and the same God because this is a supernatural mystery.

34. **What is a supernatural mystery?**

A supernatural mystery is a truth which we cannot fully understand, but which we firmly believe because we have God's word for it.

## OTHER QUESTIONS AND EXERCISES

(Answer on a separate sheet.)

1. God has (*a*) one nature; (*b*) two natures; (*c*) three natures.
2. We call the three divine Persons in one and the same God (*a*) the Blessed Trinity; (*b*) the divine nature; (*c*) the Incarnation.
3. We say that the three divine Persons are really distinct from one another because: (*a*) they are different persons; (*b*) they have the same divine nature; (*c*) they are the Blessed Trinity.
4. We cannot understand how the three divine Persons are one and the same God because it is (*a*) a supernatural mystery; (*b*) an important truth; (*c*) Divine Providence.
5. We believe that the three divine Persons are one and the same God because (*a*) we can find examples in nature; (*b*) no one understands it; (*c*) we have God's word for it.
6. I profess my faith in the Blessed Trinity when I say the (*a*) Our Father; (*b*) Confiteor; (*c*) Sign of the Cross; (*d*) Morning Offering.
7. By the Blessed Trinity we mean: (*a*) three Gods in one divine Person; (*b*) three divine Persons and three Gods; (*c*) one God in three divine Persons.
8. The word which shows that the three divine Persons are really different is (*a*) equal; (*b*) distinct; (*c*) supernatural.
9. When we say one and the same God we mean: (*a*) one and the same divine nature; (*b*) equal to each other; (*c*) distinct from one another.
10. The Sign of the Cross is (*a*) an act of faith in the unity and trinity of God; (*b*) a supernatural mystery; (*c*) a prayer honoring the Blessed Sacrament.

# Unit II. God: Creator of All Things

# Part 1.  God Created the Angelic World

## 1. God Created the Angelic World

In the lesson on the perfections of God we learned that God is almighty. This almighty power explains the act of creation. We know this from the Apostles' Creed which says that God is the Creator of heaven and earth. *When we say that God is the Creator of heaven and earth we mean that He made all things from nothing by His almighty power.*

*The chief creatures of God are angels and men.* Angels are by nature superior to men. *Angels are created spirits, without bodies, having understanding and free will.* The angels are pure spirits, that is, they have and need no bodies. They are greater than man, and yet, not equal to God. Man can think, and use his will. But God made the angels above any of His other creatures and they can know and will much better than man.

Since the angels have no bodies, we cannot see them with our bodily eyes. Neither can our human reason alone prove that angels exist. But Sacred Scripture and Tradition teach that they do exist, and that they were created by God.

*When God created the angels He bestowed on them great wisdom, power, and holiness.* Of all God's creatures angels are most like Him. The angels did not have to learn from experience. They were given knowledge and wisdom superior to that of any human being. Moreover they were given sanctifying grace and great holiness.

The angels were created to love and serve God. God created them for the same reason He created men. He created them to find eternal happiness in heaven.

## 2. Some Angels Obeyed God

The angels were holy as God created them. Like man, they were given the supernatural gift of sanctifying grace. But before God admitted the angels into His eternal presence He tested their willingness to obey and serve Him. Some obeyed; others did not.

*The angels who remained faithful to God entered into the eternal happiness of heaven, and these are called good angels.* They received the reward God promised them. They fulfill the purpose God had in creating them. *In heaven the good angels see, love, and adore God.*

Besides their duties in heaven, the angels have certain duties toward man. *The good angels help us by praying for us, by acting as messengers from God to us, and by serving as our guardian angels.* Since we are made for heaven, and heaven is the home of the angels, they are greatly interested in our salvation. They pray for us in order to help us gain heaven, where we can join them in praising God. We, in our turn should pray to them: All ye holy angels, pray for us; that we may be made worthy of the promises of Christ.

## 3. Guardian Angels

The most familiar part which angels play in our lives is that of being our guardians. When you were small you probably pictured your guardian angel in human form as you thought of your special guide beside you. Now that you are older and know that your angel does not have a body, you are likely to forget your angel's presence. Yet your angel never leaves you, in spite of your forgetfulness.

How precious each human soul must be that God would so provide for its protection. How great must God's love be to give each of us our own particular angel. St. Jerome says: "How great is the dignity of souls that each one should have from the first moment of his birth an angel delegated to guard him." Our guardian angels know better than we do just what we need. They pray not only for our bodily needs, but also for the needs of our soul. They present our prayers and good works to God, and ask favors for us. They seem to whisper in our ear to warn us of danger. Thus we see that *our guardian angels help us by praying for us, by protecting us from harm, and by inspiring us to do good.*

How grateful we should be to our guardian angels. We

owe them reverence, that is, honor and respect. As creatures closer to God than we are, they deserve our confidence and our obedience. Every Catholic child should dedicate himself to his guardian angel each morning by saying the following prayer:

> **Angel of God, my guardian dear,**
> **To whom His love commits me here**
> **Ever this day be at my side,**
> **To light and guard, to rule and guide. Amen.**

## 4. Some Angels Disobeyed God

Speaking of the good angels has been pleasant, but we must also consider the fallen angels, or the angels who disobeyed God, for we know that *not all the angels remained faithful to God; some of them sinned.* We learned long ago that *the angels who did not remain faithful to God were cast into hell, and these are called bad angels, or devils.* The bad angels, after their sin, turned completely against God, the Supreme Good, and determined to keep as many souls as possible from Him.

The fallen angels work against us in many ways.

The bad angels try to harm us. *The chief way in which the bad angels try to harm us is by tempting us to sin.* They are like hunters tracking us down, laying traps to destroy us. We must remember the devils are fallen angels with the same superior intellect they possessed before the fall. They are clever; no one escapes their hatred, but everyone can fight them with the most powerful of weapons, prayer and good works.

Christ broke the power of Satan and his followers when He died on the cross. He permits the bad angels to tempt us for our own perfection, and no temptation is too strong for us if we ask for help. God is always ready to aid us with

His divine grace. We should often pray to Michael, the leader of the good angels, in the powerful prayer: "Saint Michael the Archangel, defend us in battle, that we perish not in the fearful judgment."

## Other Sources of Temptation

The bad angels however are not the only source of our temptations. *Some temptations come from the bad angels; but other temptations come from ourselves and from the persons and things about us.* Within the nature of each of us there are certain weaknesses or inclinations to evil. These attractions toward doing wrong are the result of original sin. We must be especially careful always to guard our five senses, for it is through them that temptation enters our minds and attracts our wills.

Still other sources of temptations are the persons and things around us. There are always persons in the world who enjoy doing the devil's work. Sadly enough there are even children, Catholic children, who tempt other children to do wrong. Pictures, magazines, comic books, movies, and television shows are sometimes sources of temptations.

If the evil caused by sin and temptation were all we knew about, we would be discouraged and say it is too hard to be good. But we also know this: *We can always resist temptations, because no temptation can force us into sin, and because God will always help us if we ask Him.* This means that with grace, we have in us a power to say "no" which is stronger than the power of temptation. This power is our free will. We must use this power, and call on God often to help us keep from sin. We might picture the devil as a fierce dog that is chained securely. He might snap and snarl but he cannot harm us unless we get too close. He cannot force us into sin against our free will.

At times, when temptations come to us again and again, we may become discouraged about being good and pleasing God. We should remember at such times that temptation is not a sin unless our will freely consents to it. In other words, we must really want to commit a sin before we actually commit sin.

How can we resist the attacks of the devil? We can fight the devil and all his helpers by prayer and the sacraments. "Watch and pray lest ye enter into temptation" should be our motto. We can fight the devil by acts of mortification and by avoiding idleness. We must remember that we are not fighting alone. God is there, as are the Blessed Mother, our patron saints, our guardian angels, and many others. In the divine plan temptations are permitted by God so as to test us and to give us opportunities to gain merit. With the help of God we can resist all temptation. He says to us as He said to St. Paul, "My grace is sufficient for thee" (2 Cor. 12:9).

## REVIEW, II–1

### WORD LIST

| | | | |
|---|---|---|---|
| messengers | creation | inspiring | resist |
| dignity | creature | inspiration | bestowed |
| malice | free will | fortified | mortification |
| inclination | understanding | temptation | |

### THINGS TO REMEMBER

1. God made all things from nothing.
2. Angels and men are the chief creatures of God.
3. Angels are pure spirits having understanding and free will.
4. God created the angels to increase His own glory and to add to their happiness.

5. Our guardian angels help us win heaven; bad angels or devils try to bring us to hell.
6. Temptation is not a sin so long as our will does not consent to it.
7. Prayer and the sacraments are the chief weapons against the devil.

## THINGS TO DISCUSS AND DO

1. On Christmas night the shepherds saw the angels and heard their song, yet the angels are pure spirits. Can you explain this?
2. Do you know the prayer we say to Michael the Archangel? Say it; if you cannot, memorize it, and say it often.
3. Can we blame all temptations on the devil? Give some examples of times when we ourselves may be responsible for our temptations.
4. Name three ways in which the good angels help us.
5. Do you know the name of the angel who was the leader of the battle in heaven? The angel who brought the message to the Blessed Virgin Mary? The angel who guided Tobias on a journey? Look them up in the Bible and be ready to read the stories to the class.
6. Mention other names often given to the leader of the bad angels.
7. Name as many instances as possible where angels appeared as messengers to men.
8. How many choirs of angels are there. How many can you name?
9. If one of your companions told you that stories of angels are fairy tales, how would you answer them?
10. Say a special prayer of thanksgiving to God every day for His gift of a guardian angel.

Study Catechism Lesson 4, *Creation and the Angels*, pp. 68–70.

# Part 2. God Created the Universe

## 1. God Created the Universe by a Mere Command

God created all things by a command or an act of His almighty will. "He spoke and they were made, He commanded and they were created." God made all things without effort and without help. God does not actually speak as we do, for He has no body. He merely willed and all things were made.

## 2. God Created the Universe To Help Us Reach Heaven

Have you ever wondered why God made the world and the creatures in it? To answer this question we need only consider for a moment who God is. We know from our study of God's perfections that He is all-perfect and that nothing outside of Himself can add to His perfections. Creatures

therefore, do not add to God's perfections, but they do show
forth His glory. By doing this they fulfill the purpose for
which they were made.

While this increase of God's glory is the main purpose
of creation, the world was also created for the good of
God's creatures. Man, the chief creature of the visible world
was to make use of all other creatures in serving God. Everything on earth that God has created for man reminds us of
His goodness, and brings man closer to heaven, if properly
used.

Think of the countless things in the world as steppingstones in a brook. Each stone brings us nearer the opposite
bank. If we stay on the one stone too long, we delay our
journey. If we remain satisfied with standing on a stone
instead of continuing on, we shall never reach our goal. For
example, wealth and worldly possessions and pleasures are

creatures of God. If a person devotes himself to them without taking an interest in anything else, even in God, he is using them as the goal of his life and not as steppingstones to heaven. We must remember that we can enjoy the gifts of the earth, but that they are all only means to help us reach heaven, our final goal.

## 3. God Keeps the Universe in Existence

Have you ever heard of a baby being left on a stranger's doorstep? If so, you were probably shocked that a mother and father could do such a thing. A tiny baby is helpless. The parents should care for it by feeding, clothing, and protecting it so that the baby will become strong and healthy. The beginning of a family is important, but to keep on providing for that family is just as important.

Imagine a farmer plowing the ground on his farm, planting seeds in it, and then forgetting all about it. Imagine also, his going out of town on a two-month vacation. Such a man could not expect to find worth-while crops when he returned. A garden needs continual care.

The saying "Things well begun are half-done" is true. But a start such as planting seeds or beginning a family is only half the task. Constant care is also necessary. The act of creation was not only well begun by God but is also continued by His present care.

God not only created the universe but He also continually keeps it in existence. In addition, He cares for and watches over everything He has made, especially man. According to His divine plan the planets follow a regular course; the sun continues to give light and heat; the stars remain in their proper places in the heavens; the oceans, seas, rivers, and lakes do not ordinarily spread over the dry land. God keeps watch over the universe. He protects the things He made. He governs the world so that everything follows His plan. We recall that this care in governing the world is called God's Providence. Because God's protecting hand takes care of us and of the world, we need not fear. Let us give ourselves over completely to His care. Let us follow His plans for us with full confidence. He will always protect us.

## REVIEW, II–2

### WORD LIST

| | | | |
|---|---|---|---|
| universe | constant | material | dependent |
| providing | dominion | governs | |

### THINGS TO REMEMBER

1. God created the universe to help us reach heaven.
2. God keeps the universe in existence.
3. God watches over every one of us with infinite love.
4. God wants us to trust in Him in all our material and spiritual needs.

### THINGS TO DISCUSS AND DO

1. Read aloud the account of the creation of the universe as given in the Bible. Compare the works of the first three days with those of the second three days.
2. Name some of God's creatures that can bring you closer to Him. Choose two or three and tell how they can do this.
3. Plan and present to your class a report on: How God preserves the world He made; or better, how wonderfully God has planned everything to serve man.
4. Mother and Dad enjoy a trip to the country where they can be out in the open and enjoy themselves. Explain how they can be drawn closer to God because of this trip.
5. Do the words "create" and "make" mean different things? Explain.

# Part 3.  God Created Man

## 1. Adam and Eve Were Special Creations of God

When all the rest of the earth had been completed, God fashioned man as the lord and master of His wonderland. In the first book of the Bible the inspired writer says that God formed man's body and breathed into it a soul. God used matter already in existence to form the body of the first man.

### God Created Man's Soul Directly

Man has been called a masterpiece in God's visible world of creatures. This means that he is the greatest of all the beings on this earth. Second only to the angels he is God's most wonderful creation. Man must, however, remember that he is but dust, and that one day his body will return to dust. This truth is especially brought home to us on Ash Wednesday. The ashes placed on our foreheads that day are to remind us not to be so concerned about our body, for it will perish, or die — although it will rise again.

Our soul, however, will live forever. Into the body of Adam, formed from existing matter, God breathed an immortal soul. With this spirit man became a living creature. Now that man's material body had been joined with a life-giving spirit, he had the power to move, speak, think, will, and love. It is this spirit, or soul, that makes man different from all other creatures on earth. A plant or an animal has a life-principle or 'soul,' but it is not spiritual and it is not immortal as man's soul is.

All creatures have some likeness to God, but man resembles his creator in a special way. He is made to God's image and likeness. *Man is a creature composed of body and soul, and made to the image and likeness of God.* We can read in the Book of Genesis that before God made man He said: "Let us make mankind in our own image and likeness." It is this likeness to God that makes the soul so great in value. We might rightly ask: "How can man resemble God who is a spirit?" Man cannot resemble God with regard to his body, for God is a spirit and has no body. The body, however, does show forth the perfection of God. But the resemblance to God is chiefly in the spirit or soul. And this is exactly what the catechism says: *This likeness to God is chiefly in the soul.*

The soul has certain powers that make man able to think or reason, and to choose freely as God does. These powers we call understanding and free will. It is clear from what

**63**

we have just said about the soul that *the soul is like God because it is a spirit having understanding and free will, and is destined to live forever.*

Holy Scripture also tells us that God created the first woman. After breathing life into her body, God presented Eve to Adam. God did this to teach the human race that man is the head of the family. Although Adam is first in position and dignity in the human race, Eve is equal to man in that she has the same human nature and destiny. Finally, God wanted to show us that Eve was Adam's wife and helpmate. God united this first couple in holy matrimony, thereby teaching all human beings the importance of marriage and family life. All of us are members of the same great family and all come from the same first parents. *The first man and woman were Adam and Eve, the first parents of the whole human race.*

## 2. Adam and Eve Received Special Gifts

The human nature of our first parents reflected God's perfections. These chosen friends of God were by nature far above all other creatures on earth. But God decided to give them even greater gifts.

Can you imagine a flower moving from one place to another, or a bird telling you the things it had done? It is not within the nature of a bird or flower to do these things. These powers belong to the nature of man. Lower beings do not have the power to do certain things man can do. Man also can only act according to the powers of his nature. However, when God created Adam and Eve He intended that they and their descendants should receive powers far above their natural powers. These powers would enable them to live a life far above their nature as human beings. They would share in God's life and powers.

## Sanctifying Grace

God willed Adam and Eve to share in His divine life through the wonderful gift of sanctifying grace. Adam was given the free and undeserved privilege of taking part in God's life in addition to possessing the human life which was natural to him. This raising of the nature of man to a sharing in the life of God gave Adam and Eve the unbelievable privilege of becoming God's children by adoption. They could now act as sons of God — what dignity! What power!

You can understand how close this brought them to God. Think of the close bond between an adopted child and his new parents. Being adopted children of God, Adam and Eve had the right to inherit the kingdom of their heavenly Father. Sanctifying grace was a marvelous gift. Indeed *the chief gift bestowed on Adam and Eve by God was sanctifying grace, which made them children of God and gave them the right to heaven.* With sanctifying grace came all the great supernatural virtues.

## Other Gifts

To prepare His children to rule over His kingdom, God gave Adam and Eve other great though lesser gifts. They were given a gift of special happiness and a special gift of knowledge. Another gift was control of their animal nature, so that no passion, such as anger, revenge, lust, or greediness, would trouble them. Their wills were strong and upright, and their bodies were under easy control of their intellects and wills. They were not troubled with temptations of gluttony, anger, and impurity as we are now.

These gifts would seem enough, but God planned even more for man's happiness here on earth. Man was given perfect health, with no bodily discomforts, wants, or fears.

His body as well as his soul was to live forever. After a long life in the Garden of Paradise, man was to be taken to heaven, bodily without dying, to share God's everlasting happiness. The catechism summarizes all this when it says: *The other gifts bestowed on Adam and Eve by God were happiness in the Garden of Paradise, great knowledge, control of the passions by reason, and freedom from suffering and death.*

## 3. Adam and Eve Had To Obey God

According to God's plan, our first parents, like the angels, were required to prove themselves worthy of all the goodness already shown to them by almighty God. They realized that God was their Lord and that they were dependent on Him. Thus far they obeyed Him and loved Him. God had tested the angels for their loyalty. Now God gave Adam and Eve a trial of obedience whereby they were to earn heaven. The Bible tells of this trial with the story that *God gave Adam and Eve the commandment not to eat of the fruit of a certain tree that grew in the Garden of Paradise.*

Read the passage as it is written in the Book of Genesis, chapter 2, verses 15 to 17. By obeying God, Adam and Eve were given the chance and privilege of meriting more grace for themselves. God gave them the necessary grace to face the test.

# REVIEW, II–2

## WORD LIST

| | | | |
|---|---|---|---|
| immortal | masterpiece | privilege | undeserved |
| image | destiny | control | unruly |
| nature | inherit | loyalty | upright |
| dependent | resemblance | material | |

## THINGS TO REMEMBER

1. Man is the greatest of the creatures of the earth.
2. The soul of man makes him resemble God.
3. The soul has two important powers: understanding and free will.
4. Sanctifying grace gives us a sharing in the life of God and a supernatural resemblance to Him.
5. God shows us the importance of obedience by His command to our first parents.

## THINGS TO DISCUSS AND DO

1. Discuss how man is superior to all other creatures on earth, in his body, his imagination, his creative powers, his mind, his will.
2. Explain why your parents or superiors sometimes forbid you to do certain things.
3. Explain how you can thank God for creating you.
4. Compose a thank-you prayer to God in which you thank Him for the two special powers of understanding and free will.
5. Try to thank God for the gift of sanctifying grace received at baptism, especially after you have received Holy Communion or penance.

Study Catechism Lesson 5, *The Creation and Fall of Man*, Questions 48–54, pp. 71–72.

# End-of-Unit Review — II

## CATECHISM

### LESSON 4

#### Creation and the Angels

35. **What do we mean when we say that God is the Creator of heaven and earth?**

   When we say that God is the Creator of heaven and earth we mean that He made all things from nothing by His almighty power.

36. **Which are the chief creatures of God?**

   The chief creatures of God are angels and men.

37. **What are angels?**

   Angels are created spirits, without bodies, having understanding and free will.

38. **What gifts did God bestow on the angels when He created them?**

   When God created the angels He bestowed on them great wisdom, power, and holiness.

39. **Did all the angels remain faithful to God?**

   Not all the angels remained faithful to God; some of them sinned.

40. **What happened to the angels who remained faithful to God?**

   The angels who remained faithful to God entered into the eternal happiness of heaven, and these are called good angels.

41. **What do the good angels do in heaven?**

In heaven the good angels see, love, and adore God.

42. **How do the good angels help us?**

The good angels help us by praying for us, by acting as messengers from God to us, and by serving as our guardian angels.

43. **How do our guardian angels help us?**

Our guardian angels help us by praying for us, by protecting us from harm, and by inspiring us to do good.

44. **What happened to the angels who did not remain faithful to God?**

The angels who did not remain faithful to God were cast into hell, and these are called bad angels, or devils.

45. **What is the chief way in which the bad angels try to harm us?**

The chief way in which the bad angels try to harm us is by tempting us to sin.

46. **Do all temptations come from the bad angels?**

Some temptations come from the bad angels; but other temptations come from ourselves and from the persons and things about us.

47. **Can we always resist temptations?**

We can always resist temptations, because no temptation can force us into sin, and because God will always help us if we ask Him.

## OTHER QUESTIONS AND EXERCISES

1. In what way are the angels like God?
2. How are the angels like man and how are they different from man?
3. What three great gifts did God give the angels?
4. Why are the angels especially happy?
5. How can we be faithful to our guardian angels?
6. Is temptation a sin?

7. Explain in your own words what is meant by an occasion of sin.
8. Where can we get the help to resist temptation?
9. Number a page from 1 to 34. Write after each number the missing word for each blank from the sentences below.

The chief creatures of God are  1  and  2 .

Angels are  3  spirits, without  4  having understanding and  5 .

When God created the angels He bestowed on them great  6 ,  7 ,  8 .

Not all the angels remained  9  to God, some of them  10 .

The angels who remained  11  to God entered the  12  happiness of  13 .

In heaven the good angels  14 ,  15 , and  16  God.

The good angels help us by  17  for us, by acting as  18  from God to us, and by serving as our  19  angels.

Our guardian angels help us by  20  for us, by  21  us from harm, and by  22  us to do good.

The angels who did not remain  23  to God were cast into  24  and these are called  25  angels, or  26

The chief way the bad angels try to harm us is by  27  us to sin.

Some temptations come from the  28  angels, but other temptations come from  29  and from the  30  and  31  around us.

We can always  32  temptation, because no temptation can force us into  33  and God will always help us if we  34  Him.

## APART 2

1. Did God create the universe for the use of man?
2. Does God want us to use the things of this earth to honor Him?
3. Can television help us to honor God?
4. Does God stop watching over us after we sin?
5. Is the story of creation told in the book of Genesis?
6. Are all men dependent on God for all their needs?
7. Do creatures add to God's perfections?
8. Did God create the world without any help?
9. Does God actually speak to man?
10. Can we use all the things of the earth to help us to reach heaven?

**PART 3**

# CATECHISM
## LESSON 5

### The Creation and the Fall of Man

**48. What is man?**

Man is a creature composed of body and soul, and made to the image and likeness of God.

**49. Is this likeness to God in the body or in the soul?**

This likeness to God is chiefly in the soul.

**50. How is the soul like God?**

The soul is like God because it is a spirit having understanding and free will, and is destined to live forever.

**51. Who were the first man and woman?**

The first man and woman were Adam and Eve, the first parents of the whole human race.

**52. What was the chief gift bestowed on Adam and Eve by God?**

The chief gift bestowed on Adam and Eve by God was sanctifying grace, which made them children of God and gave them the right to heaven.

**53. What other gifts were bestowed on Adam and Eve by God?**

The other gifts bestowed on Adam and Eve by God were happiness in the Garden of Paradise, great knowledge, control of the passions by reason, and freedom from suffering and death.

**54. What commandment did God give Adam and Eve?**

God gave Adam and Eve the commandment not to eat of the fruit of a certain tree that grew in the Garden of Paradise.

## OTHER QUESTIONS AND EXERCISES

1. Is man's soul spiritual? Is it immortal? Explain.
2. Mention the many gifts God has given man.
3. Which of God's gifts were natural gifts? Which were supernatural to man?
4. Why did God command Adam and Eve not to eat the fruit of a certain tree? Does He ever give us commands similar to that?
5. What does it mean to be an adopted child of God?
6. How did God make Adam and Eve like Himself?
7. Why did God do so much for Adam and Eve? Why does He do so much for us?
8. What do we prove when we obey God's laws?

# Unit III. The Fall

## Part 1. Original Sin Comes Down to Us From Adam

Everything that God gave Adam and Eve was a gift. It was only fair that God should test them to prove their loyalty and appreciation. We already know the command He gave them. We also know that *Adam and Eve did not obey the commandment of God, but ate of the forbidden fruit*. As a fallen angel in disgrace, Satan hated God and tried to spoil His plans. We remember how Satan plotted our first parents' downfall because of his hatred and his jealousy over their happiness. The devil deceived Eve, who in turn enticed Adam to sin.

## 1. Adam and Eve Were Punished for Their Sin

The sin of our first parents was a sin of pride and disobedience. Too late did Adam and Eve realize their serious mistake in listening to Satan who said, "No, you will not die, you will be like God knowing good and evil." With this act of disobedience came the loss of sanctifying grace. As we said before, grace was God's presence in their souls. To lose grace was man's greatest punishment and misfortune. Innocence and holiness were also lost; moreover, because of their sin, the ordinary tasks which Adam and Eve were given to do became hard for them, and at times, even unpleasant and monotonous. They were subject to suffering and sickness until death claimed them. Their wills were weakened, and the attraction to sin was stronger.

You know the ending of the story. The rulers of Paradise were driven from their kingdom and the gates of heaven were also closed against them. The matter can be summed up in these words: *On account of their sin Adam and Eve lost sanctifying grace, the right to heaven, and their special gifts; they became subject to death, to suffering, and to a strong inclination to evil, and they were driven from the Garden of Paradise.*

We recall from our religion lessons of other years that *this sin in us is called original sin.* We recall too that the results of our first parents' sin are very serious for us, as well as for them. Not only were Adam and Eve punished, but all their descendants until the end of time were to suffer from the results of the sin committed by their first parents. In fact *this sin is called original sin because it comes down to us through our origin, or descent, from Adam.*

## 2. We Suffer Because of Adam and Eve's Sin

Since we came into the world with original sin on our souls we, too, are deprived of sanctifying grace. Since this was the greatest gift God gave Adam and Eve, its loss is our greatest punishment, as it was theirs.

Other punishments followed this great loss of grace. In us, as in Adam after the fall, our passions are hard to control; our intellects are less successful in attaining knowledge. We must study hard to learn the simplest things. Our wills find it difficult to keep good resolutions. You have probably often made such resolutions as "I will do my homework faithfully," or "I will help at home today." Is it easy to be faithful to these resolutions? Why not?

Besides all these punishments, man inherited another which would make life difficult. God told Adam there would often be unpleasantness, or inconvenience attached to the tasks he and his descendants would have to do to work out their salvation. You know that often when there is a difficult task to be performed, you are at first delighted at the challenge it presents. But when the difficulties are great, and the task becomes disagreeable or unpleasant, you grow weary and lose interest. This feeling of annoyance or unpleasantness or inconvenience in the work we have to do is one of the punishments which came to us as a result of Adam's sin.

If this were the end of the story, man might feel hopeless and discouraged. God, however, showed His love and mercy to Adam despite his sin. He promised to send a Redeemer. The one ray of hope for all people was faith in the Redeemer to come. The Redeemer would open the gates of heaven again for Adam and Eve and all their children. After Christ had suffered and died, God's justice would be satisfied, and man would once more enjoy the friendship of God.

On what day in your life did God make you His adopted child? On that occasion of your birthday into God's family, the supernatural gifts that were lost through Adam's sin were restored to you. With His supernatural helps, holiness is increased and the effects of original sin are decreased. To review what we have just learned, two important catechism answers should be memorized:

*On account of the sin of Adam, we, his descendants, come into the world deprived of sanctifying grace and inherit his punishment, as we would have inherited his gifts had he been obedient to God.*

*The chief punishments of Adam which we inherit through original sin are: death, suffering, ignorance, and a strong inclination to sin.*

## 3. God's Punishment Was Just

You may at times wonder about God's justice in punishing all men for Adam's sin. Of course God's infinite justice cannot be questioned by anyone.

Adam's sin was a grievous sin, committed with full consent of the will and complete knowledge. God measured out a just punishment. He had given special free gifts not necessary to man's nature. These special gifts would have been ours too, had Adam and Eve remained loyal to God. Adam held them in trust for us. When our first parents gave up the right to possess these gifts, God took His special, free gifts away from them and their descendants. He took away only the special gifts; not the gifts which were natural to man. However, God provides us with ways and means to regain the special, supernatural gifts. Can you mention some of these ways and means?

As we think over the sin of our first parents and its serious results we realize that *God is not unjust in punishing us on account of the sin of Adam, because original sin does not take away from us anything to which we have a strict right as human beings, but only the free gifts which God in His goodness would have bestowed on us if Adam had not sinned.*

In the struggle for holiness God has given us the spotless example of a perfect creature. This beautiful creature was destined for more than giving us an example of perfect God-like living. She was to be God's mother. In view of the great honor intended for Mary, as Mother of His Son, God preserved her from that blight on the human race, original sin. This privilege was earned for her by the suffering and and death, or, as we say, by the merits of Christ. According to God's plan the Mother of His Son was not to be under the power of the devil for a single instant. *The Blessed Virgin Mary was preserved from original sin in view of the merits of her divine Son; and this privilege is called her Immaculate Conception.*

O Mary, thou didst enter the world without stain; do thou obtain for me from God that I may leave it without sin.

## REVIEW, III–1

**WORD LIST**

| | | |
|---|---|---|
| descendants | original | origin |
| deprived | inherited | passions |

### THINGS TO REMEMBER

1. Through disobedience to God's law our first parents lost God's special gifts.
2. We inherit original sin because of Adam's fall.

3. God did not take away any gifts natural to man, only the free gifts which were above the natural.
4. The Blessed Virgin Mary was preserved from original sin.

## THINGS TO DISCUSS AND DO

1. Find and classify the things Adam and Eve lost and did not lose because of their sin of disobedience. Discuss the list and its classifications.
2. Name some things we must suffer as a result of our first parents' sin. Tell why this is so.
3. Prepare a paragraph entitled: The Blessed Virgin Mary and Original Sin. Read it to the class.
4. Find and report to your class the story of the Blessed Virgin Mary appearing to St. Bernadette. Be able to tell what the story has to do with the dogma of the Immaculate Conception.
5. What do we inherit because of the sin of Adam and Eve? Why?
6. It is often easier for you to do evil rather than good. Explain this.
7. Has original sin anything to do with the fact that you must study and work? Why?
8. There is a certain day of the year on which we are reminded of one penalty we are to pay for original sin. What is the day and how are we reminded?
9. Can you name three kinds of buildings and three kinds of professions that we would not find in the world if there had never been sin in the world?
10. Make a visit to the church and ask our Lord to help you choose good companions and to be a good companion, always.
11. When you prepare for confession tell God you realize all the sufferings and sorrow that sin has caused, and ask Him sincerely to help you to keep from sin.
12. Say the Act of Contrition thoughtfully, especially the last part: "I firmly resolve, with the help of thy grace, to sin no more and to avoid the near occasions of sin."
13. Say three Hail Marys every day to preserve the virtue of purity.

Study Catechism Lesson 5 (cont.), *The Creation and Fall of Man,* Questions 55–62, pp. 89–90.

THOUGHT

Actual SIN

WORD

DEED

# Part 2. Actual Sin

## 1. Actual Sin Is Sin We Commit Ourselves

Original sin, as we just studied, is inherited from Adam. *Original sin is not the only kind of sin; there is another kind, called actual sin, which we ourselves commit.* There are various kinds of actual sins for *actual sin is any willful thought, desire, word, action, or omission forbidden by the law of God.*

Planning to do some evil, or thinking how we can perform an evil deed, or rejoicing over an evil deed we have done, is a sin of thought. Some people think there is no such thing as a mortal sin of thought. They think that in order to commit a sin we must perform some action. This is not true; a *willful*, or intentional thought contrary to the law of God is an actual sin, and can be a mortal sin.

Desires, or wishes, can be sins when we wish some evil to take place, or desire to do some wrong. For instance, Jim has money in his wallet for groceries. Dan is interested in buying a catcher's glove and he knows that Jim has just the right amount of money. Carefully he plans to take the wallet and eagerly awaits his chance. However, he gets no chance to carry out his plan. Even though Dan was unable to steal the wallet, he has committed a sin of stealing in desire, and he must confess it as such.

Being careless of the use of God's name, making others unhappy by our uncharitable talk, or telling lies because we are afraid to face the truth, are examples of sinful words.

Willfully bringing harm to others, stealing, and killing are sinful deeds. These sins are usually the result of the sins of desire, but they take us one step further, to the actual doing of the sin we planned to commit.

We can also sin by neglecting to do something which God commands. Such sins are called sins of omission, as missing Mass on Sunday or holydays through our own fault, or omitting our prayers for a long time.

## 2. Mortal Sin Is the More Serious Actual Sin

*There are two kinds of actual sin: mortal sin and venial sin.* When we sin mortally we refuse to serve God in a serious matter. *Mortal sin is a grievous offense against the law of God.* The word "mortal" means deadly, and mortal sin cuts us off from sanctifying grace, which is the supernatural life of the soul. That is why *this sin is called mortal, or deadly, because it deprives the sinner of sanctifying grace, the supernatural life of the soul.*

God loves all of His creatures and wants to stay close to them. When any creature has the misfortune to sin mortally, that creature is no longer a friend of God. *Besides depriving the sinner of sanctifying grace, mortal sin makes the soul an enemy of God, takes away the merit of all its good actions, deprives it of the right to everlasting happiness in heaven, and makes it deserving of everlasting punishment in hell.* The fact that God punishes the sinner does not mean that He hates the sinner. It is true that He hates sin, but the sinner will always be His loved child.

Did you ever carry a heavy package for an older person? Surely you have given a seat to an older person on the bus. Such good acts are sometimes rewarded by a pat on the head, or even by a gift. These same acts done for the glory of God by persons in the state of grace, not only may receive an earthly reward, but also increase our store of treasures in heaven. Thus we receive merit for our good works.

But a person with mortal sin on his soul loses the merit of his good works. This is not restored to him until his mortal sins are forgiven.

Mortal sin also takes away the right to heaven. Through all the years of our lives we have been spurred on by the thought that one day we would see God. Surely this alone should be sufficient to keep us from serious sin because in hell we can never see God.

In order to commit a mortal sin, certain conditions must be present. The sin must be seriously evil; the sinner must realize the seriousness of the wrong he is doing, and he must give full consent to it.

Sometimes we think things are sinful when they are not actually so. If our conscience tells us that they are serious at the time we commit them, they are mortal sins for us even though we may find out later that such acts in themselves are not mortal sins. Giving full consent to a sin means realizing that an act is sinful and still giving in to it. Sometimes we make up our minds to do something seriously wrong, but for some reason or other we are prevented from doing it. In such cases we are actually guilty of mortal sin because our wills have chosen to commit sin.

Let us summarize: *To make a sin mortal these three things are necessary: first, the thought, desire, word, action, or omission must be seriously wrong or considered seriously wrong; second, the sinner must be mindful of the serious wrong; third, the sinner must fully consent to it.*

When Christ was hanging on the cross He forgave the Good Thief because he had shown he was sorry. We should acquire the habit of going to confession often so that we may go through life with a clear conscience and keep in God's grace. "Hail, O Cross, our only hope."

### 3. Venial Sin Is a Less Serious Actual Sin

*Venial sin is a less serious offense against the law of God, which does not deprive the soul of sanctifying grace, and which can be pardoned even without sacramental confession.*

Yet, when we commit venial sins, we are doing something so bad that there is only one worse evil — mortal sin. No matter how slight the offense, we have no excuse for offending God. Venial sin does not destroy our friendship with God, although it does lessen the warmth of our love for Him.

Sins may be venial if the acts themselves are only slightly wrong or if we think the acts are slightly wrong. When we disobey, or tell a lie we are ordinarily committing a venial sin. If we do something wrong thinking it is only a venial sin, it is usually only a venial sin. But, if we do not know it is a mortal sin because we are lazy or careless we may be more guilty than we realize. We must listen to the instructions given, and try to realize the seriousness of the circumstances so that we may form a correct conscience in regard to the sins we commit.

Briefly then, *a sin can be venial in two ways: first, when the evil done is not seriously wrong; second, when the evil done is seriously wrong, but the sinner sincerely believes it is only slightly wrong, or does not give full consent to it.*

Venial sin makes us think less often of the things of God and of the ways of serving Him. It keeps us from gaining the actual graces we need in order to overcome temptation. *Venial sin harms us by making us less fervent in the service of God, by weakening our power to resist mortal sin, and by making us deserving of God's punishments in this life or in purgatory.*

Since venial sins do not destroy our friendship with God we may be tempted to think that it does not matter whether we commit them. This would not be correct. Unless we are faithful in smaller things, we may soon sin in greater. Besides, we know that at times God has punished venial sin severely. He must, therefore, consider it a great evil.

Although we are not bound to confess our venial sins, it is well to do so. By going to confession regularly every two or three weeks, we keep ourselves very close to God. However, venial sin can be forgiven in many ways. One way is by an Act of Contrition. Expressing our sorrow for even our venial sins proves to God that we do not wish to stray from Him in even the slightest manner. Venial sin is also removed by Holy Communion, by an act of love, by works of mercy, and in other ways.

## 4. God Has Provided the Means Which Will Keep Us From Sin

We have said that this life is a journey to heaven. What are the things we need to do on this journey so that we may avoid sin and safely reach heaven, our goal? *We can keep from committing sin by praying and by receiving the sacraments; by remembering that God is always with us; by recalling that our bodies are temples of the Holy Ghost; by keeping occupied with work or play; by promptly resisting the sources of sin within us; by avoiding the near occasions of sin.*

What is meant by that phrase, "the near occasions of sin"? *The near occasions of sin are all persons, places, or things that may easily lead us into sin.*

Prayer is a very important means of reaching our goal. Even as small children we were taught to lift our minds and hearts to God often through the day. The graces obtained in this way keep us close to God. Through the sacraments we may receive more graces. Some travelers on the road of life do not know how to use the means God offers; others neglect to use them and thus have difficulty reaching heaven.

In serving God we should always have His interests in mind. That does not mean we have to be kneeling in prayer all the time. It simply means remembering that we are always in God's presence, and that no matter where we are or what we are doing He can see us, and we can praise Him. It means remembering we are temples of the Holy Ghost through the presence of sanctifying grace received at baptism.

## 5. The Chief Sources of Sin

In connection with the near occasions of sin we should know the chief sources of actual sin, called the capital sins. *The chief sources of actual sin are: pride, covetousness, lust, anger, gluttony, envy, and sloth, and these are commonly called capital sins. They are called capital sins, not because they, in themselves, are the greatest sins, but because they are the chief reasons why men commit sin.* The best way to overcome these bad habits, or vices, is to practice the virtue which is the opposite of each vice.

*Pride,* the first of these evils, may be said to be at the bottom of all sin. It means serving ourselves in preference to God. It was pride that tempted Eve in the Garden of Paradise for she could not bear to think anyone else was greater than she was. We can overcome pride by the practice of humility. This virtue helps us to see ourselves as we really are, and to realize that without God's help we can do nothing. Any success we have comes from God, and not from any power of our own.

*Covetousness* is an ugly vice. It means too great a desire for material things. The virtue of generosity, or giving, will help us to overcome a too-great desire for the things of this world.

*Lust* is a vice or bad habit of sinful acts or desires for forbidden pleasures of the body. We commit this sin when we give in to thoughts, desires, words, or actions, contrary to purity. Keeping ourselves pure and modest, and refusing to look at, read, listen to, desire, think, or do things which will be sources of temptation, help to overcome lust.

*Anger* can be a sin when it causes a person to wish great evil on another or to punish someone more than he deserves. Sometimes when a friend does things to us which we do not like, we become angry and wish for revenge. In other words we wish to "pay him back" or "get even." We should be careful, for anger is sometimes a sin. The practice of the virtue of meekness helps us to hold back our desire for revenge as well as our feelings of anger and displeasure. We should be encouraged in the practice of the virtue of meekness by our Lord's words, "Learn from me, for I am meek and humble of heart" (Mt. 11:29).

God has made His creatures in such a way that food and drink are necessary for our bodies if we are to grow, and to keep well and strong. But sometimes people get into the habit of eating and drinking too much. This excessive indulgence in eating and drinking is called *gluttony.* We can control this vice by the virtue of temperance, which means taking only a moderate amount of the things we like. If we deny ourselves some of the things we are permitted to have, it will not be so hard to keep from those which are forbidden.

*Envy* is the sin committed when we are jealous at the good fortune of others. Do you remember the story of David and Saul? David, a shepherd boy, killed the giant, Goliath, but King Saul, instead of being glad that David had killed an enemy, was jealous of the praise David received. This vice can be overcome by loving our neighbor, wishing him good luck, and rejoicing with him in his happiness.

*Sloth,* the last of the seven capital sins, is committed when we neglect the care of our souls through laziness. We can overcome this bad habit by doing our appointed tasks carefully and conscientiously, and by showing an interest in the things of God.

We mentioned before that the seven capital sins are not more serious than other sins, but that they are the chief reasons why men commit sin. Every person will find that he can trace most of his sins to one or the other of these seven capital sins. Find out your weak spot and set to work strengthening your defenses at this point.

## REVIEW, III–2

### WORD LIST

| | | | |
|---|---|---|---|
| omission | jealous | covetous | violated |
| sufficient | actual | sacramental | sloth |

### THINGS TO REMEMBER

1. Actual sin is a sin we commit ourselves.
2. The greatest evil in the world is mortal sin.
3. Venial sin makes our friendship with God less warm.
4. We must avoid the near occasions of sin, that is, the persons, places, and things which lead us to sin.

### THINGS TO DISCUSS AND DO

1. Name four things mortal sin does to the soul besides depriving it of sanctifying grace.
2. Discuss the three things necessary to make a sin mortal.
3. A sin can be venial in two ways. Name them.
4. Name as many ways as you can by which we can keep from committing sin.
5. Make a list of five near occasions of sin for boys and girls of your age. Discuss them with your classmates.
6. It is good for us to think about hell occasionally. Why?
7. After studying this lesson on sin what prayer should you remember to say every evening before going to bed. Why?
8. Does every sin deserve punishment? Explain.
9. Discuss each of the capital sins. Ask practical questions about them. For example: Do I look down on other boys and girls? Do I want everything I see? Do I go to bad movies?
10. What virtue is the direct opposite of each capital sin?

Study Catechism Lesson 6, *Actual Sin*, pp. 91–92.

**PART 1**

# CATECHISM

### LESSON 5

### Creation and the Fall of Man (Continued)

55. **Did Adam and Eve obey the commandment of God?**

Adam and Eve did not obey the commandment of God, but ate of the forbidden fruit.

56. **What happened to Adam and Eve on account of their sin?**

On account of their sin Adam and Eve lost sanctifying grace, the right to heaven, and their special gifts; they became subject to death, to suffering, and to a strong inclination to evil, and they were driven from the Garden of Paradise.

57. **What has happened to us on account of the sin of Adam?**

On account of the sin of Adam, we, his descendants, come into the world deprived of sanctifying grace and inherit his punishment, as we would have inherited his gifts had he been obedient to God.

58. **What is this sin in us called?**

This sin in us is called original sin.

59. **Why is this sin called original?**

This sin is called original because it comes down to us through our origin, or descent, from Adam.

60. **What are the chief punishments of Adam which we inherit through original sin?**

The chief punishments of Adam which we inherit through original sin are: death, suffering, ignorance, and a strong inclination to sin.

**89**

**61. Is God unjust in punishing us on account of the sin of Adam?**

God is not unjust in punishing us on account of the sin of Adam, because original sin does not take away from us anything to which we have a strict right as human beings, but only the free gifts which God in His goodness would have bestowed on us if Adam had not sinned.

**62. Was any human person ever preserved from original sin?**

The Blessed Virgin Mary was preserved from original sin in view of the merits of her divine Son; and this privilege is called her Immaculate Conception.

## OTHER QUESTIONS AND EXERCISES

1. Did God love Adam and Eve after their sin? Does He love us after we have sinned?
2. Why do we share in Adam's punishment?
3. What promise made at baptism should we think of when tempted to sin?
4. Which punishment of Adam do we suffer every day?
5. What should we think of, from this lesson, when our daily tasks seem hard to do?
6. How would you answer someone who said God is not just in punishing us for Adam's sin?
7. How would you explain to a non-Catholic friend what is meant by the Immaculate Conception?
8. When was the Immaculate Conception proclaimed a dogma of the Church?
9. If Adam and Eve had practiced two important virtues they might not have sinned. What are these virtues?

# CATECHISM

## PART 2

### LESSON 6

#### Actual Sin

63. **Is original sin the only kind of sin?**

    Original sin is not the only kind of sin; there is another kind, called actual sin, which we ourselves commit.

64. **What is actual sin?**

    Actual sin is any willful thought, desire, word, action, or omission forbidden by the law of God.

65. **How many kinds of actual sin are there?**

    There are two kinds of actual sin: mortal sin and venial sin.

66. **What is mortal sin?**

    Mortal sin is a grievous offense against the law of God.

67. **Why is this sin called mortal?**

    This sin is called mortal, or deadly, because it deprives the sinner of sanctifying grace, the supernatural life of the soul.

68. **Besides depriving the sinner of sanctifying grace, what else does mortal sin do to the soul?**

    Besides depriving the sinner of sanctifying grace, mortal sin makes the soul an enemy of God, takes away the merit of all its good actions, deprives it of the right to everlasting happiness in heaven, and makes it deserving of everlasting punishment in hell.

69. **What three things are necessary to make a sin mortal?**

    To make a sin mortal these three things are necessary:
    *first,* the thought, desire, word, action, or omission must be seriously wrong or considered seriously wrong;
    *second,* the sinner must be mindful of the serious wrong;
    *third,* the sinner must fully consent to it.

### 70. What is venial sin?

Venial sin is a less serious offense against the law of God, which does not deprive the soul of sanctifying grace, and which can be pardoned even without sacramental confession.

### 71. How can a sin be venial?

A sin can be venial in two ways:
> *first,* when the evil done is not seriously wrong;
> *second,* when the evil done is seriously wrong, but the sinner sincerely believes it is only slightly wrong, or does not give full consent to it.

### 72. How does venial sin harm us?

Venial sin harms us by making us less fervent in the service of God, by weakening our power to resist mortal sin, and by making us deserving of God's punishments in this life or in purgatory.

### 73. How can we keep from committing sin?

We can keep from committting sin by praying and by receiving the sacraments; by remembering that God is always with us; by recalling that our bodies are temples of the Holy Ghost; by keeping occupied with work or play; by promptly resisting the sources of sin within us; by avoiding the near occasions of sin.

### 74. What are the chief sources of actual sin?

The chief sources of actual sin are: pride, covetousness, lust, anger, gluttony, envy, and sloth, and these are commonly called capital sins.

### 75. Why are these called capital sins?

They are called capital sins, not because they, in themselves, are the greatest sins, but because they are the chief reasons why men commit sin.

### 76. What are the near occasions of sin?

The near occasions of sin are all persons, places, or things that may easily lead us into sin.

## OTHER QUESTIONS AND EXERCISES

1. Why should we try to receive as many graces as possible?
2. What should we do as soon as we realize we have committed a sin?
3. Where can we receive the strength to obey God's laws?
4. Will we receive a punishment for venial sins?
5. How can we atone for venial sins?
6. Why should we confess our venial sins?
7. Should we be just as sorry for our venial sins as for our mortal sins?
8. What is the worst thing that can happen to a person on this earth?
9. Why should we try to remain in the state of grace?
10. Why should we be faithful to our morning and night prayers?
11. What does the word mortal mean? Why is this a good name for this sin?
12. How many kinds of actual sin are there?
13. What is the supernatural life of the soul called?
14. Can venial sin be pardoned without sacramental confession?
15. What do we call persons, places, and things which may easily lead us to sin?
16. When any one of the three conditions for a mortal sin is not present, do we commit a mortal sin?
17. How can we protect ourselves against mortal sin?
18. Which of the chief sources of sin make us neglect our religious duties?
19. What source of sin makes us dislike people who have some things we would like to have?
20. Why is anger so dangerous?
21. Write your answers on a separate sheet of paper.

Actual sin is any willful  1 ,  2 ,  3 ,  4 , or  5
There are two kinds of actual sins:  6 , and  7  sin.
Mortal sin is a  8  offense against the law of God.
Venial sin is  9  serious offense against the law of God. It does not  10  the soul of  11  grace, and it can be  12  without sacramental  13
This sin is called mortal, or deadly, because it  14  the sinner of  15  grace, the  16  life of the soul.

Venial sin harms us by making us   17   fervent in the service of God, by weakening our power to resist   18  , and by making us deserving of   19   punishments in this life or in   20

Match the following on a separate paper.

1. a chief source of sin
2. actual sin
3. mortal sin
4. near occasion of sin
5. original sin
6. venial sin

(A) any willful thought, desire, word, action, or omission forbidden by the law of God
(B) a very great offense against the law of God
(C) pride
(D) a bad comic book or movie
(E) weakens our power to resist mortal sin
(F) deprives the soul of sanctifying grace
(G) makes us less fervent in God's service
(H) anger
(I) a playmate who uses sinful words
(J) takes away the merit of all good actions
(K) must be pardoned through sacramental confession

## Section Review

Now we should take a general review of Section I

*God, the Father Almighty, One in Three*

using the End of Unit Tests on pages 42, 67, 88. as a guide to locate the most important points.

## SECTION II

# God the Son, Our Redeemer

*I believe . . .*

**in Jesus Christ, His only Son, our Lord, who was conceived by the Holy Ghost, born of the Virgin Mary, suffered under Pontius Pilate, was crucified, died and was buried. He descended into hell, the third day He arose again from the dead. He ascended into heaven, sitteth at the right hand of God, the Father Almighty, from thence He shall come to judge the living and the dead.**

## Overview

In Section I we learned many things about God and His perfections and about the work of the first person of the Blessed Trinity, God the Father. Now in this Section we shall turn our minds to God the Son, how He became man, how He lived on earth, how He suffered and died for us and rose from the dead that we might gain eternal life.

# Unit IV. The Birth and Public Life of Christ

# Part 1.  God Prepared the World for the Coming of the Redeemer

### 1. God Promised a Redeemer

After the disobedience of Adam and Eve, man lost sanctifying grace, that is, friendship with God. As a result our first parents and all their descendants lost the right to everlasting happiness.

It would have been fair and just, if God had closed the gates of heaven forever, as He had done to the disobedient angels. He knew, however, man's weakness and the power of the devil. In His deep love and mercy, God promised to send a Redeemer whose blood would wash away the guilt of man's sin.

God's justice demanded that satisfaction for sin come from a human being because a human being had offended Him. The sin was a serious offense against the infinite God, and, so, in a certain sense, infinite. Therefore divine justice required infinite satisfaction. No created being could make such satisfaction because all creatures are finite. So God sent His only-begotten Son to be our Redeemer, God-made-man. As the Son of God He could offer infinite satisfaction; and as a human being He could offer the sacrifice for the human race.

### 2. God Made the World Wait for the Redeemer

We know that God has a reason for everything He does. He had reasons for making the world wait for the Redeemer. He permitted His creatures to suffer from the misery of sin because this suffering would help them to understand how much they needed a Redeemer. God also wished to show man how helpless he was without divine aid. In addition,

man was to realize the great dignity of God who has been offended. Besides this, God planned to prepare the world for the great event that was to come.

The people of the Old Testament awaited the Promised Redeemer; some, like the Chosen People, waited eagerly; others with more or less indifference. God repeatedly renewed the promise made to our first parents after their fall. He sent His prophets to the Hebrews, to remind them of the promise. During this time, many who believed in God's promises and followed their conscience in the love and service of the one true God were saved. Since the work of redemption was still to be accomplished, these souls remained in limbo, a place of waiting, where the souls of the just remained until Christ ascended into heaven.

### 3. God Used Certain Means in Preparing the World for the Promised Redeemer

Have you ever gone with your father on an early morning fishing trip? Perhaps it was still dark as you settled in your boat hoping for a good catch of fish. While you waited for the first nibble on your line you probably noticed that the night sky seemed to fade away as if in preparation for the first faint streaks of light. Little by little these rays broadened until suddenly before your eyes the sun burst forth, a golden ball, shedding its bright rays over the awakening earth.

We can compare the darkness of the night sky to the misery and sin brought into the world by our first parents. Just as the first streaks of dawn announce the light of day, so the promises contained in the prophecies about the Redeemer prepared for His actual coming. We can trace these promises in the Old Testament through the history of the Chosen People.

All through history the Hebrews were made to feel, more or less strongly, the need of a Redeemer. To keep them mindful of this need, God frequently repeated His promise to send a Redeemer. He gave Adam this promise in the Garden of Eden. After God had tested Abraham's faith He renewed the promise. Again God repeated His promise to David. The repetition of this promise to His Chosen People was one way in which God prepared the world for the coming of His Son.

God also prepared the world for the Redeemer by raising up many prophets who continually reminded the people of these promises. They also foretold many things about Christ.

As the time approached for the coming of the Saviour, the air seemed to be filled with expectancy.

In addition to prophecies, God used types and figures to foreshadow the coming of Christ. A type or a figure of Christ was any person or thing which helped the people to understand what the Redeemer would be like. For example, Adam, the father of the human race, is a figure of Christ, the Father of the Redeemed race. Noah's building of the Ark to save the members of his family from the deluge is a type of Christ's founding the Church to save all men. The Paschal Lamb, the victim of sacrifice in the Old Law, is a figure of Christ, the Lamb of God who is the victim of sacrifice in the New Law. The manna, provided by God as food for the Chosen People while they were wandering in the desert, prefigured Christ in the Holy Eucharist in which He supplies us spiritual food for the journey through life.

God used the prophecies to keep alive the faith and hope of His people and to render them ever mindful of His love. He enlightened the leaders of the Chosen Race so that they could better explain the meaning of these prophecies. Their instructions were a source of great comfort to the people who awaited the Saviour. The promise of a Redeemer encouraged men to keep faithful to the one true God. Thus we see that *God did not abandon man after Adam fell into sin, but promised to send into the world a Saviour to free man from his sins and to reopen to him the gates of heaven.*

## REVIEW, IV–1

**WORD LIST**

| begotten | Redeemer | foretold | dignity |
| satisfaction | Redemption | type | prefigured |
| excluded | fulfillment | prediction | expectancy |
| figure | renewed | redeem | anticipation |

## THINGS TO REMEMBER

1. Original sin destroyed the friendship between God and man.
2. This infinite injury caused by original sin demanded infinite satisfaction.
3. The long wait between the fall of man and the Redemption taught man the wickedness of sin, the dignity of God, and the need of a Redeemer.
4. God prepared the world for the coming of the Redeemer by means of prophetic words and signs concerning the birth, public life, death, resurrection, and ascension of Christ.
5. God made use of persons and things to prefigure the Redeemer.

## THINGS TO DISCUSS AND DO

1. Prepare a talk on one of the following Old Testament characters showing how he reminds us of the Redeemer: Adam, Noah, Abraham, Moses, Jonas.
2. Pretend that you were one of the Israelites. Write a letter to a Gentile friend, telling him about the manna in the desert.
3. Explain the statement: "The greater the dignity of the person offended, the greater becomes the injury."
4. Prepare a skit to express your idea of how our first parents felt when they were expelled from Paradise.
5. To whom was the Redeemer first promised?
6. To whom was the promise of the Redeemer repeated?
7. Explain how it was just for God to send the good people of the Old Testament to Limbo.
8. Why could not Noah or Abraham have offered themselves in satisfaction for the sin of Adam?
9. How could the people who lived before the Redeemer be saved?

Study Catechism Lesson 7, *The Incarnation*, Question 77, p. 122.

# Part 2. God Sent His Divine Son as the Promised Redeemer

Did anyone ever promise you a special present several months before your birthday? You were probably so anxious to get it that the period of waiting seemed endless. The closer the day, the more excited you became.

This anxious waiting resembles the expectancy of the Jewish people before the birth of Christ. God had promised Adam and Eve a Redeemer. The exact time the promise was to be fulfilled was left uncertain. God waited thousands of years before sending His beloved Son because He wanted to prepare the world to receive its Redeemer. The prophecies indicated that the time was finally at hand.

## 1. The Incarnation Was the Beginning of the Fulfillment of God's Promise

At last God the Father decided that the world was ready. He sent the Redeemer, the Saviour of the human race. Who was this Saviour of all men? *The Saviour of all men is Jesus Christ.* Who is Jesus Christ? He is the divine Son, made man, that is the second Person of the Blessed Trinity in human flesh. He is the God-man: God-made-man. Indeed, *the chief teaching of the Catholic Church about Jesus Christ is that He is God made man.* The Son of God was always God. But *the Son of God was not always man, but became man at the time of the Incarnation.* Let us make an act of faith in Him: "Jesus, Son of the living God, have mercy on us."

God chose Mary, a spotless, humble girl of Nazareth, for the great privilege of being the Mother of Christ, that is, the Mother of the God made man. How did God bring this about? By the power of the Holy Spirit the Son of God began His earthly life as man beneath the most pure heart of Mary.

Another way of expressing this truth is as follows: *The Son of God was conceived and made man by the power of the Holy Ghost in the womb of the Blessed Virgin Mary.* We call this the Incarnation. *By the Incarnation is meant that the Son of God, retaining His divine nature, took to Himself a human nature, that is, a body and soul like ours.*

Let us never forget what St. Louis-Marie de Montfort said: "It was through Mary that Jesus Christ came to us and it is through her that we must go to Him."

### The Visit of the Angel

Let us recall the story of the visit of the Archangel Gabriel to Mary. It was during this visit that the Incarnation took place.

If you had been in Mary's place how surprised you would have been at the sight of the heavenly visitor. However, as soon as she learned the reason for this unusual visit, Mary's fear disappeared, and she was willing to do whatever God asked of her. We know that this was so from her answer to the Archangel Gabriel: "Behold, the handmaid of the Lord; be it done unto me according to Thy word." At these words the Son of God became man.

The Church commemorates the visit of the angel to Mary on a special day, Annunciation Day. The word "annunciation" comes from the verb "announce," which means "tell" or "make known." While we celebrate the birthday of Christ on Christmas Day, let us not forget that *the Son of God was conceived and made man on Annunciation Day, the day on which the Angel Gabriel announced to the Blessed Virgin Mary that she was to be the Mother of God.* The feast of the Annunciation is March 25. This is a feast we should celebrate with gratitude and deep devotion.

## Titles of the Redeemer

Our Blessed Redeemer, who began to live in this world at the moment of the Incarnation is known by several names. We call Him "Jesus" which means Saviour. We also call Him "Christ," which means "anointed one." The Hebrew word for "anointed one" is "Messias."

Another title given to Jesus is "our Lord." We call Him our Lord because He is our ruler, both as God and as man. When we think of the human nature of Christ, that is, His birth in Bethlehem and His early life with Mary and Joseph, it is easier to ask God for favors, and to beg His forgiveness. The fact that Jesus Christ is man as well as God helps to bring us closer to Him.

## Two Natures in Christ — One Person

*Jesus Christ has two natures: the nature of God and the nature of man.* That is, He is divine and also human. He has a divine nature and a human nature. This mystery, like that of the Blessed Trinity, we accept by faith. Each nature is perfect. Our Lord is both God and man.

Although our Lord has two natures is He two persons? *No. Jesus Christ is only one Person; and that Person is the second Person of the Blessed Trinity.*

*Jesus Christ is God because He is the only Son of God, having the same divine nature as His Father.* As God, Jesus has the greatest and highest nature possible. He has every perfection in an infinite degree. Mention some of the perfections of God. Sometimes we think of these divine perfections as belonging only to the Father, but they belong equally to God the Son and to the Holy Spirit. The miracles of Christ show His divinity because He performed them by His divine nature. He showed His divine power when He said to the daughter of Jairus, "Girl, I say to thee arise" (Mk. 5:41). The miracles are a proof that Christ is the Son of God, because only God can work a miracle.

But Jesus Christ is also man. *Jesus Christ is man because He is the Son of the Blessed Virgin Mary and has a body and soul like ours.* As man, Christ is like us in everything except sin. He had a human body which needed food and rest. He also had a human soul, with an intellect or mind, and a human will. The Son of God made man did all the things we read about in the Gospels. These records of Christ's birth, of His manner of living, His conversations, and the human sympathy He so often showed, give proofs of His humanity.

So again we can say that *Jesus Christ has two natures:*

*the nature of God and the nature of man.* Each of these natures is whole and entire. The nature of God, or the divine nature, Christ has from His heavenly Father from eternity. Through this divine nature He forgave sins and brought the dead to life. The Son of God was not always incarnate, but became man at the time of the Incarnation when He received His human nature through Mary, His earthly mother.

Christ did not lose His divine nature when He took up a human nature, but He did hide His divine nature His childhood actions did not appear much different from those of any other Jewish boy of the time.

Christ knew that many of the people would doubt that He was God. They might agree that He was a very unusual child and man, but not have faith in Him as God. Christ also knew that He could win many more souls for His Father's kingdom by coming into this world as a tiny infant whom all men could love if they would. He chose, therefore, to be born in poverty and simplicity.

## 2. Mary and Joseph Prepared for the Coming of Christ

At the time when Christ was born, unmarried people were a disgrace to the nation. Furthermore, it was looked on as a curse to be married and not have children. Mary, although she knew that she would be criticized, had promised to remain a virgin. This promise meant that she, of her own free will, gave up the privilege of ever becoming a mother. She observed, however, one custom of the time and betrothed herself, that is, promised herself in marriage to Joseph, a descendant of the royal house of David. This ceremony bound Mary to Joseph for life. It was during the time of betrothal that the angel appeared to Mary. Mary gave her consent to become the Mother of God after the angel had explained to her how this would be done without loss of her virginity.

Sometime later, an angel informed Joseph, who also had taken a vow of virginity, that Mary was to become the Mother of God through the power of the Holy Spirit. As the spouse and the protector of Mary, Joseph accepted the guardianship of the Christ Child thus becoming His foster father. *Jesus Christ had no human father, but St. Joseph was the spouse of the Blessed Virgin Mary and the guardian, or foster father, of Christ.*

"O St. Joseph, foster father of our Lord Jesus Christ and true spouse of Mary, the Virgin, pray for us."

### John's Mother and Mary

The angel, at the Annunciation, told Mary that her cousin Elizabeth was to have a son. Mary decided to visit Elizabeth and set out for the hill country of Judea. As she approached the doorway of Elizabeth's home her cousin greeted her with great happiness. Filled with the Holy Ghost, Elizabeth spoke the beautiful words, "And how have I deserved that the Mother of my Lord should come to me?" (Lk. 1:43.) At this moment John the Baptist, whom Elizabeth was carrying beneath her heart, was cleansed from original sin by Christ resting beneath Mary's Immaculate Heart.

The Eastern people chanted hymns at times of great joy or sorrow. Mary was so overjoyed by what had happened that her heart sang out the beautiful words of the "Magnificat" (Lk. 1:46–55). Let us read it from the New Testament trying to realize the meaning of the words.

Mary, the most perfect of all creatures, was humble. She gave praise to God for honoring her. How much more should we remember that everything we have, all the graces we have received, all the good things we can do, all come from God. Of ourselves, we have nothing, of ourselves we can desire nothing and without God's divine Providence, and His loving assistance, we could not accomplish anything. In thanksgiving for all these favors, and knowing our dependence on God, let us often repeat this prayer: "Lord, I am nothing, but, although nothing, I adore thee."

After visiting Elizabeth, Mary went back to Nazareth. She and Joseph spent their time preparing for the coming of the Promised Redeemer. Imagine Mary getting the baby clothes ready for Him, perhaps spinning and weaving things for Him to wear. Picture Joseph in the carpenter shop, perhaps making a little crib so that the divine Infant would be comfortable.

Caesar Augustus interrupted these preparations. Anxious to know the number of people over whom he ruled, Caesar Augustus ordered a census. When a census is taken today, census takers go from door to door to get their information. In the time of Caesar Augustus the people went to be enrolled in the cities of their ancestors. Thus Joseph had to go to Bethlehem because he was of the house of David, and Bethlehem was David's town.

The trip to Bethlehem at that time meant several days' journey on foot. Because Joseph and Mary knew that this journey was God's will for them, they did not complain about it. They accepted Caesar's command and obeyed it humbly and willingly.

Many times God's will is made known to us through the commands of our superiors. Who are our superiors? Name some ways in which we can serve God by obeying our country's commands. Are you cheerful when you are asked to obey some law you consider difficult to observe?

### 3. Events Surrounding the Birth of Christ

Mary and Joseph fulfilled many prophecies which foretold the coming of Christ when they carried out the decree of Caesar Augustus. You remember the story of the journey to Bethlehem and how they could find no shelter there.

You can picture the stable on the hillside in which the infinite, eternal, all-knowing, all-wise, Son of God came into this world in human form. The angels sang the beautiful hymn of praise and glory, "Glory to God in the highest."

The shepherds who were watching their flocks on the hillside heard these words. As the angels' message was made clear to them, the shepherds hastened to see the wonder which the angels announced. They hurried over to Bethlehem repeating in their hearts the song of the angels. This joyful song is part of the Mass and it takes us back in spirit to the little stable, on the hillside where *Christ was born of the Blessed Virgin Mary on Christmas Day, in Bethlehem, more than nineteen hundred years ago.*

## REVIEW, IV–2

**WORD LIST**

| | | |
|---|---|---|
| Incarnation | human nature | divine nature |
| reparation | infinite satisfaction | |

**THINGS TO REMEMBER**

1. Christ is the Promised Redeemer.
2. The Incarnation means God the Son was made man.
3. God retained His divine nature as Son of God when He became the Son of the Blessed Virgin Mary.
4. God intended the Blessed Virgin Mary to be the Mother of Jesus from all eternity.

5. Mary teaches us how to co-operate with God's grace.
6. The feast of the Annunciation, March 25, commemorates the message of the Archangel Gabriel to Mary.
7. Jesus is only one Person although He has two natures.
8. All men are brothers of Christ: We must respect others' rights.
9. Mary and Joseph give us the example of respect and obedience to divine and civil authority.

## THINGS TO DISCUSS AND DO

1. Explain how we live our Faith in the doctrines we are learning in this unit by joining with the Church during Advent and at Christmas.
2. Learn the names of the four great empires which existed before the birth of Christ. What part did they play in God's preparation of the world for the Saviour?
3. Look up the story of the birth of Christ in the New Testament. Which Evangelist tells us most about it?
4. Make an acrostic using the word Bethlehem.
5. Make a chart listing some incidents in the life of Christ. Indicate whether they reveal His human nature or His divine nature.
6. Write a conversation which might have taken place between Mary and Joseph on the way to Bethlehem.
7. Illustrate the visit of Gabriel to Mary.
8. How would you answer a non-Catholic friend who said that Mary is not the Mother of God?
9. Who were the first to adore the infant Christ?
10. Why did God so often remind the Chosen People of His promise?
11. Which of the three Persons of the Blessed Trinity became man?
12. Why do you think Christ chose to be born in Bethlehem?
13. What does the name "Jesus" mean?
14. What does the name "Christ" mean?
15. What is the second article of the Apostles' Creed?
16. As man, in what way is Christ unlike us?
17. How do the wine and the water at Mass represent the two natures of Christ?

Study Catechism Lesson 7, *The Incarnation*, Questions 78–89, on pp. 122–124.

# Part 3.  The Early Life of Christ

### 1. Jesus Is Circumcised

Let us recall how Jesus received His name. Among the Jews, at the circumcision ceremony the father of the family named the child. This took place eight days after the birth of a child. The feast of the Circumcision is on January 1. We celebrate this day as a holyday of obligation.

God the Father chose the name "Jesus," which means Saviour, for His Son. In this way God made known to the world that the work of His Son was to be the saving of mankind from the cruel slavery of sin.

This name of Jesus is so sacred that the Church has set aside a special day, usually January 2, to honor the Holy Name. We show our deep respect and reverence for this name by calling on Jesus often to help us. Since He so faithfully lived up to His name and proved Himself a Saviour we can ask Christ to help us to live up to our name of Christian. Should we celebrate these two feasts with great devotion this year?

"Blessed be the most holy Name of Jesus without end."

## 2. The Presentation in the Temple

The next event in the life of Christ was the Presentation. Under the Law of Moses first-born sons were consecrated to the Lord and had to be bought back at a set price. This was to be done on the fortieth day after Christ was born. On this occasion, the Law also required a ceremony of purification for the mother. She was to bring an offering of a lamb and a dove or, in the case of the poor, two doves.

Think about Mary and Joseph with the Child entering the Temple. They did not look any different from any other young couple bringing their baby to be presented to the Lord. But to two people in the Temple, they were different. The Holy Spirit had revealed to Simeon that he would not die before he saw the Child who was to redeem the world. The Holy Spirit directed Simeon to the Temple on this day. As Joseph and Mary approached the Temple, Simeon realized who was entering. Taking the Child in his arms and filled with deep love of God Simeon recited a beautiful prayer of thanksgiving that he had lived to see the Redeemer.

"Now thou dost dismiss thy servant, O Lord, according to thy word in peace: Because my eyes have seen thy salvation, which thou hast prepared before the face of all peoples: a light of revelation to the gentiles, and a glory for thy people Israel."

Simeon, after he had said this wonderful prayer, turned to Mary and prophesied that a sword of sorrow would one day pierce her heart. He was trying to tell her that she would be united with Christ in saving the world, by suffering with Him.

Simeon had the privilege of holding the Christ Child in his arms. But this same Christ lives in our souls through sanctifying grace. We receive the same Christ in Holy Communion. Are we as fervent after Communion as Simeon was when he held Christ?

A prophetess, Anna, also happened to be in the Temple at the time when the Holy Family entered. She, too, realized who this Child was, and leaving the Temple, she spoke about Him to all who were awaiting the coming of the Redeemer.

Just as Anna, the prophetess, drew attention to Christ, so also our good conduct leads other people to follow Christ, our Friend and Leader. We can take Anna for our example and pray often to Christ that the entire world may accept Him. "Sacred Heart of Jesus, Thy Kingdom Come." We celebrate the Presentation and the feast of the Purification on February 2, Candlemas Day.

### 3. The Magi Visit Jesus

The angels announced the birth of Christ to the Jews through the shepherds, but a star, as had been prophesied, announced Christ's birth to the rest of the world. The people of the Orient knew of the prophecy. When the Magi, or Wise Men, saw the star they set out to find the new King of the Jews. The star led them to Jerusalem, and here King Herod questioned them. He was afraid that this newborn

King would take his throne. Herod told the Magi to go to Bethlehem and come back to tell him where they had found the newborn King of the Jews.

Since it was a king they were visiting the Magi brought gifts worthy of a king: gold, frankincense, and myrrh. After offering their gifts and adoring the Child the Magi returned to their own country, without going back to Jerusalem to see Herod. They had been warned by God that the wicked King planned to harm the Child.

## 4. A Wicked King Is Surprised

When the Magi did not return to Jerusalem to report about the King they had visited, Herod realized they had outwitted him. He, therefore, ordered all baby boys under two years of age in Bethlehem and the surrounding country to be put to death. He thought in this way he would surely manage to kill the Child who threatened his throne. But before Herod's soldiers could harm the Holy Family, an angel appeared to Joseph and told him to flee to Egypt with Jesus and Mary. Joseph did not question the angel. Without a word of complaint he, Mary, and Jesus set out for Egypt over the desert sands.

After some time in Egypt, an angel again appeared to Joseph and told him to take the Child and His mother back to the land of Israel, because Herod was dead.

Are we jealous and afraid of rivals as Herod was? Do we obey the command of God as willingly as Joseph? Especially when we think the commands are difficult, do we still obey?

"Joseph most obedient, pray for us."

## 5. The Holy Family Is a Model of Obedience

We have seen how the parents of Jesus obeyed the Law

of Moses in presenting the Child Jesus in the Temple. Twelve years later Mary and Joseph gave another example of their obedience to this law when they took Jesus to Jerusalem to celebrate the feast of the Pasch. Jesus would not have had to attend this feast until He was thirteen years old. Respect for the Law prompted the Holy Family to attend. For eight days they took part in the services. Then, when the celebration was over, they started for home. They traveled in a large caravan. At the end of the day, as they arrived at the stopping place for the night, both Mary and Joseph looked for Jesus. When they did not find Him they returned to Jerusalem to search for Him.

On the third day they found Jesus in the Temple amid a group of doctors, amazing them with His understanding and His questions. When Mary questioned Him about His delay in returning home, He answered with that question we all remember. "Did you not know that I must be about My Father's business?" At their command, Jesus went home with His parents, and, as the Gospel says, "He was subject to them."

How does this incident in the life of Christ apply to us? Like Jesus we must be willing to fulfill God's laws of prayer and worship. We must be willing to do God's will at all times. Especially we must be obedient to our parents and do all in our power to make our own family life happy. Celebrating the Feast of the Holy Family properly will help us in this.

## REVIEW, IV–3

### WORD LIST

| | | | |
|---|---|---|---|
| Circumcision | prophetess | solitary | personality |
| Presentation | Orient | purification | |

## THINGS TO REMEMBER

1. The word "Jesus" means Saviour.
2. Christ always did His Father's will.
3. The experience of Simeon and Anna on seeing the Saviour teaches us the reward of earnest prayer.
4. The Holy Family at Nazareth is the model of the Christian home.

## THINGS TO DISCUSS AND DO

1. List ways in which the example of the Child Jesus helps us to do the will of God.
2. Write a paragraph on the Nativity story as it might be told by the shepherds, or the innkeeper.
3. Draw two pictures: (a) the Magi offering gold, frankincense, and myrrh; (b) boys and girls offering their prayers, good deeds, and sufferings to the Infant.
4. Dramatize the Presentation, with Simeon and Anna.
5. Tell how to baptize in case of necessity.
6. Explain: Christ led a hidden life at Nazareth.
7. Examine the liturgy of the Christmas season and find out how we can and should re-live the life of Christ with the Church.
8. What were the duties of each member of the Holy Family; of your family?

# Part 4. Christ's Public Life

The hidden life of Jesus came to an end at the marriage feast of Cana. We are now going to begin a very brief outline of the public life of Christ.

## 1. The Preparation for the Public Life of Christ

What are some of the things we remember about John the Baptist, who was Jesus' cousin? During Jesus' hidden life, John lived alone in the desert. He spent much of his time in prayer and penance, making himself ready for his great work of preparing the people to receive the Redeemer.

One day a group of men from Galilee who had heard of John's work came to the Jordan to be baptized. Among them was Jesus. As John caught sight of Jesus the Holy Spirit made known to him that He was the Messias. At first John refused to baptize Jesus, because he felt unworthy. Jesus, however, commanded him to do it. While Jesus was coming out of the water after the baptism, the heavens opened and the Holy Spirit came down upon Him in the form of a dove. The voice of the Father said, "This is my beloved Son, in whom I am well pleased" (Lk. 3:22).

## The Devil Tries to Tempt Jesus

After His baptism Christ went into the desert where He spent forty days and nights praying and fasting, in preparation for His public life. During this time the devil tempted Him three times but Jesus quickly and firmly resisted his attacks. The devil then left Jesus and angels came and ministered to Him.

Jesus allowed Himself to be tempted to show us that we cannot expect to go through life without temptations. Although temptations in themselves are not sinful, we must resist them as strongly as Christ did. We, therefore, should receive the sacraments often in order to obtain God's grace; they are our greatest weapons against temptations.

## Jesus Begins to Choose His Disciples

Jesus now returned to the region around the Jordan River. The time had come for John to announce who Jesus was. John was speaking to two of his disciples when he saw Jesus coming toward him. How did he let the two disciples know that this man was Jesus? He used the words, "Behold the Lamb of God" so that these two disciples would realize that here was no ordinary man. The priest repeats these words in every Holy Mass.

The disciples were so overcome by the personality and power of Jesus that they left John and followed Christ. Andrew especially was so happy that he could not keep his joy to himself and hastened to tell his brother Simon. Simon at once went to Jesus.

Jesus returned to Galilee with His disciples. In time He attracted other men, among them Philip and Nathaniel. To answer Christ's call some, like the fishermen James and John, the sons of Zebedee, left their boats and all their possessions. As other Apostles joined the little band, it grew to be twelve. Most of them were very ordinary men. But they loved Christ so much that they were willing to leave everything to follow Him. With such men Christ could do much.

## 2. The Beginning of the Public Life

The public life of Christ began at the marriage feast of Cana where He performed His first miracle. After it, He went to Jerusalem for the Passover and then returned to Galilee where most of His public life was spent, especially at Capharnaum.

He preached His Gospel to the people, beginning with the famous Sermon on the Mount which opened with the Eight Beatitudes. He worked miracles, including the raising of more than one person to life, and showed divine power over all the forces of nature. He lived a life of perfect virtue.

## 3. The Envy of the Jewish Leaders

During His public life Christ traveled far and wide in the Holy Land: in Judea, in Samaria, and particularly in Galilee. He preached and did good wherever He went.

Our Lord quickly became very popular among the people, and this caused the leaders of the Jews to be envious of Him and to oppose Him. In spite of this Christ went on preaching, using many parables, to reveal, and at the same time partly to conceal His meaning. As He was preaching and performing His miracles, the prophecies concerning Him were being fulfilled in His person and in His actions.

In addition He Himself made prophecies, for instance concerning the Holy Eucharist, when He multiplied the loaves and the fishes; and about His own death, which He prophesied three times, His resurrection from the dead, and the establishment of His kingdom on earth — the Church.

## 4. Revealing Himself as the Promised Redeemer

In all this our Lord was revealing Himself as the Redeemer promised by God to our first parents. His preaching was such that He left room for faith in those who heard and saw Him, so that He might reward them if they freely turned to Him.

After three years of preaching, teaching, and working miracles the time had arrived for our Lord to offer to God the Father that great sacrifice of Himself for which He had come to earth. We shall study this in the next unit.

### REVIEW, IV–4

**WORD LIST**

| | | |
|---|---|---|
| preparation | Galileans | hidden life |
| solitary | Messias | public life |
| penance | descended | resisted |
| resist | Passover | ordinary |
| ministry | prophecies | establishment |
| disciples | personality | |

## THINGS TO REMEMBER

1. Christ was baptized by His cousin John in the Jordan River.
2. The three Persons of the Blessed Trinity were sensibly present at the baptism of Christ.
3. Christ set us an example in the way He overcame temptation.
4. Christ chose simple men as His helpers.
5. Christ lived all the things He preached.

## THINGS TO DISCUSS AND DO

1. Did Jesus and John prepare for their work in the same way? Explain your answer telling what the work of each was.
2. What could you imitate in the life of St. John?
3. When the devil tempts you, do you act as our Lord did?
4. At what part of the Mass does the priest use the words of St. John? What do they mean? Why is the word "Lamb" used?
5. Does Christ call us as He called the Apostles?
6. What is the one virtue we need more than all others in order to follow Jesus?
7. Look up the Sermon on the Mount in the Bible. Tell why it could be called a lesson in good conduct.
8. The text mentions that Christ's preaching left room for faith. What does this mean?
9. Say a prayer every day that you may learn what God wants you to do and will prepare yourself for your lifework as Christ did.
10. Write a letter to a friend explaining one of Christ's parables or miracles.

# End-of-Unit Review — Unit IV

**PART 1**

## CATECHISM

### LESSON 7

#### The Incarnation

77. Did God abandon man after Adam fell into sin?

God did not abandon man after Adam fell into sin, but promised to send into the world a Saviour to free man from his sins and to reopen to him the gates of heaven.

## OTHER QUESTIONS AND EXERCISES

1. Tell in your own words why God did not punish man's disobedience as He punished that of the angels.
2. Why was it possible for Jesus Christ to offer satisfaction to God and at the same time offer it for the human race?
3. Why did God wait so long before sending the Redeemer?
4. What did the people of the Old Testament have to do in order to be saved?
5. Why did God remind the people often of the promise of a Redeemer?

**PART 2**

## CATECHISM

### LESSON 7

#### The Incarnation (Cont.)

78. Who is the Saviour of all men?

The Saviour of all men is Jesus Christ.

**79. What is the chief teaching of the Catholic Church about Jesus Christ?**

The chief teaching of the Catholic Church about Jesus Christ is that He is God made man.

**80. Why is Jesus Christ God?**

Jesus Christ is God because He is the only Son of God, having the same divine nature as His Father.

**81. Why is Jesus Christ man?**

Jesus Christ is man because He is the Son of the Blessed Virgin Mary and has a body and soul like ours.

**82. Is Jesus Christ more than one Person?**

No, Jesus Christ is only one Person; and that Person is the second Person of the Blessed Trinity.

**83. How many natures has Jesus Christ?**

Jesus Christ has two natures: the nature of God and the nature of man.

**84. Was the Son of God always man?**

The Son of God was not always man, but became man at the time of the Incarnation.

**85. What is meant by the Incarnation?**

By the Incarnation is meant that the Son of God, retaining His divine nature, took to Himself a human nature, that is, a body and soul like ours.

**86. How was the Son of God made man?**

The Son of God was conceived and made man by the power of the Holy Ghost in the womb of the Blessed Virgin Mary.

**87. When was the Son of God conceived and made man?**

The Son of God was conceived and made man on Annunciation Day, the day on which the Angel Gabriel announced to the Blessed Virgin Mary that she was to be the Mother of God.

**123**

**88. Is St. Joseph the father of Jesus Christ?**

Jesus Christ had no human father, but St. Joseph was the spouse of the Blessed Virgin Mary and the guardian, or foster father, of Christ.

**89. When was Christ born?**

Christ was born of the Blessed Virgin Mary on Christmas Day, in Bethlehem, more than nineteen hundred years ago.

## OTHER QUESTIONS AND EXERCISES

1. On what day did the angel announce to Mary that she was to be the Mother of God?
2. Who is the promised Redeemer?
3. How many natures has Christ?
4. What word means "God became man"?
5. Was Jesus the Son of God after He became the Son of Mary?
6. In what city was Jesus born?
7. Who is the foster father of Christ?
8. What is the name of the hymn which Mary chanted when she went to visit Elizabeth?
9. Name three virtues Mary practiced when the angel gave her the message, or when Christ was born. Tell how she practiced them.
10. What is the name of the angel who told Mary that she was to be God's Mother?
11. How many Persons are there in God?
12. What is the nature of God called?
13. In what particular way is Jesus different from us?
14. From what royal family was Joseph descended?
15. How do Mary and Joseph teach us to respect our country's laws?

## PART 3

## QUESTIONS AND EXERCISES

1. What does the name Jesus mean?
2. What do we call the ceremony at which the Hebrew fathers in the Old Testament named their sons?

3. What ceremony took place forty days after Christ's birth?
4. What other ceremony took place at the Presentation?
5. In what ways can we imitate the example of Simeon and Anna?
6. What are the three worshipers from the east called?
7. What lessons can we learn from the incident in the temple when Christ was twelve?
8. How did Jesus prepare for His great work?
9. How can we imitate Christ's example in preparing for our work in life?

## PART 4

### QUESTIONS AND EXERCISES

1. How did Christ redeem us?
2. What kind of men did Jesus choose as leaders of His Church?
3. When did Christ's hidden life come to an end?
4. Who baptized Jesus? Where?
5. What happened at the baptism of Jesus?
6. How did the devil tempt Jesus?
7. Why did Jesus suffer these temptations?
8. What is our greatest help in time of temptation?
9. Where was most of Christ's public life spent?
10. What was Christ's method of teaching?
11. What are some prophecies which Christ made?
12. What virtue did Christ particularly require of men in His preaching?
13. Name some prophecies which Christ fulfilled.

# Unit V.  Christ Redeems Us by His Passion, Death, and Resurrection

"Jesus Christ . . . suffered under Pontius Pilate, was crucified, died, and was buried."

# Part 1. The Redemption

## 1. Our Redemption by Christ Means Salvation

God the Son did not have to take our human nature and save us. Man had sinned through his own weakness and malice and not because God had neglected him. But God saw the misery sin had brought into the world and was merciful to fallen man. It was His love for us that made Christ, of His own free will, offer Himself to the eternal Father as the victim to atone, or make up, for man's sinfulness. This offering of Himself by Christ to God is the Redemption. *By the Redemption is meant that Jesus Christ, as the Redeemer of the whole human race, offered His sufferings and death to God as a fitting sacrifice in satisfaction for the sins of men, and regained for them the right to be children of God and heirs of heaven.*

> "Hail precious blood flowing from the wounds of our crucified Lord Jesus Christ and washing away the sins of the whole world."

Thus Christ's sacrifice is the cause of our salvation. The Passion of our Lord was the highest and most perfect act of His life. This voluntary offering of His sufferings and death fully paid the debt that mankind owed to God for sin. The payment of this debt meant the difference between heaven and hell for us. If Christ had not suffered, heaven could never be ours.

But did Christ need to suffer as much as He did? Even though the debt was so great, Christ could have paid it by shedding only one tear or one drop of blood. This is told very well in the beautiful hymn of St. Thomas Aquinas in honor of the Blessed Sacrament: *"Adoro Te Devote."* We

**127**

ought to spend some time thinking over the words of this verse:

> O Loving Pelican! O Jesus, Lord!
> Unclean I am, but cleanse me in Thy Blood;
> Of which a single drop, for sinners spilt,
> Is ransom for a world's entire guilt.

Since every act of Christ had infinite value why did He have to suffer so much? Our Lord suffered as much as He did for several reasons. First, Christ wanted to show us what a terrible evil sin is, and how necessary it is for us to avoid it. Second, He wanted to teach us His way of living, that is, carrying on bravely in the trials of life. He is our model in every type of suffering. Third, He wanted to show us His infinite love.

As we follow our Lord step by step, the truth will become clearer to us. Christ's example not only teaches us the value of willing service of God, but also that the sorrow which we must bear from time to time can easily be made to atone for temporal punishment due to our sins. Suffering borne for Christ can have untold value.

## 2. The Redemption by Christ Fulfills God's Promise

Christ, in His last days on earth, fulfilled God's promise to give mankind a chance to regain heaven. Following the story of Christ and His disciples in the Gospels brings you close to His sufferings. If you do not have a Bible, a Lenten Missal contains the whole story of the Passion. Although you know much of this story, it will be good for you to review the events of our Lord's last days on earth. These events are one part of the great act of Redemption, one of the chief truths mentioned in the Creed.

## The First Palm Sunday

Did you ever stop to think that the most sorrowful and solemn of all the weeks of the year, Holy Week, begins joyfully? There is a note of joy in the ceremony of the palms on Palm Sunday. "Hosanna!" the Church sings. Did this ever strike you as strange?

Christ accepted the honor paid Him by the people on Palm Sunday as a tribute to His divinity. At the same time He knew that according to the prophecy these same people would cry for His blood before the end of the week. This quick change of heart shows the influence of others on our actions. Many of these excited admirers of Jesus turned against Him because they listened to the words of His enemies. We should pray for the courage to do what is right no matter what others may urge us to do.

## Two Gifts From the God-Man

Jesus remained near Jerusalem for the rest of the week after Palm Sunday teaching and preparing His followers for the great events to come. The time came when Jesus must make ready for the Great Supper. He told a few chosen Apostles where they were to eat the supper and how to get ready for it. No one was to spoil this last Passover with His beloved disciples. However, Christ knew one of His disciples wanted to betray Him to the Jews. Judas would do this evil deed, but not until after the Last Supper.

The feast of the Passover, as you recall, commemorated the sacrifice and eating of the Paschal Lamb just before the Hebrews escaped from the slavery of Egypt. It also foreshadowed our delivery from sin. The Passover was a very solemn feast for the Jews. The food and the special ways of preparing it had deep meaning. Christ carried out the

ceremonies prescribed by the Law to the last detail.

When all the Apostles were reclining at the table, Jesus took a towel, poured water into a basin, and began to wash the feet of His disciples, drying them with the towel. Usually a servant did this service. Jesus did it Himself to teach an important lesson to His twelve chosen followers. The lesson was that of humility; to serve others is never a lowly task. That is why Christ washed the feet of His creatures.

As the Last Supper went on, the Apostles saw that this was no ordinary feast. Toward the end of the meal, Jesus took bread, blessed and broke it and gave it to His Apostles saying, "Take, this is My body." Then He took a cup of wine and giving thanks, He gave it to them, and said, "This is My blood of the new covenant, which is being shed for many" (Mk. 14:22, 24). These words fulfilled the promise which Christ had made during His public life.

Christ had planned for His ministry to continue on earth. Men were to take His place. They were to be other Christs, chosen from among ordinary men. They were to be priests, exercising His priesthood. The Apostles were the first priests. With the words, "Do this in remembrance of Me," Christ gave these humble fishermen the power to change bread and wine into His own body and blood. At the Last Supper the Catholic priesthood began.

The Church was to have a human leader. Christ had to prepare this supreme head of His Church. He had taught Peter many lessons during the time they spent together. He had promised that He would make Peter the head of His Church.

At the Last Supper, our Lord reminded Peter that he must trust Him completely. He predicted that before the next day, Peter would deny Him. Peter protested he would never do such a terrible thing. Then Christ told His friends that He would soon die, but promised them that the Holy Spirit would come to them. The Master knew that the Apostles had not understood much of what He had said. He told them, however, that when the Holy Spirit came upon them, they would understand everything.

Christ's Passion was now to begin. We shall review His chief sufferings.

## REVIEW, V–1

**WORD LIST**

| sublime | voluntary | Passion | service |

1. Jesus Christ redeemed the entire human race.
2. Christ redeemed the world through His Passion and death.
3. Christ paid the debt for Adam's sin.
4. Christ gave us the Holy Eucharist and the priesthood at the Last Supper.

## THINGS TO DISCUSS AND DO

1. Plan a panel discussion on: Christ's Part in My Redemption.
2. What is meant by the statement, "There is much wasted suffering in the world"?
3. What lesson about human conduct does the triumphal entry into Jerusalem teach us?
4. Learn and dramatize the ceremonies of the Jewish Passover.
5. What lesson did Jesus wish to teach the Apostles by the washing of the feet?
6. What personal fault did Peter fail to overcome?

Study Catechism Lesson 8, *The Redemption*, Question 90, p. 153.

# Part 2. The Passion

## 1. The Agony in the Garden

After the Last Supper Jesus and the Apostles went to a favorite place of prayer, the Garden of Gethsemani. Here, Christ underwent the most extreme suffering of mind and body. He was taking upon His shoulders the sins of every man and woman ever born. He knew what He would have to suffer to atone for them and He broke out into a bloody sweat. The Apostles, instead of praying with Him, fell asleep. God sent an angel to comfort Christ. After receiving this comfort, Christ made an act of resignation to His Father's will.

"Sacred Heart of Jesus, strengthened in Thine agony by an Angel, strengthen us in our agony."

Jesus then left the Garden and went forth to meet the soldiers who were coming to arrest Him. His heart was heavy as He saw Judas, the betrayer, leading the approaching mob. Imagine a man preferring money to the friendship of Christ! Peter bravely drew his sword and cut off the ear of the servant, Malchus. But Christ rebuked Peter and healed the ear. The Apostles then fled like children who scatter for fear of being blamed for someone else's mischief. They were not strong enough to bear the trial with their Master.

## 2. Insults and Accusations Against Christ

The soldiers led Christ to the high priest. We know how the entire night was spent. The rulers sent Christ from one to another. He listened to their insults and accusations mostly in silence. Pontius Pilate tried to save Jesus by letting the people choose to face either Barabbas, a criminal, or Christ, the Saviour. He was sure they would want Christ freed rather than Barabbas. But the people cried for the blood of Christ, and Pilate ordered our King to be scourged, that is, beaten with heavy whips. This punishment was usually inflicted before a prisoner was crucified. The cruel soldiers took turns in beating Christ, until His body was a mass of bleeding wounds. Then they placed a crown of thorns upon His head, struck it, and mocked Him saying, "Hail, King of the Jews." When the soldiers became tired of tormenting Jesus, Pilate sentenced Him to death because he feared to lose his position if he released Him.

## 3. The Journey to Calvary

*Christ died on Good Friday.* They placed a heavy cross on the bleeding shoulders of our Lord, and He carried it to the place where criminals were executed. Our Lord did not complain. He was eager to bear the cross that would save mankind and give infinite glory to His heavenly Father. Do we accept unpleasant things as tiny crosses that will make us more like Jesus? We all have crosses to bear, the cross of sickness or poverty, the cross of misfortune or disappointment, or the cross of penance. We only make ourselves unhappy by not accepting willingly the cross God places on our shoulders — for then we carry it alone and without merit.

## 4. The Final Suffering of Christ

*Christ died on Golgotha, a place outside the city of Jerusalem.* Here with a crowd looking on, the soldiers stripped off His garments. The pain of the torn flesh was nothing to the shame His pure heart suffered at His nakedness. Jesus, the pure Son of God, suffered this humiliation to atone for our sins of impurity. We cause our Saviour much pain by immodestly showing or uncovering our bodies, by causing others to commit sins of thought, desire, or deed, and by each immodest or impure act we are guilty of.

The willing Victim offered Himself meekly to the soldiers to be nailed to the cross. Hanging here between heaven and earth with outstretched arms Christ offered His final sufferings to His heavenly Father for all men.

To say this all briefly, *the chief sufferings of Christ were His bitter agony of soul, His bloody sweat, His cruel scourging, His crowning with thorns, His crucifixion, and His death on the cross.*

Christ preached His greatest sermon from this cross. We call the brief statements uttered by Christ during His three hours' agony, "The Seven Last Words." If you are unable to list these seven important sentences, you should try to find them in the gospel stories of the Passion.

"We, therefore, pray Thee help Thy servants: whom Thou hast redeemed with Thy precious blood."

### 5. Christ Dies for Us

The last three hours of agony were finally over. Christ had promised heaven to the good thief; He had given Mary to us as a Mother. With infinite resignation, Christ spoke His final words, "Father, into Thy hands I commend my spirit." Then He died. The great act of Redemption was over. Man was freed from the power of the devil at that awful moment. A man who was God had died to save men. Nature bore witness to this great event by covering the land with darkness, splitting the veil of the Temple in two, and by an earthquake that terrified those who saw the sad events of Calvary.

"Be mindful, O Lord, of Thy creatures whom Thou hast redeemed by Thy precious blood."

The silence of death remained on Calvary after Christ had breathed His last. Later the centurion opened Christ's side with a spear, and blood and water flowed from the wound. Then His lifeless body was taken down from the cross, and placed in the arms of His dear grieving Mother. What have these great sufferings meant to each of us? Every one of us can say at least that *from the sufferings and death of Christ we learn God's love for man and the evil of sin, for which God, who is all-just, demands such great satisfaction.*

In the Passion we recognize the two natures in Jesus Christ. It was Christ's human nature that suffered, but it was His divine nature and Person which gave every act infinite value. Through the merits gained by Christ, our acts performed in the state of grace and especially out of love for God, are made meritorious for eternity. Our suffering Saviour not only merited God's love for us, but also taught us, how to gain this love.

You know that Christ gives all men a chance to make use of the merits He gained for them on Calvary. Sanctifying grace, which Christ merited for us, is within the reach of everyone. Christ suffered for all. This is a very great truth! Why did Christ suffer and die for us? You remember that redemption means "a buying back." Through His suffering and death, Christ bought back the right to heaven for all mankind. Pause a moment and offer thanks to Jesus crucified. You were a slave and He freed you; a prisoner and He released you — by dying for you.

**136**

"Hail saving Victim offered for me and for all mankind upon the gibbet of the cross."

Resolve to be a true follower of Christ. Unite with Him in atoning for your own sins and those of others. Share His sufferings. Do not let Him suffer alone. During Holy Week especially live with Christ in the liturgy of the Church.

## REVIEW, V–2

### WORD LIST

| centurion | complete | gibbet |
| Golgotha | merit | humiliation |

### THINGS TO REMEMBER

1. Every act in the Passion and death of Christ was infinite in value.
2. The suffering and death of Christ are proof of His love for man.
3. The sorrowful mysteries of the Rosary remind us of Christ's sacrifice for us.
4. We can atone for sins by uniting ourselves with Christ in His sufferings, especially in the liturgy of Holy Week.

### THINGS TO DISCUSS AND DO

1. Discuss how a good Catholic unites himself to Christ in His sufferings especially by celebrating the last three days of Holy Week with the Church in the sacred liturgy.
2. Write a newspaper article dated the year of our Lord's death. Suggested headline:

   Death of a Prophet       Body Stolen?
   Verdict: Guilty          Empty Tomb

3. Plan a radio broadcast on the Seven Last Words.

4. When did Christ speak during His trial?
5. Why was Christ silent before Herod?
6. Explain how Peter lied, denied his faith, and swore falsely, the night of Christ's arrest.
7. Mention three of Christ's worst sufferings.
8. On a map of Jerusalem follow Christ during His Passion.
9. Who were the people who tried to comfort Christ along His way to Calvary?
10. Describe the earth at the moment of Christ's death.
11. Who was the rich man who helped bury our Lord?
12. During what week do we especially commemorate Christ's sufferings and death?

Study Catechism Lesson 8, *The Redemption*, Questions 91–94, p. 154.

# Part 3.  Christ Renews the Sacrifice of Golgotha in the Mass

## 1. The Sacrifice of the Mass and the Sacrifice of Golgotha Are the Same

The death of our loving Saviour, Jesus Christ, on Golgotha was the key act in our redemption. We remember, that only a divine Person could fully atone for the great wrong done by our first parents, and through this atonement, reopen to us the gates of heaven. God the Father willed that this atonement be made by the death of Christ.

We share in the benefits of this death through the Holy Sacrifice of the Mass. Christ is God. That is why He could tell His Apostles and their successors to do as He had done the evening before His death. They were to take bread and

wine and change them into His body and blood, the Body
that had been slain, the Blood that had been spilt. They were
to offer them again and again, day after day, from the rising
of the sun to its going down. This is the Mass. Every Mass is
the repeated offering of the crucified Christ to the heavenly
Father. Thus the sacrifice of Calvary and the sacrifice of the
Mass are the same sacrifice, though Calvary was bloody and
the Mass is unbloody.

## 2. The Sacrifice of the Mass Has Many Effects

You help to supply the bread and wine by your offertory
gift. As the priest offers this bread and wine, put your whole
self on the paten. This means your joys, prayers, works, and
sufferings. Your little offering is like a drop of water compared to the boundless ocean of Christ's infinite gift to God.

But just as your little drop is lost in the great ocean, so your little gift of self is lost in Christ's infinite gift. Yet you join yourself with Him as He produces the many effects of the Mass.

You join with Him as He gives glory, praise, and thanks to God. You join with Him as He offers satisfaction for sins. You join with Him as He asks God for the graces men need; as He prays for His Church, for sinners, for all men. Indeed you join yourself with Christ as He produces all the effects of the Mass, all the effects of the Redemption.

## 3. We Must Take Part in the Sacrifice of the Mass

Each year we learn to know our religion better. So each year we should learn to appreciate more the chances this religion gives us to increase our store of grace. We know that the greatest prayer we can offer is the Mass, so why not assist at Mass often and devoutly?

During the Mass we should try to keep our minds on the Holy Sacrifice as the renewal of Calvary takes place before us. Using the Missal will help us to follow the Mass along with the priest, but we may also be united with Christ by thinking over His Passion and death, or by saying the rosary Receiving Holy Communion with devotion during the Mass makes our sacrifice even more profitable, and increases the grace already existing in our souls.

If we realize what the Mass is, we will be deeply recollected during it. We will not be tempted to misbehave, or to talk and laugh in church. Non-Catholics are often astonished at the large number of Catholics who go to church every Sunday. On the other hand, they are often surprised that other Catholics believe all they say they do about the Mass and yet are so careless about assisting at it. Let us ask God to give us the faith and the courage to attend daily Mass whenever possible. But most of all let us ask Him for the grace of assisting at Mass as Mary assisted at the foot of the Cross, suffering every pain with Christ.

## REVIEW, V–3

### WORD LIST

| | | |
|---|---|---|
| renews | atonement | slain |
| bloody | unbloody | offertory |
| infinite | boundless | paten |
| participate | profitable | Missal |

### THINGS TO REMEMBER

1. The sacrifice of the Mass and the sacrifice of Golgotha are the same sacrifice.
2. A bloody sacrifice was offered on Calvary; an unbloody sacrifice is offered in the Mass.
3. The Mass is the greatest prayer we can offer.

### THINGS TO DISCUSS AND DO

1. How can you show that you realize the value of Holy Mass?
2. Set aside one day of the week besides Sunday on which you will assist at Mass. Be there on time, and try to receive Holy Communion.
3. How do you help supply the bread and wine?
4. Name some ways in which you should assist at Mass.

# Part 4. The Resurrection of Christ — a Proof of His Divinity

### 1. Christ Descends Into Limbo

As we knelt in spirit before the tomb of Christ on Good Friday, and in our minds watched the guards seal the stone, the sight should have comforted rather than grieved us. For the sealed tomb is a gateway to the most glorious proof of Christ's divinity, and instead of being sad, we should rejoice with the Son of God. We should rejoice too, with the just people who lived before the coming of Christ. They had waited long for this great day when Christ would lead them to their heavenly home. Do you recall where these just souls were waiting?

In the Apostles' Creed we say that Christ "descended into hell." Do you know what this means? *When we say that Christ descended into hell we mean that, after He died, the soul of Christ descended into a place or state of rest called limbo, where the souls of the just were waiting for Him.* This "hell" was not that of the damned, but a place of natural happiness free from torments, yet without the supernatural happiness of heaven. Can you name some of the holy people who were waiting in limbo?

These souls in limbo were looking forward to the reopening of the gates of heaven. They were faithful friends of God who had heard His word and kept it. Their one hope of release from the prison of limbo was the Promised Redeemer. *Christ went to limbo to announce to the souls waiting there the joyful news that He had reopened heaven to mankind.* How happy these souls must have been at the sight of their Master!

*While His soul was in limbo, Christ's body was in the holy sepulcher.* There it remained under guard in the place where the Apostles had laid it after His death.

## 2. Christ Rises From the Dead

Holy Scripture tells us what we know of Christ's resurrection from the dead. One of the most important reasons for the resurrection is this: it shows that Christ is divine. It was the greatest of His miracles, and the one which He foretold as proof of His divine mission. When the Jews asked for a sign from our Lord to show that He came from God, Jesus answered: " 'Destroy this temple, and in three days I will raise it up.' The Jews therefore said, 'Forty-six years has this temple been in building, and wilt thou raise it up in three days?' But he was speaking of the temple of His body.

**143**

When, accordingly, he had risen from the dead, his disciples remembered that he had said this, and they believed . . . the word that Jesus had spoken" (Jn. 2:19–22).

The Resurrection of Christ is the most important teaching of the Catholic Church. The Church has realized this from the very beginning, for the great Apostle, St. Paul, wrote to His followers: "If Christ has not risen, vain is our preaching, vain too is your faith" (1 Cor. 15:14).

The New Testament tells us what happened after Christ's resurrection. In the Gospel we read what the angel said to Mary Magdalen and the holy women who had come to the tomb on the third day after the burial of Jesus: "He is not here: He is risen." The same Man who had died on the cross arose from the tomb that first Easter morning. This we learned long ago. Our catechism tells us: *Christ rose from the dead, glorious and immortal, on Easter Sunday, the third day after His death.*

There is no mention of Christ's visiting His Mother, but we know that He must have paid her a visit soon after His resurrection. The Gospels, however, do tell us of Christ's appearance to Mary Magdalen. We can imagine her joy in discovering that the man she thought was the gardener was her beloved Master. The Gospels also tell us of Christ's meeting with the holy women, of His journey to Emmaus in company with His disciples, and of His meeting with Peter.

During the forty days after the Resurrection, Christ appeared many times to the Apostles, talking to them, eating and drinking with them. We like especially to recall two of these appearances: first, when Christ entered the Upper Room through closed doors, and second, when He performed the miracle of the fishes on the shores of the Lake of Galilee. If you do not remember these stories read them either in the New Testament or in a Bible History.

### 3. The Resurrection Proves That Christ Is God

Christ wanted to prove that He was what He claimed to be. Coming back to life through His own power, as He predicted, after He was known certainly to be dead, was the supreme proof that He was divine. He also wanted us to understand that death is not the end of all things, but only the beginning. One day we too, if we have been faithful, shall rise from the dead, to begin a new life with Christ in heaven. Let us remember then, that *Christ rose from the dead to show that He is true God and to teach us that we, too, shall rise from the dead.*

The Church teaches us that *all men will rise from the dead, but only those who have been faithful to Christ will share in His glory.* Those who have been unfaithful, and have not repented, will be denied the special privileges reserved for the chosen friends of God. Those who have been faithful will join the company of the angels and will see God face to face forever. The hope of one day joining the heavenly hosts who continually praise God, should encourage us to persevere to the end in doing good.

### 4. The Resurrection Is the Greatest of All Miracles

The Resurrection is the greatest of all miracles because Christ raised Himself from the dead as He had foretold He would. No other dead person has ever been able to perform such a miracle. It is true that Lazarus arose from the dead, but it was not through his own power. Lazarus arose at the command of Christ. Besides, Lazarus had to die again later. But Christ arose from the dead never to die again. The God-Man really conquered death and secured for us a share in His victory.

## 5. The Feast of the Resurrection Ranks as the Highest of All Feasts

No doubt, your first choice of feast days would be Christmas. But the feast that commemorates Christ's great victory over sin and the redemption of the human race is even more important. Easter Sunday gives proof beyond all doubt that Jesus Christ was divine. It assures man of his redemption. The feast of the Resurrection, therefore, holds the central position in the church year.

## 6. Christ's Reasons for Remaining on Earth After His Resurrection

*Christ remained on earth forty days after His Resurrection to prove that He had truly risen from the dead, and to complete the instruction of the Apostles.*

It might seem to us that Christ's resurrection was a fitting end to His life here on earth. Why then did He not return at once to heaven to His Father? Christ did not return to heaven at once for several reasons. By staying on earth after His Resurrection, and by appearing to His Apostles and disciples and even eating with them, Christ proved that He had truly risen and made the Apostles witnesses for Him. To see Him alive after His cruel death was for them a proof beyond doubt that Jesus Christ had truly risen from the dead.

Then too, Christ had some last instructions to give to His Apostles. Now that they had witnessed many of the things foretold by Christ, the Apostles were ready for more profound teachings. The divine Teacher had taught slowly during the three years the Apostles were with Him. The time had finally come to confirm and complete these teachings.

# REVIEW, V–4

## WORD LIST

| | | | |
|---|---|---|---|
| limbo | visible | glorious | profound |
| torments | immortal | sepulchre | hell |

## THINGS TO REMEMBER

1. "Christ descended into hell" means Christ descended into the limbo of the Patriarchs, a place where the souls of the just awaited the Redeemer.
2. The Resurrection is the great proof of Christ's divinity.
3. The Resurrection is the greatest feast of the Church year.
4. The Apostles were Christ's first missionaries.

## THINGS TO DISCUSS AND DO

1. Talk about some Old Testament persons who were waiting in limbo for the Redeemer.
2. Why is the Resurrection the greatest of Christ's miracles?
3. Memorize the words of Christ that made the Apostles missionaries. Where are they to be found?
4. Imagine you were one of the persons to whom Christ appeared after He rose from the dead. Write a letter to a friend describing the meeting.
5. Illustrate one of the following scenes: the sealed tomb with the guards before it; the holy women on their way to the sepulcher; Christ and Mary Magdalen; Christ and Peter; Christ in limbo.
6. Report on the new Easter vigil service and show how it helps us to know and to live our faith in Christ.
7. What proof do we have that Christ rose from the dead?
8. What is meant by the expression "Death is a beginning"?
9. Which Apostle at first doubted our Lord's Resurrection?
10. What must we do if we want our bodies to rise gloriously at the end of the world?

Study Catechism Lesson 8, *The Redemption* (Con't.), Questions 95–100, pp. 155–156.

# Part 5.   Christ Ascends Into Heaven

### 1. Why Christ Ascended Into Heaven

After spending forty days on earth proving that He had truly risen, and giving further instructions to His Apostles, the time came for Jesus to return to heaven, body and soul, humanity and divinity. In His last talk with His Apostles, Jesus explained to them that it was necessary that He go to prepare a place for them and for us. He told them that, just as He had come from heaven to do a certain work on earth, He now must return to heaven. He also told the Apostles that He would send the Paraclete, the Holy Spirit, the third Person of the Blessed Trinity, who would sanctify them and who would be with them always.

After finishing His talk, Christ led the Apostles up the Mount of Olives overlooking Jerusalem. There He blessed them with uplifted hands, and the Gospel tells us that He "departed from them and was carried up into heaven" (Lk. 24:51).

What feelings must have filled the Apostles as they watched Christ ascend higher and higher until a cloud received Him out of their sight. The gates of heaven were at last opened! The angels joyously greeted their triumphant Lord, who entered, body and soul, by His own power into His heavenly home. The souls from limbo accompanied Him.

*Christ ascended, body and soul, into heaven on Ascension Day, forty days after His Resurrection.* The day on which we commemorate this event is Ascension Day, and it is a holyday of obligation.

Let us now turn to the last article of the part of the Creed we are studying. Notice that it says that Jesus Christ sits "at the right hand of God the Father" in heaven, and that "from thence He shall come to judge the living and the dead."

*When we say that Christ sits at the right hand of God, the Father Almighty, we mean that our Lord as God is equal to the Father and that as man He shares above all the saints in the glory of His Father and exercises for all eternity the supreme authority of a king over all creatures.*

## 2. Christ Gives Us the Means to Attain Heaven

Now that we know so much of Christ's life on earth, His sufferings, death, resurrection and ascension, we have many added graces to help us reach our heavenly goal, to see Him forever. God has given us many means to come closer to Him. Prayer is one. Good works another. The best way is to receive the sacraments of Penance and Holy Eucharist frequently. Our life on earth is but a place of waiting and of preparation, where we should do everything possible to make our eternity happy with God. And, of course, the most important of all means of attaining heaven is faithfulness to God's commandments. Our good example which results from regularly keeping these commandments will also lead other souls closer to Him. Lastly, we can be sure of a high place in heaven by surrendering ourselves to God's will, and by leaving everything in His hands since He knows better than we do the things which will help us to reach heaven.

### 3. Christ Will Come Again From Heaven to Judge All Men

We read that as the Apostles watched Christ go up into heaven, two men in white garments suddenly stood by them and said, "Men of Galilee, why do you stand looking up to heaven? This Jesus who has been taken from you into heaven will come in the same way as you have seen Him going up into heaven." These words refer to Christ's coming to judge mankind at the end of the world. What does that mean? *When we say that Christ will come from thence to judge the living and the dead, we mean that on the last day our Lord will come to pronounce a sentence of eternal reward or of eternal punishment on everyone who has ever lived in this world.*

> "Lord, I fear Thy justice, I implore Thy mercy; deliver me not to everlasting pains, grant that I may possess Thee in the midst of everlasting joys."

How different will be this second coming! The first time Jesus came to redeem fallen man He appeared meek and humble, a little Babe in Bethlehem. In His second coming,

He will appear mighty and majestic, as a King and a just Judge having power to judge all men. Everyone who has ever lived will stand before Christ on that day to receive a final sentence of reward or punishment.

No one knows exactly when this day will come. We must live each day as though it were our last, so that on the day of judgment we will hear the consoling words of our Lord, "Come, ye blessed of my Father, possess you the kingdom which is prepared for you."

## 4. Christ Has a Purpose in Judging All Men

Let us note two definite reasons for the General Judgment. First, the honor and glory of Jesus Christ will be made known at that time; His supreme power and authority over the universe will be recognized by everyone. Second, at the General Judgment, all men will receive their just reward or punishment, both as individuals and as members of the human race.

If we expect to hear the consoling message that we are saved, we must live this present life according to the teachings of our faith. We must love and serve God and never cut ourselves off from Him by sin. We should often think of the last judgment and prepare each day to meet our just and merciful King.

## REVIEW, V–5

**WORD LIST**

sanctify          Paraclete          uplifted          triumphant

## THINGS TO REMEMBER

1. Christ had His human body when He ascended to His Father.
2. The final phrase in many prayers "Through Christ our Lord" teaches us that the surest way to God the Father is through His divine Son.
3. Christ is the judge of the living and the dead.
4. "Christ sitteth at the right hand of God the Father" means He is equal to the Father and the Holy Spirit in all things.

## THINGS TO DISCUSS AND DO

1. Explain what Christ meant when He said, "In my Father's house there are many mansions."
2. Be ready to explain to the class the need for a second judgment: the general judgment.
3. Explain how your conscience can act as a judge.
4. Find scripture passages about the end of the world and the Last Judgment.
5. How will Christ's second coming differ from His first coming?
6. What is the best way to reach our heavenly goal?

Study Catechism Lesson 8, *The Redemption* (Con't.), Questions 101–104, pp. 156–157.

# End-of-Unit Review — V

## PART 1

## CATECHISM

### LESSON 8

#### The Redemption

90. What is meant by the Redemption?

By the Redemption is meant that Jesus Christ, as the Redeemer of the whole human race, offered His sufferings and death to God as a fitting sacrifice in satisfaction for the sins of men, and regained for them the right to be children of God and heirs of heaven.

## OTHER QUESTIONS AND EXERCISES

Write 1 to 10 on a paper. After each number write the letter of the answer which matches it in the exercise below.

1. Redemption
2. Redeemer
3. human race
4. salvation
5. Passion
6. Holy Week
7. Jerusalem
8. Passover
9. Peter
10. Palm Sunday

A. all men, women, and children
B. the most solemn time of the year
C. the first pope
D. the regaining of heaven for all men
E. saving our souls
F. city in and near which Jesus spent His last days
G. the day Jesus triumphantly entered the Holy City
H. our Lord Jesus Christ
I. sufferings of Christ
J. the feast on which the Paschal Lamb was eaten

# CATECHISM

## LESSON 8

### The Redemption (Cont.)

91. **What were the chief sufferings of Christ?**

    The chief sufferings of Christ were His bitter agony of soul, His bloody sweat, His cruel scourging, His crowning with thorns, His crucifixion, and His death on the cross.

92. **When did Christ die?**

    Christ died on Good Friday.

93. **Where did Christ die?**

    Christ died on Golgotha, a place outside the city of Jerusalem.

94. **What do we learn from the sufferings and death of Christ?**

    From the sufferings and death of Christ we learn God's love for man and the evil of sin, for which God, who is all-just, demands such great satisfaction.

## OTHER QUESTIONS AND EXERCISES

1. Did Jesus complain about His sufferings?
2. Was Jesus glad when Peter cut off the servant's ear?
3. Were the Apostles frightened when they saw the soldiers?
4. Did Pilate try to release Jesus?
5. Explain how we might sometimes act like Peter when he cut off the servant's ear, or like Pilate when he sentenced Christ to death.
6. Was Barabbas freed because he was innocent?
7. Did Christ preach a sermon from the cross?
8. Does Christ's death on the cross prove He hated sin?
9. Does Christ love us?
10. Can we share in the merits of Christ?

## PART 3

1. How do we share in the merits of Christ's death?
2. How do we supply the bread and wine for the Mass?
3. What should we place on the paten at Mass?
4. What happens to our gift at the Consecration?
5. What is the greatest prayer we can offer?
6. Why is the Mass more powerful than any private prayer?
7. Who offers each Mass?
8. What is the best way to assist at Mass?
9. Why could Christ tell the Apostles to continue offering sacrifice?
10. How does Christ in the Mass show us He is pleased with our gift?

## PART 4

## CATECHISM

### LESSON 8

#### The Redemption (Cont.)

95. **What do we mean when we say in the Apostles' Creed that Christ descended into hell?**

    When we say that Christ descended into hell we mean that, after He died, the soul of Christ descended into a place or state of rest, called limbo, where the souls of the just were waiting for Him.

96. **Why did Christ go to limbo?**

    Christ went to limbo to announce to the souls waiting there the joyful news that He had reopened heaven to mankind.

97. **Where was Christ's body while His soul was in limbo?**

    While His soul was in limbo, Christ's body was in the holy sepulcher.

98. **When did Christ rise from the dead?**

    Christ rose from the dead, glorious and immortal, on Easter Sunday, the third day after His death.

### 99. Why did Christ rise from the dead?

Christ rose from the dead to show that He is true God and to teach us that we, too, shall rise from the dead.

### 100. Will all men rise from the dead?

All men will rise from the dead, but only those who have been faithful to Christ will share in His glory.

## OTHER QUESTIONS AND EXERCISES

1. Where did Christ's soul go immediately after death?
2. Where was Christ's body placed after His death?
3. How have we learned of Christ's Resurrection?
4. On what day did Christ rise from the dead?
5. Who thought Christ was the gardener when she met Him?
6. What did Christ's Resurrection prove?
7. Who will share in Christ's glory?
8. How does the Resurrection rank as a miracle? Why?
9. Why did Christ remain on earth after His Resurrection?
10. How did Lazarus rise from the dead?

## PART 5

## CATECHISM

### LESSON 8

#### The Redemption (Cont.)

### 101. When did Christ ascend into heaven?

Christ ascended, body and soul, into heaven on Ascension Day, forty days after His Resurrection.

### 102. Why did Christ remain on earth forty days after His Resurrection?

Christ remained on earth forty days after His Resurrection to prove that He had truly risen from the dead and to complete the instruction of the Apostles.

103. **What do we mean when we say that Christ sits at the right hand of God, the Father Almighty?**

When we say that Christ sits at the right hand of God, the Father Almighty, we mean that our Lord as God is equal to the Father, and that as man He shares above all the saints in the glory of His Father and exercises for all eternity the supreme authority of a king over all creatures.

104. **What do we mean when we say that Christ will come from thence to judge the living and the dead?**

When we say that Christ will come from thence to judge the living and the dead, we mean that on the last day our Lord will come to pronounce a sentence of eternal reward or of eternal punishment on everyone who has ever lived in this world.

## OTHER QUESTIONS AND EXERCISES

1. Who is the Paraclete?
2. What is the name of the mount from which Christ ascended into heaven?
3. How long after the Resurrection did Christ ascend into heaven?
4. What is the day on which Christ ascended into heaven called?
5. What authority does Christ hold over all creatures?
6. How will Christ appear in His second coming?
7. Why will there be a general judgment?
8. What will be the words of reward Christ uses at the last judgment?
9. How did Christ ascend into heaven?
10. What does Christ's Ascension into heaven mean to us personally?

### Section Review

Now we should take a general review of SECTION II
*God the Son, our Redeemer*
using the End of Unit Tests as a guide to locate the most important points.

# The Holy Ghost and the Church

*I believe in the Holy Ghost, the Holy Catholic Church, the communion of saints, the forgiveness of sins, the resurrection of the body, and life everlasting. Amen.*

## Overview

We now come to the third Person of the Blessed Trinity, the Holy Spirit. We shall study Him in Himself (Unit VI), in the grace He brings, and in His works (Unit VII), especially in the Church (Unit VIII).

In connection with the power of the Holy Spirit in the Church we shall study the forgiveness of sins, the four last things, and our eternal life with God (Unit IX).

# Unit VI.  I Believe in the Holy Ghost

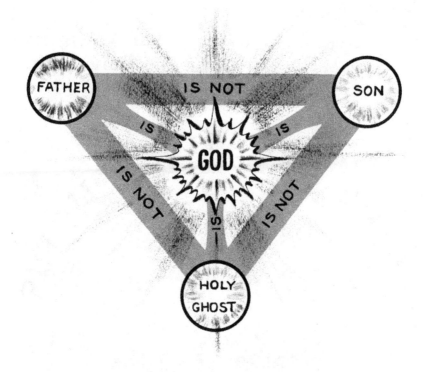

# Part 1. The Holy Ghost Is God, Third Person of the Blessed Trinity

Which Persons of the Blessed Trinity have we studied thus far? Which divine Person remains to be studied? What knowledge do we have of the Holy Spirit? In which prayers have we invoked Him? In which Bible references have we met Him?

Before we begin to learn more about the Holy Spirit let us recite or sing the following hymn that we may gain His grace to help us:

> Come, Holy Ghost, Creator blest,
> And in our souls take up Thy rest,
> Come with Thy grace and heavenly aid,
> And fill the hearts which Thou hast made.

## 1. The Holy Ghost Is God

Long ago we learned that the *Holy Ghost is God and the third Person of the Blessed Trinity.* Who is God? We remember that God is the Supreme Being. He is infinitely perfect. He made all things and keeps them in existence. The Holy Ghost is the third Person in God, the Supreme Being. He, too, is above all creatures. He, too, is the self-existing and infinitely perfect Spirit. He is eternal, all-good, all-knowing, all-present, and almighty. He is all-wise, all-holy, all-merciful, and all-just.

Let us make the sign of the cross and thoughtfully pray these words, "In the name of the Father, and of the Son, and of the Holy Ghost. Amen." When did we name the Holy Ghost? Recite the "Glory Be to the Father." When did we call upon the Holy Ghost?

We call the third Person the "Holy Ghost" or the "Holy Spirit." The word "ghost" is an old English word which means "spirit." We use the word "holy" because the Holy Ghost is holy and because He makes our souls holy.

Why do we call the Holy Spirit the third Person of the Blessed Trinity? We call the Holy Spirit the third Person of the Blessed Trinity because Christ Himself mentioned the Holy Spirit third when He told the Apostles to baptize ". . . in the name of the Father, and of the Son, and of the Holy Spirit" (Mt. 28:19). We call the Holy Ghost the third Person also because He goes out from, or proceeds from, the Father and the Son.

## 2. The Holy Ghost Proceeds From the Father and the Son

A missionary Father explained to the natives in the Belgian Congo in Africa that in the far North water freezes and becomes like rock so that elephants can walk upon it. The natives shook their heads. They could not understand this, because they had never seen ice. It is even more difficult for us to understand the relations of the three Persons in the Blessed Trinity.

We can never fully understand how the Holy Ghost proceeds from the Father and the Son because this is a supernatural mystery, a truth which our minds can know when God reveals it, but cannot understand even after it has been revealed. Yet we believe it because the Church teaches it. We can, however, learn something about this truth.

God the Father knew that He was God from all eternity. This eternal knowledge was not like a thought of ours, by which, for example, we know a tall tree. Nor was it simply a thought in the mind of God. This eternal knowledge generated or begot a living, distinct Person, God the Son. The two Persons, God the Father and God the Son, loved each other. But this love they had for one another was not like ours, a feeling or a well-wishing. This mutual love of Father and Son is a third person, the Holy Spirit. That is what we mean when we say *the Holy Ghost proceeds from the Father and the Son.* All three Persons are equal; all three are co-eternal. And what we must not forget: God is a most pure spirit. He has no body. Our human minds can never completely grasp what He is.

## 3. The Holy Ghost Is Equal to the Father and the Son

Why is the Holy Ghost equal to the Father and the Son? *The Holy Ghost is equal to the Father and the Son, because He is God.* He has the same divine nature as they have.

## 4. Various Names Are Used for the Holy Ghost

In Holy Scripture various names are given to the Holy Spirit. Find some of these titles in the following passages, and discuss what they mean.

"And I will ask the Father and he will give you another Advocate to dwell with you forever, the Spirit of truth whom the world cannot receive, because it neither sees Him nor knows Him. But you shall know Him, because He will dwell with you, and be in you" (Jn. 14:16–17).

"Do you not know that you are the temple of God and that the Spirit of God dwells in you?" (1 Cor. 3:16.)

What do the titles tell you about the Holy Spirit? As our Advocate, the Holy Spirit pleads for us, protects, assists, and defends us. We may also call the Holy Spirit a Consoler because He consoles us; and an Intercessor because He intercedes for us. As the Spirit of truth, He shows us the truth and protects us in it.

Let us make an act of faith in the Holy Spirit as we find it in the Nicene Creed of the Mass. "I believe . . . in the Holy Ghost, the Lord and giver of life; who proceedeth from the Father and the Son. Who together with the Father and the Son is adored and glorified."

## 5. Various Symbols Represent the Holy Ghost

There are some symbols which are often used to represent the Holy Ghost. These will help us to remember Him. Among them are water, fire, wind, the dove, and oil.

Why does water remind us of the Holy Spirit? Without water living things wither and die. Water reminds us of life and freshness. The Holy Spirit brings supernatural life with the waters of baptism and renews and refreshes our souls with grace.

A second symbol is fire. Why does fire remind us of the Holy Spirit? He descended in tongues of fire on the first Pentecost. Fire gives light, warmth, and makes a great change in anything it touches. Like a flaming fire the Holy Spirit kindles fresh light in discouraged hearts, and burns away what is evil. A forest fire is irresistible. So too are Christians who have been genuinely inflamed with the spiritual fire of the Holy Ghost.

Why is wind a symbol of the Holy Spirit? On the first Pentecost there was a sound of a mighty wind as the Holy Ghost came upon the Apostles. The Holy Spirit purifies souls and like a powerful wind sometimes brings sudden conversions.

The dove symbolizes the Holy Spirit because it gives an idea of rest, joy, and gentleness. When did the Holy Spirit appear in the form of a dove?

For which sacraments does the Church use holy oils? Why? Oil softens, strengthens, cures, heals wounds, and takes away stiffness. The Holy Spirit gives joy and strength to souls, softens what is hard, and cures and heals.

Say a little "thank you" prayer in your heart to the Holy Spirit. Promise Him that you will remember that He is dwelling in your soul.

## REVIEW, VI–1

**WORD LIST**

| proceeds | supernatural | Advocate |
|----------|--------------|----------|
| Consoler | conversions  |          |

## THINGS TO REMEMBER

1. We call the Holy Ghost the Holy Spirit, the Spirit of Truth, the Spirit of God, the Advocate, the Consoler.
2. Water, fire, wind, oil, and the dove are symbols of the Holy Ghost.
3. The Holy Ghost is God, and is equal to the Father and the Son.

## THINGS TO DISCUSS AND DO

1. Write a prayer to the Holy Spirit. Use as many names for Him as you understand.
2. Make a symbol of the Holy Ghost and write several sentences to explain it.
3. Write a letter to a younger friend or relative explaining just how the Holy Spirit helps him every day.
4. Make a visit to Christ in the Blessed Sacrament. Ask Him to increase your devotion to the Holy Ghost.
5. Whenever we want to make an important decision we should pray especially to the Holy Ghost. Why?
6. Say the prayer to the Holy Ghost every day.
7. Make a list of the times when you might need the help of the Holy Ghost.

Study Catechism Lesson 9, *The Holy Ghost and Grace*, Questions 105–107, p. 207.

# Part 2. The Holy Ghost Dwells in the Church and Sanctifies Souls — Grace

### 1. The Holy Ghost — Source of Life in the Church

Ten days after Christ had ascended into heaven, He sent the Holy Ghost upon the Apostles and disciples gathered together in the Upper Room. At once the Apostles, the first bishops of the Catholic Church, began to preach and baptize. They were not afraid to carry out Christ's command because the Holy Ghost gave them courage. They and their successors have carried out the command of Christ even though they met great hardships and persecutions. The successors of the Apostles will continue to teach Christ's truths until the end of time because the Holy Ghost who came on that first Pentecost day will stay with the Church forever.

This is the first work of the Holy Ghost. He abides, or dwells, in the Church. He is the soul of the Church.

Christ established His Church to lead us all to heaven. None of us can get to heaven by our own human powers. None of us can enter heaven unless we are holy. Another big work of the Holy Ghost is to make each one of us holy through the gift of grace. This, then, is His twofold work: *The Holy Ghost dwells in the Church as the source of its life and sanctifies souls through the gift of grace.*

## 2. Grace, a Supernatural Gift

We must now study carefully the important and not easy topic of grace. You have all seen butterflies. Did you ever hear one of them speak? Why can it not speak? It is beyond the nature of a butterfly to speak.

Johnny Jones is a husky eleven-year-old boy. He has a human nature. What are some of the things Johnny Jones can do? Johnny can think and choose just as the angels can. He can feel, see, hear, touch, and move. Johnny can grow and live like the grass that his father plants on his front lawn. Like a baseball or a stone, Johnny also exists. Johnny is a whole wonderful little world by himself.

Despite all his powers, there are some things Johnny cannot do. No matter what Johnny can do, or think, or invent, he cannot gain supernatural life by himself. Of and by himself he cannot become a child of God. He is a creature. He cannot get grace by himself. It is beyond his human nature. But God can give grace to him as a special gift if He wishes.

God has made Johnny and therefore loves him more than any one of us could even understand. He sent His only Son, Jesus Christ, into the world. Every act and word of Jesus on earth was an eternal, infinite, and divine act because Jesus is God. Every act of Jesus earned eternal, boundless merits for us. Through His death on the cross Jesus paid the full price of our redemption. These merits gained grace for men. The Holy Spirit distributes these graces, to Johnny and to all of us. We call these graces gifts because God gives them freely. Johnny and the rest of us neither deserve them nor can we ever earn them by ourselves. This should help us understand that *grace is a supernatural gift of God bestowed on us through the merits of Jesus Christ for our salvation.*

Let us thank God the Father, the Son, and the Holy Spirit for the wonderful gift of grace. When we glance at the crucifix and remember what Christ suffered to earn grace, let us pray, "We adore Thee, O Christ, and we bless Thee; because by Thy holy Cross Thou hast redeemed the world."

## 3. There Are Two Kinds of Grace

*There are two kinds of grace: sanctifying grace and actual grace.* Christ earned both for us and the Holy Spirit distributes them. First let us study carefully what sanctifying grace is and does.

1. *Sanctifying grace is the supernatural life of the soul.*

Do you remember the fairy tale about King Midas who was supposed to have the power of turning into gold everything he touched? The gift of sanctifying grace which the

Holy Spirit brings into a person's soul when he is baptized does a far more wonderful thing than this. To the natural life of the soul it adds a supernatural life — a sharing in the very life of God.

God can do all things. He can give us a supernatural, divine life by the gift of grace, while at the same time we remain true human beings. St. Thomas Aquinas says that, "By the action of the Holy Spirit we are transformed into gods." Briefly then, *sanctifying grace is that grace which confers on our souls a new life, that is, a sharing in the life of God Himself.*

To help us to understand what sanctifying grace is, Jesus used a little comparison. He said, "I am the vine, you are the branches. He who abides in me, and I in him, he bears much fruit; for without me you can do nothing" (Jn. 15:5). By grace we live in Jesus, in God. We live by His divine life. Life-giving sap flows from the vine to the branches making them live and produce fruit. Sanctifying grace, like the sap in a vine, brings God's life. When Johnny Jones receives sanctifying grace, he shares in the life that God lives.

With sanctifying grace, the soul of Johnny Jones not only becomes God's dwelling place, it becomes holy and pleasing to God as well. When iron is in fire, it looks like fire, and is as hot as fire. With sanctifying grace Johnny's soul is supernaturally like to God, who is infinitely holy.

Besides, by grace God adopts Johnny into His family. This adoption into God's family is different from the adoption of an orphan child. Adopted children do not resemble their foster parents, but those whom God has adopted actually become like God. Their holiness is a share of God's holiness. They become God's sons by grace, as Jesus is God's Son by nature. A wonderful inheritance comes with adoption into God's family. This inheritance is the right to heaven.

To put it briefly *the chief effects of sanctifying grace are: first, it makes us holy and pleasing to God; second, it makes us adopted children of God; third, it makes us temples of the Holy Ghost; fourth, it gives us the right to heaven.*

> "O Holy Spirit, sweet Guest of my soul, abide in me and grant that I may ever abide in Thee."

Why is sanctifying grace necessary for salvation? Sanctifying grace is necessary because there is no natural power on earth that can help us to get to heaven. We can attain the happiness of heaven only through God's grace which Jesus Christ earned for us and which the Holy Ghost distributes. *Sanctifying grace is necessary for salvation because it is the supernatural life, which alone enables us to attain the supernatural happiness of heaven.*

2. *Actual grace is a supernatural help to do good and avoid evil.*

The supernatural life of sanctifying grace must be kept alive. Just as we must fight germs and disease if our bodies are to be healthy and live, so also we must fight temptations and sin if we are to have the supernatural life of grace in our souls. To help us to attain or keep supernatural life, the Holy Spirit offers another special supernatural gift called actual grace. The word explains itself. It is the grace that helps us see which acts are good and pleasing to God and urges our wills to choose those good acts and to keep away from evil.

Actual grace is different from sanctifying grace because we have it only for a time. It is a passing help. Sanctifying grace, on the contrary, remains as long as we do not commit mortal sin.

Some holy people, like St. Aloysius, never committed a mortal sin. They had sanctifying grace from the time of their baptism until they died, and they will have it for all eternity.

Actual graces, however, come and go. The Holy Spirit gives us many actual graces all during life. We receive actual grace, for example, when our parents give us good advice, while we are reading good books, when we see others acting kindly and properly, when we are tempted and discouraged, and at many other times. Some actual graces that we have received are a Catholic home, a Catholic school, and the continual presence of Jesus in our churches. *Actual grace is a supernatural help of God which enlightens our mind and strengthens our will to do good and to avoid evil.*

## 4. We Can Refuse or Resist Grace

Have you seen the picture of Christ knocking at a door? When the artist painted this picture he called his friends together to ask them what they thought about it. One of his friends wondered why the door did not have a knob. The artist explained that the door which he had painted represented the human heart. The knob is only on the inside. Each person opens his heart only to the one he chooses to love.

God gives us the grace to let Him in, but He does not force His way into our hearts. God gave us a free will. He will not force His gifts upon us. We can accept them or refuse them. How did St. Peter act when Christ glanced at him as he was warming himself by the fire the night of our Lord's arrest? With what words did Christ offer actual grace to Judas in the Garden of Gethsemani? (Mt. 26:50.) The Angel Gabriel greeted Mary with the words, "Full of

**171**

grace!" What do you think Mary did with every actual grace that God offered to her?

Can we resist the grace of God? *We can resist the grace of God, for our will is free, and God does not force us to accept His grace.* Do you remember Judas?

It is just as impossible for Johnny Jones to remain in sanctifying grace without the accompanying actual grace as it is for a man to stay alive without breathing. Actual grace helps us keep, develop, and increase the virtues and gifts, and thereby, protects our supernatural life and makes it strong. Therefore, *actual grace is necessary for all who have attained the use of reason, because without it we cannot long resist the power of temptation or perform other actions which merit a reward in heaven.*

A person is considered to have the use of reason when he has reached the age of seven. Some people reach it sooner and others later. The Little Flower must have reached it at the age of three years because later she wrote that from that time on she had never refused Christ a sacrifice. At the age of reason we know the difference between good and evil. It is then that we begin to need actual grace.

## REVIEW, VI–2

**WORD LIST**

| | | | |
|---|---|---|---|
| Pentecost | inheritance | successors | persecutions |
| abides | human powers | finite | boundless |
| resist | transformed | resemble | original |
| merits | actual | reason | attain |

## THINGS TO REMEMBER

1. Sanctifying grace is the greatest treasure in the world. We must rather die, like Maria Goretti, than lose it by committing mortal sin.
2. The Holy Ghost gave the Apostles, who were the first members of the Catholic Church, the courage to preach and baptize.
3. We receive grace through the merits of Christ.
4. Sanctifying grace gives us the right to heaven.
5. The Holy Ghost gives us actual graces many times during life.

## THINGS TO DISCUSS AND DO

1. Number your paper from 1 to 16. Write S on your paper for each phrase that describes sanctifying grace, A for actual grace.
   1) Shares in the life of God.
   2) Received first in baptism.
   3) Helps one to know right from wrong.
   4) Makes one a child of God.
   5) Helps one to avoid evil.
   6) Helps one to do good.
   7) Is lost by mortal sin.
   8) Passes when a good deed is performed.
   9) Is offered to a person many times a day.
   10) Gives a desire to do good.
   11) Is the supernatural life of the soul.
   12) Makes my soul God's dwelling place.
   13) Makes me holy and pleasing to God.
   14) Stays at all times until mortal sin is committed.
   15) Makes one an heir to heaven.
   16) Is given to all to help them to get to heaven.

2. Number your paper from 1 to 12. After each number write the letter in front of the words in Column One, which best match the explanation in Column Two.

| *Column One* | *Column Two* |
|---|---|
| A. Holy Ghost | 1. Not belonging to nature, but above it |
| B. Proceeds | |
| C. Grace | 2. Power to choose |
| D. Actual Grace | 3. Go against, refuse, reject |
| E. Sanctifying Grace | 4. Sanctifier |
| F. Supernatural | 5. Goes out from |
| G. Use of Reason | 6. Reward |
| H. Resist | 7. Third Person of the Blessed Trinity |
| I. Free Will | |
| J. Merit | 8. Supernatural gift |
| | 9. Holy-making gift |
| | 10. An urge or prompting to do good |
| | 11. Distributor of grace |
| | 12. Power to think |

3. Discuss the advantages of living in the state of sanctifying grace.
4. Tell about the descent of the Holy Ghost. Explain how He helped the Apostles and how He helps us every day.
5. Kneel before a crucifix. Look at our Lord and think how His sufferings on the cross brought the Holy Ghost to us.
6. Try to call on the Holy Ghost every day to help you out in some difficulty, however small.
7. How do you prove that you believe your body is a temple of the Holy Ghost?
8. Could you prove that one of the greatest graces is the keeping of our souls in the state of sanctifying grace?
9. Explain how the merits of Christ bring grace to our souls.

Study Catechism Lesson IX, *The Holy Ghost and Grace* (Con't.), Questions, 108–116, pp. 208–209.

# Part 3. Prayer and the Sacraments, Especially the Holy Eucharist, Are the Principal Means to Obtain Grace

Since actual grace and sanctifying grace are absolutely necessary for us, how can we obtain these graces from God? *The principal ways of obtaining grace are prayer and the sacraments, especially the Holy Eucharist.*

## 1. Prayer Brings Grace

To speak to God in prayer we need only our mind and our will. No matter where I am, or where I go, or what I am doing I can pray. I can pray anywhere and at any time. When I am in the state of grace God is in my soul. I need only to think of God with love and gratitude, begging forgiveness and asking His help. God will not let even a little prayer go unanswered. A poet once very truthfully stated, "More things are wrought by prayer than this earth dreams of."

To help us pray better we could use some of the following hints. In church it will help to keep our eyes on the tabernacle or a statue. In a more public place, it is helpful to keep our eyes cast down. Kneeling shows our acknowledgment of God's greatness and help us to be humble. An erect posture at prayer shows reverence, respect, and love.

Some people in the Old and New Testament have spoken so beautifully to God that their conversations have come down to us through long ages, for example, the Psalms of King David. Let us try to talk worthily to God. We need His graces, His gifts, His heavenly home. We want others to get there, too. We want to know the language of heaven

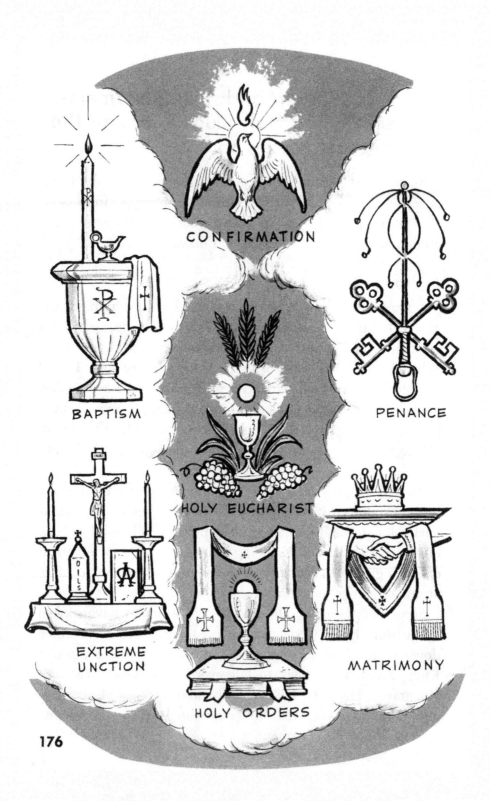

CONFIRMATION

BAPTISM

PENANCE

HOLY EUCHARIST

EXTREME
UNCTION

HOLY ORDERS

MATRIMONY

176

even here on earth. But we should learn to talk to God in our own words, too.

## 2. The Sacraments Bring Grace

Another way to obtain God's supernatural gifts, besides prayer, is by receiving the sacraments. Can you name the seven sacraments? Which brings the most grace? The Holy Eucharist brings the most grace because it contains Christ Himself, the source of all grace. Some sacraments give sanctifying grace while others increase it in our soul. Besides sanctifying grace each sacrament also gives sacramental grace which provides special help to achieve the purpose of that sacrament.

We must not forget that the Eucharist is both a sacrament and a sacrifice. We can receive great graces from the Holy Eucharist as a sacrifice just as the good thief did. He prayed devoutly and contritely at the bloody sacrifice on Calvary and entered Paradise that very day. We, too, can assist devoutly at Mass. We can go to Mass every day. When we go to Mass, why should we be on time? Why should we stay for the entire Mass?

Other ways of obtaining grace are by performing good works, and using sacramentals. *Sacramentals are holy things or actions of which the Church makes use to obtain for us from God, through her intercession, spiritual and temporal favors.* God gives us grace when we perform good acts for His honor and our neighbor's good.

## 3. We Must Be Grateful for the Gift of Grace

Do you recall the story of the five wise and the five foolish virgins? There are many foolish boys and girls who do not realize the value of keeping in the state of grace. We should feel sorry for them because they do not know what they are losing. The wise persons are those who keep in the state of grace. They are wise because even their ordinary good actions, like eating, playing, and sleeping can give them double pay. While they are growing physically they can merit eternal rewards. The greater their love of God is, the more these wise people merit for heaven. They make certain that their acts gain more supernatural merit by daily praying the Morning Offering.

The least that we can do to show our gratitude for the gift of grace is to remain in the state of grace. We should try to increase grace by prayer and by receiving the sacraments, and do everything God wants us to do. There is no limit to the holiness God wants us to strive for, because to each one our Lord has said, "You therefore are to be perfect, even as your heavenly Father is perfect" (Mt. 5:48).

*We can make our most ordinary actions merit a heavenly reward by doing them for the love of God and by keeping ourselves in the state of grace.*

## REVIEW, VI–3

### WORD LIST

| | | | |
|---|---|---|---|
| unanswered | King David | acknowledgment | gratitude |
| increase | source | reverence | posture |
| sacramental | | | psalms |

### THINGS TO REMEMBER

1. Receiving the Holy Eucharist is the principal way of obtaining grace.
2. Sacramental grace is a special grace which accompanies each sacrament.

3. We must try to be recollected in prayer; that is, we must try to keep our minds on what we are saying when we talk to God.
4. We should thank God every day for His gift of grace.

## THINGS TO DISCUSS AND DO

1. Explain to the class how you can keep in the state of grace.
2. How can you gain grace while you are playing?
3. Assist at Mass more devoutly in thanksgiving for the sacrifice which made grace possible to you.
4. Why do we need God's graces?
5. Compose a prayer to our Blessed Mother in which you ask her to keep you close to her Son through His gift of grace.
6. If you do not already know the prayer to the Holy Ghost, learn it, and say it at least once each day.
7. Read the story of the Wedding Garment (Mt. 22). Explain to the class how it is related to this lesson.

Study Catechism Lesson 9, *The Holy Ghost and Grace*, Questions 117–118, pp. 209–210.

# Part 4. The Holy Spirit Also Brings or Infuses Supernatural Gifts — The Theological Virtues, the Gifts, Fruits, and Beatitudes

We have been studying about the Holy Ghost. Who is the Holy Ghost? What is His main work? When Christ told His Apostles He was going to leave them and go to the Father, they were troubled. In order to comfort them He made a promise to them. What was it? Yes, Christ told them He would send them an Advocate, a Comforter. This was the Holy Ghost. Tell the story of the coming of the Holy Ghost. Why did His coming have such a great effect on the Apostles?

FAITH     HOPE     CHARITY

## 1. The Holy Ghost Bestows Theological Virtues on the Soul

*The three theological virtues are faith, hope, and charity.* These virtues make us able to direct our minds and hearts to God. They help us to believe in God, to hope in Him, and to love Him with all our hearts for His own sake, and our neighbor as ourselves for the love of God. These virtues are powers for doing good which are infused or poured into the soul by God. They give our minds and wills *supernatural* power. They come from God as special supernatural helps to lead us back to Him. In order to have merit before God all other virtues must spring from these three.

*These virtues are called theological virtues because they have God for their proper object.* God is the One whom we believe, trust, and love. Although all virtues are directed to God, still, they do not all deal *directly* with Him, as for example, the virtue of justice, which deals directly with human rights and property. Because faith, hope, and love have God for their object or end they get the name, theological, which comes from the Greek word which means God.

We know that this first coming of the Holy Ghost took place on Pentecost. When do we first receive the Holy Ghost? The Holy Ghost comes to us for the first time in baptism. Because His chief work is to make us holy, He brings with Him sanctifying grace. This grace gives us a new life and nature. It gives us a part in the nature of God Himself. It also brings some very wonderful powers that help the soul to produce fruits. These powers are supernatural, that is, they are above our natural capacity of willing, thinking, acting. *The chief supernatural powers that are bestowed on our souls with sanctifying grace are the three theological virtues and the seven gifts of the Holy Ghost.* They help produce the fruits of the Holy Ghost and the beatitudes in our lives. First let us look at the three theological virtues.

## 2. Faith Is the Virtue of Belief

The first supernatural power which sanctifying grace brings is the gift of faith. Faith gives our intellect or understanding the power to know, and to believe in a supernatural way.

Since faith is a gift of God, we can obtain this power to believe only through God's grace. We might say, this virtue impels the soul to believe the truths which God has revealed. Faith is very necessary in the life of every Christian for it is the foundation of all other virtues. Although we do not fully understand the mysteries in the Apostles' Creed, faith makes it possible for us to believe firmly in the Creation, Redemption, and all other doctrines of the Church. *Faith is the virtue by which we firmly believe all the truths God has revealed, on the word of God revealing them, who can neither deceive nor be deceived.*

We say that faith is the virtue by which we "believe." This means that we do not know or understand completely. A fact, such as "one and one are two," we accept or understand. But through the gift of faith we accept all the doctrines of the Church, all the truths that God has revealed, even though we do not understand them. God cannot deceive. Furthermore, no one can deceive Him. Why not? God is all-knowing. No one can hide anything from Him.

How can we strengthen our faith right now? We develop our muscles by using them regularly; so too, we must develop our faith by frequently making acts of faith. Let us review our Act of Faith as it is written in this text. In this prayer, let us find a definition for the virtue of faith.

We should often thank God for the gift of faith. We can show that we appreciate it by living it in our daily lives. This means that we should see God's loving Providence in everything that happens to us. In the pleasant and unpleasant happenings of the day, let us learn to say, "Thank You, God." What are some daily occurrences that may demand the exercise of our virtue of faith?

When we find it hard to see God's loving plan for us, let us pray, "Lord, increase our faith." Let us also remember, "For he who comes to God must believe that God exists and is a rewarder to those who seek him" (Hebr. 11:6).

## 3. Hope Is the Virtue of Trust

Are we sure of getting what we hope for from human beings: our parents, teachers, friends? How does this hope differ from that which we place in God? When we place our hope in God, we practice the supernatural virtue of hope. The virtue of hope gives our will the supernatural power to put our complete trust in God. It gives us the supernatural habit of firmly trusting God, depending on Him to fulfill His promises. Why? Because He is all-powerful. There is nothing He cannot do. Furthermore, He is faithful to His promises. "Heaven and earth will pass away, but my words will not pass away" (Mt. 24:35).

For what do we hope? The most important thing of course, is our eternal salvation and the means to obtain it. We are certain that God will give us all the means and graces we need to get to heaven. Why, then, do some people go to hell? They go there because they neglect or refuse to use the means to get to heaven, which are prayer and the sacraments.

Simeon, the prophet, who foretold the great sorrows of our Lady, is an excellent example of the practice of the virtue of hope. God had made a promise to him. Simeon waited many years before he saw the promised Redeemer. A legend says that he was so overjoyed at having seen Jesus that he died that very day.

Often we hear people say, "I have no confidence in myself." If these people practiced the virtue of hope, they would realize that with God's help they can do all things. St. Paul said, in the midst of most difficult work, "I can do all things in him who strengthens me" (Phil. 4:13). We know, too, from our own experience that if we really believe people are truthful, we are confident that they will keep the promises they make to us. Certainly God is more worthy of our trust than any human person. Therefore, we should seek God's help in everything we do. We should try to be patient and brave, for *hope is the virtue by which we firmly trust that*

*God, who is all-powerful and faithful to His promises, will in His mercy give us eternal happiness and the means to obtain it.*

We have all heard the saying, "While there is life, there is hope." In eternity there is no need for hope. Why is there no hope in heaven? In hell?

Because we can strengthen ourselves in the practice of the virtue of hope by frequently making acts of hope, let us review, at this point, the Act of Hope so that we know it by heart.

### 4. Charity Is the Virtue of Love

Before beginning the study of the third theological virtue, let us ask ourselves some very important questions. Why did the second Person of the Blessed Trinity live on earth for thirty-three years? It is because God loves us infinitely that He became man. Why do so many missionaries leave their native lands to live in a foreign country among people whom they do not know? Why do so many priests and religious leave everything that is dear to them? It is charity, or love of God and neighbor, that prompts these people to make such heroic sacrifices.

There are many saints whose lives are outstanding examples of the practice of the virtue of love. You remember how much St. Maria Goretti loved God. When a cruel death threatened her, she would not turn her back on Him. Again and again she repeated the prayer, "My God, I love Thee." Are we willing to suffer anything rather than commit a mortal sin? Is our charity equal to hers?

The virtue of charity gives our wills the supernatural power to love God and our neighbor in a supernatural way. The virtue of love is a supernatural gift which accompanies sanctifying grace. It has nothing to do with our feelings, which are natural. We may not like a certain individual, but by exercising this supernatural gift of love we can truly say that we love him because he is our neighbor and a child of God like ourselves. We wish him well because God made him to His own image and likeness. We must even love those who treat us unjustly because our Lord said, "Do good to those who hate you" (Mt. 5:44).

The following definition for the virtue of charity may help us to understand it better and lead us to practice charity toward God and men. *Charity is the virtue by which we love God above all things for His own sake, and our neighbor as ourselves for the love of God.*

We can increase the virtue of charity by receiving the sacraments. How can we strengthen this virtue when we are in the state of grace? Every time we have kind thoughts, every time we speak kind words, every time we perform good deeds for someone, realizing we are doing them for the love of God, we can strengthen the virtue of charity. But we must remember that the motive is an important thing in any of our actions. What does "motive" mean? The motive of an act means the reason why we do that act. For example: two students may perform the very same kind deed; one may greatly strengthen the virtue of charity by his action and the other may not. How can this happen? The motive or reason why we perform an action is important.

## REVIEW, VI–4

### WORD LIST

| | | | |
|---|---|---|---|
| Advocate | partake | theological | legend |
| doctrines | confidence | revealing | virtue |
| deceive | proper object | motivate | motive |

## THINGS TO REMEMBER

1. The three theological virtues are faith, hope, and charity.
2. The Holy Ghost infuses the theological virtues into our souls at baptism.
3. We cannot truly love God unless we love our neighbor.
4. Even the most difficult task can be performed with God's help.
5. Through the gift of faith, we believe all that God has revealed even though we cannot always understand it.

## THINGS TO DISCUSS AND DO

1. Compose an Act of Love including love of God and neighbor.
2. How is love of neighbor a proof of our love for God?
3. After receiving Holy Communion say a special prayer to our Lord, asking Him to increase your faith, hope, and love.
4. Recall the story of Jesus and St. Peter when Jesus asked Peter three times if he loved Him. Show what lesson you can take from this Gospel.
5. Find and explain the symbols of faith, hope, and charity. Draw them.
6. Why can the supernatural power to believe be given only by the grace of God?
7. What is the difference between knowing and believing?
8. What are some of the truths of our religion which we believe without understanding them fully?
9. What are some ways in which we can increase and strengthen the theological virtues?
10. Why is charity called the queen of virtues?

Study Catechism Lesson 10, *The Virtues and Gifts of the Holy Ghost*, Questions 119–124, pp. 210–211.

# Part 5.  The Holy Ghost Bestows His Seven Gifts

## 1. The Seven Gifts of the Holy Ghost

Besides the three theological virtues which we receive with sanctifying grace we also receive seven other gifts. These gifts provide additional assistance which helps us to live a life of grace. Since they come with sanctifying grace, they can be lost through mortal sin. We can strengthen and increase the gifts by using them.

*The seven gifts of the Holy Ghost are: wisdom, understanding, counsel, fortitude, knowledge, piety, and fear of the Lord.* Four of these gifts, wisdom, understanding, counsel, and knowledge enlighten our minds, that is, they help us to understand God's will. The other three, fortitude, piety, and fear of the Lord, strengthen our will and help us to heal the wounds of sin in our souls.

BLESSED ARE THE POOR IN SPIRIT... THE MEEK... THEY WHO MOURN...THEY WHO HUNGER AND THIRST FOR JUSTICE... THE MERCIFUL...THE CLEAN OF HEART...THE PEACEMAKERS...THEY WHO SUFFER'

In a general way, then, *the gifts of the Holy Ghost help us by making us more alert to discern and more ready to do the will of God.* "Now we have received not the spirit of the world, but the spirit that is from God, that we may know the things that have been given us by God" (1 Cor. 2:12). Let us now learn something about each gift of the Holy Ghost.

## Wisdom

We all like stories from the life of Christ. In the story of Mary and Martha, Christ said, "Martha, Martha, thou art anxious and troubled about many things; and yet only one thing is needful. Mary has chosen the best part, and it will not be taken away from her" (Lk. 10:41–42). What did our Lord mean by the best part? Had Mary shown real wisdom?

Wisdom, we know, helps us to put first things first; to think about eternal truths, to place a correct value on our salvation, and to love the things of God. Isn't this what Mary was doing? That is what our Lord meant by the best part.

People often say, "Put first things first," or "He has absolutely no sense of values." The gift of wisdom helps us to know that the first things, that is the most important things, are the things of God because He made us and we are His creatures. Our Christian sense of values should lead us to choose the things that will help us save our souls rather than those which might lead us to sin.

## Understanding

Pope Pius XI once had an audience with a group of pilgrims. As he was passing among the group, his eyes fell on a blind boy. He paused before Him and raised his ring to the boy's lips. Immediately the blind boy sensed what was happening. His lips trembled and his eyes filled with tears. Sympathetically, the Pope told the boy that his blindness was only physical and that we all experience spiritual blindness when we consider the truths of religion.

Only the Holy Ghost can help us to understand the teachings of the Church. It is His gift of understanding that helps us grasp in a small way an explanation of the meaning of the mysteries of faith.

God gives us the means to increase the gift of understanding. Some of the means are: listening attentively to sermons, earnestly studying our religion, and reading good Catholic books, magazines, and pamphlets. Can you think of other ways?

The better we understand our religion, the more capable we are of helping to spread God's kingdom here on earth. St. Thomas and St. Augustine, great doctors and teachers of the Church, used this gift of understanding to draw others to Christ and to increase the honor and glory of God.

## Counsel

Counsel is the gift by which the Holy Ghost helps us to make wise decisions and puts us on our guard against the attacks of the devil. Our Lord told many parables while He was on earth to explain how we are to use the gift of counsel. He gave us His own example on how to meet the attacks of the devil at the time He was tempted in the desert.

In one of His parables He said that the Kingdom of Heaven is like a treasure which a man found in a field. He then hid the treasure. He was so happy at finding such a treasure that he sold all he had to buy the field.

Again Christ said the Kingdom of Heaven is like a precious

pearl. A merchant seeking for precious pearls found one. At once he sold everything he had to get money to buy the precious pearl.

We, too, using our gift of counsel, can ward off the deceits of the devil and the world. We can choose those things that are going to lead us on the way of eternal salvation and give greater glory to God. We can give up the things that are of little value in order to win heaven.

## Fortitude

Fortitude is the gift of firmness of soul in bearing all difficulties. It is the gift of the Holy Ghost which helps us to practice constant patience and self-denial, to withstand persecution, and to carry out good resolutions regardless of the difficulties we may meet. We might call it spiritual bravery.

There are many examples of the practice of fortitude in the lives of the saints. One story is that of St. John Nepomucene. Over 500 years ago, King Wenceslaus IV of Bohemia appointed St. John as court preacher. Recognizing St. John's holiness, Queen Johanna chose him as her confessor. The King became madly jealous of his wife. One day he summoned St. John and demanded that he repeat what the Queen had told him in confession. Without hesitation, the confessor refused the King's request. The King, thinking he could win over St. John, promised him honors and riches. Seeing that this had no effect on the Saint, he began to threaten him, and finally imprisoned and tortured him on the rack. Still the priest remained firm in his refusal. Then the King granted him freedom. St. John spent this time preparing himself for the death he was sure would follow.

Several days later the King saw St. John walking in the

garden. He called him and again tried to get him to reveal the Queen's confession. Because St. John would not do so, the King condemned him to death. At the King's command, soldiers put a wooden gag into the saint's mouth, bound his hands and feet, and threw his body into the river at night. A bright light appeared and surrounded the body as it floated. By means of this light the Christians on the shore were able to find the body and give it Christian burial.

Many years later they opened the casket, and found only the tongue of the Saint. The rest of the body had decayed. God has preserved his tongue because St. John practiced great fortitude in keeping the seal of confession.

Although most of us will never have to practice fortitude in the heroic degree of St. John, we have many opportunities during the day to practice this virtue. Can you mention some? How can we be practicing fortitude right now? Are Catholics in other countries practicing fortitude in a heroic degree?

## Knowledge

The gift of knowledge helps us to recognize the things that will lead us to salvation. It assists us in using everything we meet in this world to help us to get to heaven.

The great St. Dominic, while still a youth, was a university student during a famine. In order to give a little help to the starving people, Dominic sold all of his furniture. Realizing that the people still needed help, he sold his most precious possession, his books. When a fellow student visited him he saw the empty bookshelves.

"What sort of knowledge should I get out of dead books," said Dominic, "while living men, brethren of mine, are dying of hunger?"

True knowledge is knowledge of God's will. Let us pray for true knowledge in this little prayer, "Teach me, O Lord, to do Thy will, for Thou art my God."

## Piety

St. Thérèse of Lisieux, a saint of our times, taught us much about the gift of piety. In her "little way" she always tried to please God by giving Him as much love as possible. "From the age of three, I have not refused the good God anything," she said. How many of us are able to say the same thing? Do our lives show that God and His interests are important to us? If we try to please God more and more, we are using our gift of piety. This gift helps us at all times to find joy in humble prayer and in performing our actions only to please God.

## Fear of the Lord

Fear of the Lord is a reverence for God which leads us to avoid offending our loving Father. St. Rose of Lima, the first canonized saint of the New World, was a very beautiful child. Instead of being proud of her beauty she feared that it might cause her or others to offend God. To prevent this, she cut off her curls and made herself unattractive to keep others from admiring her. Thus she was willing to sacrifice a natural gift to prevent an offense against God.

"Fear of the Lord is the beginning of wisdom," says the scripture. The thought of God's justice in rewarding good and punishing evil is a wholesome thought. There is a saying that the thought of hell has filled heaven. Christ Himself often mentioned hell and God's eternal punishment to His listeners.

## 2. The Virtues and Gifts Help To Produce the Twelve Fruits of the Holy Ghost

*Some of the effects in us of the gifts of the Holy Ghost are the fruits of the Holy Ghost and the beatitudes.* The fruits of the Holy Ghost carry a reward even here on earth, in the peace of soul which we enjoy when we practice the virtues. *The twelve fruits of the Holy Ghost are: charity, joy, peace, patience, benignity, goodness, long-suffering, mildness, faith, modesty, continency, and chastity.*

A chart of these fruits and their explanations might appear somewhat as follows:

| Fruits of the Holy Ghost | Practiced by: |
|---|---|
| 1. Charity | Love of God and neighbor |
| 2. Joy | Happiness of mind and heart in serving God; realization of God's goodness |
| 3. Peace | A joyful state of mind; the perfection of joy |
| 4. Patience | Calmness in trials and troubles |
| 5. Benignity | Sweetness of temper and disposition; a gentle kindness |
| 6. Goodness | Wishing, thinking, and doing what is right |
| 7. Long-suffering | Calmness or patience in long trials |
| 8. Mildness | Meekness and forbearance |
| 9. Faith | Truthfulness and veracity; belief in all the truths of God |
| 10. Modesty | Reverence of self; acceptance of praise in a balanced way |
| 11. Continency | Control of anger, impatience, evil desires and actions |
| 12. Chastity | Purity of soul and body |

## 3. The Theological Virtues and the Seven Gifts Help Produce the Eight Beatitudes

Another effect of the gifts of the Holy Ghost is mentioned in Christ's Sermon on the Mount. Great crowds of people came to hear Christ. When He saw the multitude so eager to learn, He began to teach them the rules of conduct which lead to true happiness. We call them the eight beatitudes.

The eight beatitudes are:

1. *Blessed are the poor in spirit, for theirs is the kingdom of heaven.*
2. *Blessed are the meek, for they shall possess the earth.*
3. *Blessed are they who mourn, for they shall be comforted.*
4. *Blessed are they who hunger and thirst for justice, for they shall be satisfied.*
5. *Blessed are the merciful, for they shall obtain mercy.*
6. *Blessed are the clean of heart, for they shall see God.*
7. *Blessed are the peacemakers, for they shall be called children of God.*
8. *Blessed are they who suffer persecution for justice' sake, for theirs is the kingdom of heaven (Mt. 5:3–10).*

God expects us to co-operate with grace and to produce within ourselves the fruits of the Holy Ghost. In the Gospel He tells us, "Every tree that does not bear good fruit is cut down and thrown into the fire" (Mt. 7:19).

Besides using these gifts as a means to gain our own salvation, God wants us to use them to attract others into His fold. The power of example is great. We should use as our motto the saying, "Don't go to heaven alone." We never know when our smallest act may influence others and lead them to eternal happiness. Let us pray many times, "Sacred Heart of Jesus, let me love Thee and make Thee loved."

# REVIEW, VI–5

spiritual blindness     eternal salvation     natural gifts
self-denial     discern     audience
alert     veracity     beatitudes
physical     pilgrims
deceits     enlighten

## THINGS TO REMEMBER

1. The Holy Ghost infused the seven gifts into our souls at baptism. These gifts are increased at confirmation.
2. When we use the seven gifts they produce the twelve fruits of the Holy Ghost.
3. The eight beatitudes are rules of conduct which form a perfect Christian character.

## THINGS TO DISCUSS AND DO

1. Number your paper from one to seven. Write the letter of the word in Column One which is explained in Column Two.

| Column One | Column Two |
|---|---|
| A. Wisdom | 1. Helps me to avoid sin through fear of offending God. |
| B. Understanding | 2. Helps me to love the things of God. |
| | 3. Gives me strength and courage to resist temptations. |
| C. Counsel | 4. Helps me to grasp in a small way an explanation of the meaning of the mysteries of faith. |
| D. Fortitude | 5. Shows me how to offer due worship and service to God. |
| E. Knowledge | 6. Puts me on guard against the deceits of the devil. |
| F. Piety | 7. Helps me to distinguish rightly between what I should and should not believe, and shows me what God wants me to do. |
| G. Fear of the Lord | |

2. Write a letter to a friend. In it explain how the seven gifts of the Holy Ghost help us.
3. Prepare a report on the Gifts of the Holy Ghost. Show how the use of these gifts results in the fruits of the Holy Ghost and the Beatitudes.
4. Make a chart of the twelve Fruits of the Holy Ghost. Using the chart give a talk to the class showing how each of these twelve fruits can be applied to our daily life.
5. Find saints to exemplify each of the Beatitudes.
6. Explain how a person who is wealthy can be poor in spirit.
7. Explain how a person who has little material wealth might not be poor in spirit.

Study Catechism Lesson 10, *The Virtues and Gifts of the Holy Ghost*, Questions 125–129, p. 212.

# Part 6.  The Holy Ghost Also Bestows Moral Virtues

*Besides the theological virtues of faith, hope, and charity there are other virtues, called moral virtues.* The theological virtues and the moral virtues in our souls grow more intense with every increase of sanctifying grace. These virtues become easier to exercise each time we practice them.

While the theological virtues deal directly with God, the moral virtues have to do with created things. *These virtues are called moral virtues because they dispose us to lead moral, or good, lives by aiding us to treat persons and things in the right way, that is, according to the will of God.*

A moral virtue or action may be either natural or supernatural. For example, a man pities a beggar. He gives him some money because he feels sorry for him. Was this a natural or a supernatural act? On another occasion he gives help to a beggar. This time, however, the man is in the state of grace and he looks upon the beggar as his brother whom Christ has redeemed. He gives the beggar

**197**

an alms because he knows Christ commanded him to love his brother as himself for God's sake. In this case his act is supernatural. He practiced divine charity, Christlike charity.

In order to gain merit for heaven a good act must be supernatural. It must be performed while in the state of grace.

A natural moral virtue can have only a natural reward. Moral supernatural virtues, however, help us to win merit and to gain heaven. Thus we can make our ordinary actions merit eternal reward for us by performing them in the state of grace and especially with the intention of pleasing God.

*The chief moral virtues are prudence, justice, fortitude, and temperance; these are called cardinal virtues.*

*These virtues are called cardinal virtues because they are like hinges on which hang all the other moral virtues and our whole moral life. The word "cardinal" is derived from the Latin word "cardo" meaning hinge.*

Let us learn the nature of these four moral virtues.

*Prudence disposes us in all circumstances to form right judgments about what we must do or not do.*

*Justice disposes us to give everyone what belongs to him.*

*Fortitude disposes us to do what is good in spite of any difficulty.*

*Temperance disposes us to control our desires and to use rightly the things which please our senses.*

## 1. Prudence Is Knowing What To Do or Not To Do

This virtue does two things. It helps us to see clearly what is right and what is wrong. It also helps to find the best means to do good and avoid evil.

Prudent boys and girls are those who not only "use their heads" but also pray that they may do good and avoid evil. Prudence tells us to think before we act. It urges us to seek the advice of our parents, priests, and teachers before we decide on important actions.

If we are prudent and know that certain persons, places, or things are occasions of sin for us, or cause scandal to others, we avoid them. If it is our habit to come late for Mass, prudence would lead us to set the alarm ten or fifteen minutes earlier or have someone call us.

If we realize that sanctifying grace makes every good act meritorious for heaven, then we should be prudent and remain in the state of grace. Some good words to remember are the words of the Psalmist: "Your ways, O Lord, make known to me; teach me your paths" (Ps. 24:4).

## 2. Justice Is the Habit of Being Fair To Everyone

First, justice is being fair to God: We must love, and serve God. We must worship Him as the Supreme Being both in private and in public. We should make every effort to keep His commandments, to pray to Him, and to do penance for having offended Him by our sins.

Second, justice is being fair to our neighbor: God gave us parents to love, reverence, and obey. He wishes us to be respectful, obedient, and loyal to our priests, teachers, civil authorities, and all others whom He has placed over us. He wants us to study well and be honest in our schoolwork. He expects us to be kind, just, and honest with our companions. He expects us to play fair and observe the rules in our games and social activities. He expects nations, like neighbors, to practice justice among themselves.

Third, justice is being fair to ourselves. We must be just to ourselves by trying to save our souls, by taking care of our health, by mixing play with work, and by being truthful, pure, and honorable in all our actions.

Justice demands that we respect and protect all God-given rights of man such as those that are written in our Declaration of Independence and in our just laws. There was peace in King Solomon's kingdom because he insisted that every man be given his just due. Let us ask God to help us to be just in every way, especially to Him.

### 3. Fortitude Is Strength in Doing Hard Things

Fortitude is another word for strength. It is the virtue which overcomes fear and directs our conduct to endure difficulties for God. We need courage to help us to save our souls. We must pray for it. It takes strength from God to obey, to be truthful, to be patient, to suffer disappointment, sickness, and the like, and to resist temptation.

In one of his letters, St. Paul tells us about his difficulties and hardships (2 Cor. 11:22–31). He triumphed over all his troubles, however, and died a martyr. It is heroic to overcome difficulties for God. Christ said about such conduct, "Therefore, everyone who acknowledges me before men, I also will acknowledge him before my Father in heaven" (Mt. 10:32) and again, ". . . he who loses his life for my sake, will find it" (Mt. 10:39). As Christ told the Apostles, so He tells us that He is returning to heaven to send the Spirit of Fortitude, the Spirit of Courage, to every one of us. When we need to be brave during temptation, trouble, or sickness, or when problems face us, let us ask the Holy Spirit for this gift of strength.

### 4. Temperance Is the Habit of Control of Self

Everything which God made is good, but sometimes men make bad use of the things He created. They overeat or overdrink and in other ways misuse His gifts, and thus break His laws. Temperance means not going too far in anything. It helps us to control our habits of eating, drinking, speaking, dressing, playing, and working.

Temperance is not easy. Christ, however, promised that He will change into joy the sorrow we endure in doing His will.

Let us imitate the Blessed Virgin and good St. Joseph

**201**

who practiced the supernatural moral virtues perfectly. Then we will become Christlike, holy and pleasing to God, with a guaranteed right to heaven.

## 5. Other Moral Virtues

There are also other moral virtues which the Holy Ghost gives to us. Besides the cardinal virtues, *some of the other moral virtues are: Filial piety and patriotism, which dispose us to honor, love, and respect our parents and our country.* Charity, however, commands us to think of others also. We should be able to see good in every human being and to wish for the welfare of all other nations as well as our own. Our charity should therefore be universal and exclude no one. Only then is it Catholic.

We remember Tobias, the younger, particularly for his filial piety, because he obeyed his father in all things and had a great reverence for him.

Under justice we consider the virtue of *obedience, which disposes us to do the will of our superiors.* By this we mean that it helps us obey those who have a right to command us or who have responsibility for us, as our parents, teachers, priests, and others. We should train ourselves to do what they command us promptly and cheerfully. Christ is the Model of obedience. It made no difference whether He was to help His mother in the house or His foster father in the carpenter shop. In doing their will He realized He was doing the will of His Father in heaven. He obeyed completely and lovingly even to the death on the cross.

Under justice also comes truthfulness or *veracity, which disposes us to tell the truth.* We need not tell everything we know. In fact there are times when we should not tell what we know. But we should always be truthful because we are children of God who is Truth itself. The boy Samuel practiced the virtue of veracity. Although greatly frightened, he told Heli, the high priest, that God was about to punish his two sons.

Justice also includes *liberality, which disposes us rightly to use worldly goods.* We should always be ready to give generously to those in need. Many American boys and girls give some of their spending money to the missions. Their parents give clothes to those who are needy. Some families share their homes with orphan children. They help the poor; make their holidays cheerful. These people know that what they give and do for the poor, they give and do to Christ.

A part of the virtue and gift of fortitude is *patience, which disposes us to bear up under trials and difficulties.* Job practiced the virtue of patience. God had blessed him with wealth, friends, a good family, and many other things which make life enjoyable on this earth. To try Job, however, God allowed the devil to take all these good things away from him and replaced them with sorrow and suffering. But despite his misfortune, Job did not complain. He continued to praise God (Job 19:25–26).

Temperance includes *humility, which disposes us to acknowledge our limitations.* Compared to God, who are we? What do we have that is our very own? Our wealth, appearance, dress, abilities, or what others think of us, these are not the most important things in life. The virtues that we practice to please God are the only treasures we can take with us when we die. Christ said, ". . . learn from me, for I am meek and humble of heart; and you will find rest for your souls" (Mt. 11:29). He also said: "Seek first the kingdom of God and His justice, and all these things shall be given you besides" (Mt. 6:33).

Temperance includes *chastity, or purity, which disposes us to be pure in soul and body.* Many martyrs died to keep the virtue of chastity. Recall the stories of the martyrdom of St. Agnes and St. Maria Goretti. Let us have a special devotion to the Blessed Virgin and ask her daily to help us to be pure. Memorize this prayer, "My Queen! my Mother! I give thee all myself, and, to show my devotion to thee, I consecrate to thee my eyes, my ears, my mouth, my heart, my entire self. Wherefore, O loving Mother, as I am thine own, keep me, defend me, as thy property and possession."

*Besides these, there are many other moral virtues.* We must remember, however, that the virtue of religion, which is a part of the virtue of justice, is the highest moral virtue. By practicing it we give God the worship that belongs to Him. We practice this virtue especially when we unite with Christ in His perfect prayer and sacrifice, the Holy Mass. "Blessing and glory and wisdom and thanksgiving, honor, might and power be unto our God for ever and ever. Amen."

## REVIEW, VI–6

### WORD LIST

| | | |
|---|---|---|
| moral | interior | civil authorities |
| dispose | patriotism | cause of scandal |
| virtue | limitations | welfare of other nations |
| liberality | veracity | meritorious |

### THINGS TO REMEMBER

1. The moral virtues are of two kinds, natural and supernatural.
2. We receive the supernatural moral virtues at baptism.
3. The supernatural moral virtues increase in our souls with the increase of sanctifying grace.

4. The Blessed Virgin Mary and St. Joseph possessed the supernatural moral virtues in their entirety.
5. The practice of the moral supernatural virtues keeps us on the right road to God.

## THINGS TO DISCUSS AND DO

1. Write an original prayer in which you ask God to increase the moral supernatural virtues in your soul.
2. Play a guessing game on the cardinal virtues listed in this lesson.
3. Make a visit to St. Joseph and ask him to help you practice that moral virtue which you think you need most.
4. Discuss how St. Joseph practiced faith, obedience, charity, humility, courage, prudence, and other virtues.
5. Read the life of St. Martin de Porres and tell the class how he practiced the moral virtues.
6. Tell how the two kinds of moral virtues differ.
7. Name the virtues we practice when we:
   are fair to everyone,
   control ourselves,
   are strong in doing hard things,
   know what to do or not to do,
   tell the truth,
   are pure in soul and body,
   see how weak we are and how great God is,
   honor and respect our parents,
   use money for good purposes,
   do not complain when we are hurt or when we suffer.
8. On a separate paper write the numbers from one to ten and write the moral virtues which are practiced in the following acts.
   1) Promptly answering your mother when she calls.
   2) Never cheating in schoolwork.
   3) Showing respect and regard for traffic officers and patrol boys.
   4) Thinking before acting.
   5) Not doing a wrong act when the gang thinks it is a clever thing to do.

6) Letting others use your baseball glove, or ball and bat.
7) Contributing to the support of the Church in the Sunday collection.
8) Taking time out to greet Mother and telling her about the day, before joining the neighborhood crowd after school.
9) Consulting the list of approved movies before going to the theater.
10) Knowing when to stop whether eating, playing, joking, or working.

Study Catechism Lesson 10, *The Virtues and Gifts of the Holy Ghost*, Questions 130–135, pp. 214–215.

# End-of-Unit Review — Unit VI

**PART 1**

## CATECHISM

### LESSON 9

#### The Holy Ghost and Grace

105. **Who is the Holy Ghost?**

The Holy Ghost is God and the third Person of the Blessed Trinity.

106. **From whom does the Holy Ghost proceed?**

The Holy Ghost proceeds from the Father and the Son.

107. **Is the Holy Ghost equal to the Father and the Son?**

The Holy Ghost is equal to the Father and the Son, because He is God.

## OTHER QUESTIONS AND EXERCISES

1. Is the Holy Ghost true God?
2. How does the work of the Holy Ghost prove God's love for us?
3. Why should Catholics practice devotion to the Holy Ghost?
4. Why do we call the third Person of the Blessed Trinity the Holy Ghost?
5. How are we temples of God?
6. How does the Holy Ghost dwell in us?
7. What is the work of the Holy Ghost as our advocate?
8. How is the Holy Ghost mentioned in the Nicene Creed?
9. Why is belief in the Holy Ghost a test of our faith?
10. How could you express your thanks to the Holy Ghost in prayer?

# CATECHISM

## LESSON 9 (Cont.)

### The Holy Ghost and Grace

**108. What does the Holy Ghost do for the salvation of mankind?**

The Holy Ghost dwells in the Church as the source of its life and sanctifies souls through the gift of grace.

**109. What is grace?**

Grace is a supernatural gift of God bestowed on us through the merits of Jesus Christ for our salvation.

**110. How many kinds of grace are there?**

There are two kinds of grace: sanctifying grace and actual grace.

**111. What is sanctifying grace?**

Sanctifying grace is that grace which confers on our souls a new life, that is, a sharing in the life of God Himself.

**112. What are the chief effects of sanctifying grace?**

The chief effects of sanctifying grace are:
*first,* it makes us holy and pleasing to God;
*second,* it makes us adopted children of God;
*third,* it makes us temples of the Holy Ghost;
*fourth,* it gives us the right to heaven.

**113. What is actual grace?**

Actual grace is a supernatural help of God which enlightens our mind and strengthens our will to do good and to avoid evil.

**114. Can we resist the grace of God?**

We can resist the grace of God, for our will is free, and God does not force us to accept His grace.

**115. Why is sanctifying grace necessary for salvation?**

Sanctifying grace is necessary for salvation because it is the supernatural life, which alone enables us to attain the supernatural happiness of heaven.

**116. Is actual grace necessary for all who have attained the use of reason?**

Actual grace is necessary for all who have attained the use of reason, because without it we cannot long resist the power of temptation or perform other actions which merit a reward in heaven.

## OTHER QUESTIONS AND EXERCISES

1. Why does God give us grace?
2. Why should we pray to the Holy Ghost before confession?
3. Tom says we should pray to the Holy Ghost especially before tests. Do you agree with him? Why?
4. In what two ways can we increase the supernatural life received at baptism?
5. If we really appreciate sanctifying grace, what resolution would we make?
6. Why should we accept the actual grace God offers us?
7. Name some actual graces you receive every day.
8. Do we sometimes act like the young man to whom Jesus said, "If thou wilt be perfect sell what thou hast and follow me." How did this young man refuse actual grace?
9. Does God force us to accept His grace? How could you prove this?
10. Why is actual grace so important in our daily life?

**PART 3**

# CATECHISM

### LESSON 9 (Cont.)

#### The Holy Ghost and Grace

**117. What are the principal ways of obtaining grace?**

The principal ways of obtaining grace are prayer and the sacraments, especially the Holy Eucharist.

118. How can we make our most ordinary actions merit a heavenly reward?

We can make our most ordinary actions merit a heavenly reward by doing them for the love of God and by keeping ourselves in the state of grace.

## OTHER QUESTIONS AND EXERCISES

1. What kind of prayer is most pleasing to God?
2. What is the simplest kind of prayer?
3. Is just reminding ourselves that we are in the presence of God a prayer? How?
4. Why should we receive Holy Communion frequently?
5. What value is there in ejaculatory prayer?
6. How does the Holy Eucharist especially give grace?
7. Does having sanctifying grace in our souls mean the same thing as being free from mortal sin? Explain.
8. How can we receive grace from the Holy Eucharist as a sacrifice?
9. Is overcoming temptation a means of gaining grace? How?
10. What is the best way to show our gratitude for the gift of grace?

**PART 4**

## CATECHISM

### LESSON 10

#### The Virtues and the Gifts of the Holy Ghost

119. What are the chief supernatural powers that are bestowed on our souls with sanctifying grace?

The chief supernatural powers that are bestowed on our souls with sanctifying grace are the three theological virtues and the seven gifts of the Holy Ghost.

120. Why are these virtues called theological virtues?

These virtues are called theological virtues because they have God for their proper object.

**121. What are the three theological virtues?**

The three theological virtues are faith, hope, and charity.

**122. What is faith?**

Faith is the virtue by which we firmly believe all the truths God has revealed, on the word of God revealing them, who can neither deceive nor be deceived.

**123. What is hope?**

Hope is the virtue by which we firmly trust that God, who is all-powerful and faithful to His promises, will in His mercy give us eternal happiness and the means to obtain it.

**124. What is charity?**

Charity is the virtue by which we love God above all things for His own sake, and our neighbor as ourselves for the love of God.

## OTHER QUESTIONS AND EXERCISES

1. How do we partake of the nature of God?
2. Why is faith necessary in the life of every Christian?
3. How should we develop our faith?
4. When is hope a supernatural virtue? When is it a natural virtue?
5. How do we practice the virtue of hope in our daily lives?
6. Why is there no need for hope in heaven?
7. What do we mean when we say we must love our neighbor as ourselves for the love of God?
8. Why should we pray for our enemies?
9. What does the word "neighbor" mean?
10. What motive, or reason, should we have for all we do?

## PART 5

# CATECHISM

### LESSON 10 (Cont.)

#### The Virtues and Gifts of the Holy Ghost

**125. Which are the seven gifts of the Holy Ghost?**

The seven gifts of the Holy Ghost are: wisdom, understanding, counsel, fortitude, knowledge, piety, and fear of the Lord.

**126. How do the gifts of the Holy Ghost help us?**

The gifts of the Holy Ghost help us by making us more alert to discern and more ready to do the will of God.

**127. Which are some of the effects in us of the gifts of the Holy Ghost?**

Some of the effects in us of the gifts of the Holy Ghost are the fruits of the Holy Ghost and the beatitudes.

**128. Which are the twelve fruits of the Holy Ghost?**

The twelve fruits of the Holy Ghost are: charity, joy, peace, patience, benignity, goodness, long-suffering, mildness, faith, modesty, continency, and chastity.

**129. Which are the eight beatitudes?**

The eight beatitudes are:
1. Blessed are the poor in spirit, for theirs is the kingdom of heaven.
2. Blessed are the meek, for they shall possess the earth.
3. Blessed are they who mourn, for they shall be comforted.
4. Blessed are they who hunger and thirst for justice, for they shall be satisfied.

5. Blessed are the merciful, for they shall obtain mercy.
6. Blessed are the clean of heart, for they shall see God.
7. Blessed are the peacemakers, for they shall be called children of God.
8. Blessed are they who suffer persecution for justice' sake, for theirs is the kingdom of heaven.

## OTHER QUESTIONS AND EXERCISES

1. How are the seven gifts of the Holy Ghost lost?
2. What is the best way to strengthen and increase the seven gifts?
3. Give an example from daily life showing how you use each of the seven gifts.
4. To whom especially should we pray to understand the teachings of the Church?
5. Why is there such great need for every Catholic to understand his religion?
6. How do the little acts of self-denial we practice every day help us gain the gift of fortitude?
7. What other virtues besides fortitude did St. John Nepomucene practice? What lesson does that teach us?
8. The religion text says: "True knowledge is knowledge of God's will." Explain in your own words what this means and tell how it applies to you.
9. How do we use the gift of piety?
10. What is meant by peace of soul? How can we obtain it?
11. How can we be poor in spirit?
12. How can we apply to ourselves the quotation from the Gospel, "Every tree that does not bear good fruit is cut down and thrown into the fire"?

## PART 6

# CATECHISM

## LESSON 10 (Cont.)

### The Virtues and Gifts of the Holy Ghost

**130. Are there any other virtues besides the theological virtues of faith, hope, and charity?**

Besides the theological virtues of faith, hope, and charity there are other virtues, called moral virtues.

**131. Why are these virtues called moral virtues?**

These virtues are called moral virtues because they dispose us to lead moral, or good, lives by aiding us to treat persons and things in the right way, that is, according to the will of God.

**132. Which are the moral virtues?**

The chief moral virtues are prudence, justice, fortitude, and temperance; these are called cardinal virtues.

**133. Why are these virtues called cardinal virtues?**

These virtues are called cardinal virtues because they are like hinges on which hang all the other moral virtues and our whole moral life. The word "cardinal" is derived from the Latin word "cardo" meaning hinge.

**134. How do prudence, justice, fortitude, and temperance dispose us to lead good lives?**

Prudence disposes us in all circumstances to form right judgments about what we must do or not do.

Justice disposes us to give everyone what belongs to him.

Fortitude disposes us to do what is good in spite of any difficulty.

Temperance disposes us to control our desires and to use rightly the things which please our senses.

### 135. Which are some of the other moral virtues?

Some of the other moral virtues are:

Filial piety and patriotism, which dispose us to honor, love, and respect our parents and our country.

Obedience, which disposes us to do the will of our superiors.

Veracity, which disposes us to tell the truth.

Liberality, which disposes us rightly to use worldly goods.

Patience, which disposes us to bear up under trials and difficulties.

Humility, which disposes us to acknowledge our limitations.

Chastity, or purity, which disposes us to be pure in soul and body.

Besides these, there are many other moral virtues.

## OTHER QUESTIONS AND EXERCISES

1. Explain how the practice of the moral virtues will make you a better American as well as a better Catholic.
2. Are the moral virtues meant only for Catholics? Explain your answer.
3. When are the moral virtues supernatural?
4. In what sense are the cardinal moral virtues hinges?
5. How do we practice justice toward God?
6. How can we practice the virtue of liberality?
7. Mention three ways in which you can practice patience.
8. Why should St. Maria Goretti have a special appeal for boys and girls your age?
9. What is meant by the virtue of religion?

# Unit VII.  Christ Sends the Holy Spirit To Guide His Church

# Part 1. The Church Leads All Men to Salvation

In the unit we have just completed we learned that the Holy Ghost loves us so much that He remains with us when we are in the state of sanctifying grace, and always helps us with actual grace. In gratitude we certainly have promised to show our love for Him by praying to Him before confession, before study or big undertakings, in temptation, and at many other times.

Now we shall review what we know about the Church and learn many new things about how the Holy Ghost gives us His grace through the Church. We shall then better appreciate our belonging to the Church. We will also do all we can to help others to find the true Church.

## 1. Christ Promised To Send the Holy Ghost

Just as the Father sent His divine Son into the world to save sinful men, so Christ together with the Father sent the Holy Ghost to continue the work of salvation. Before Christ ascended into heaven He organized His Church, and promised to send the Holy Ghost, to dwell in the Church until the end of time. It is through the Holy Ghost that the Church brings all men to salvation (Jn. 16:7–15).

## 2. The Apostles Prepared for the Coming of the Holy Ghost

Just before His Ascension, Christ told His Apostles to stay in the city, ". . . until you are clothed with power from on high" (Lk. 24:49). So they went back from Mount Olivet to Jerusalem and hid themselves in the Upper Room. The Blessed Virgin and the other disciples were with them. Here

**217**

they waited in prayer for nine days, making the first novena in the Church.

### 3. The Church Is the Congregation of All Baptized People

The Catholic Church is Christ's society which trains men for heaven. It is a supernatural society, because its founder, Jesus Christ, was true God. It is a supernatural society, because its purpose is to give all men the supernatural life of sanctifying grace and to enable them to attain eternal happiness in union with the Triune God in heaven. It is a supernatural society, because it administers the seven sacraments or seven channels of divine grace established by Jesus Christ to allow men to share in the fruits of His redemption.

Besides this, the Church is a visible society. It is a visible society because it is made up of men and women of flesh and blood. It has a visible head, the pope, who acts as the vicar of Christ, its invisible head. The supernatural life of sanctifying grace, which the Church brings to men through the sacraments, makes use of visible, sensible signs: water in baptism, bread and wine for the Eucharist, oil for Confirmation and Extreme Unction.

The members of this society must do the following: they must receive the sacrament of baptism and believe the teachings of the Church. They must assist at the Holy Mass and receive the sacraments. They must obey the Holy Father and the bishops who are united with him.

Our Lord often spoke of the Church He was establishing. In His parables He compared it with the things the people saw about them, such as a sheepfold, a kingdom, a grain of mustard seed, a city placed on a mountain, a light on a candlestick. Christ also likened His Church to a vine. He said, "I am the vine, you are the branches" (Jn. 15:5).

In other parts of the Bible, there are other names for the Church. These are "a body" (Eph. 1:23); "the house of God" (Tim. 3:15); and "a holy city" (Apoc. 21:10). A symbol for the Church is the ark. If you know the story of Noah and the Ark you will be able to understand why the ark is a symbol of the Church.

When we say "Catholic Church" we do not mean a building of stone or wood, even though we find this comparison in Scripture (Eph. 2:21). When we speak of the Catholic Church we mean that *the Church is the congregation of all* baptized persons united in the same true faith, the same sacrifice, and the same sacraments, under the authority of the Sovereign Pontiff and the bishops in communion with him.

Jesus Christ founded the Church. Jesus Christ founded the Church to bring all men to eternal salvation.

The Church instructs us in our duties to God, our neighbor, and ourselves. It provides us with the sacraments which make us pure, strong, and holy.

## 4. The Holy Spirit Dwells in the Church

The Church is enabled to lead men to salvation by the indwelling of the Holy Ghost, who gives it life. We mentioned before how the Holy Ghost dwells in the Church. God the Father and God the Son sent the Holy Ghost to dwell in the Church. The dwelling of the Holy Ghost in the Church was first visibly manifested on Pentecost Sunday, when He came down upon the Apostles in the form of tongues of fire. It will last as long as the world exists, for the Holy Ghost will dwell in the Church until the end of time.

As the soul in the human body helps it to grow, act, and become perfect, so the Holy Spirit dwells and works in the Church and all its members. The Holy Ghost is the soul of the Church.

The indwelling of the Holy Ghost enables the Church to teach, to sanctify, and to rule the faithful in the name of Christ. These are the three great works or missions of the Church. By teaching, sanctifying, and ruling in the name of Christ is meant that the Church always does the will of its divine Founder, who remains forever its invisible Head.

## The Church Teaches Its Members

The Church has power to do Christ's work in His name. Christ said to the Apostles He had chosen: "As the Father has sent me, I also send you" (Jn. 20:22). He bade them teach the doctrine He had taught. He gave them all power saying, "He who hears you, hears me; and he who rejects you, rejects me" (Lk. 10:16). He sent them to all nations and promised to be with them until the end of the world (Mt. 28:20).

## The Church Sanctifies Its Members

The Church sanctifies its members by uniting them to Christ. It does this through the Mass, the sacraments, especially the Holy Eucharist, and by the many opportunities it offers for practicing the supernatural virtues.

## The Church Rules Its Members

Before He ascended into heaven, our divine Lord told His Apostles, who were the first bishops of the Catholic Church, "Go, therefore, and make disciples of all nations . . . teaching them to observe all that I have commanded you" (Mt. 28:18, 20). He thereby gave His Apostles and their successors, the bishops of the Catholic Church, the power to rule the members of His Church.

Any organization or society needs law if it is to carry out its work. The Church also, the supernatural society founded by Christ, has laws and rules which its members must obey. The laws of the Church are intended to help men reach heaven. They help us know what we must believe and what we must do if we are to be happy forever with God.

Since the Church can make laws, it can also punish us if we disobey them. In very serious cases, the Church can even punish us by excommunication. This means that a person is no longer a member of the Church. Because of his disobedience he has been cut off from the society founded by Jesus Christ. He has revolted against Christ and deprived himself of the full use of the means to attain salvation. Even when the Church excommunicates a person, however, she is always ready to welcome him back. Like Christ, the Church rejoices at the return of repentant sinners.

## 6. Christ Is the Invisible Head of the Church

Christ had told His Apostles that even though He would ascend to His Father, He would be with them always: ". . . and behold, I am with you all days, even unto the consummation of the world" (Mt. 28:20). This is what we mean when we say Christ is the invisible Head of the Church.

With Christ, the Apostles became the governing members of the Church. There is no Church without them, just as there is no Church without Christ. For, *Christ gave the power to teach, to sanctify, and to rule the members of His Church to the Apostles, the first bishops of the Church.*

Christ commanded the Apostles to teach all nations, but He did not intend that the Apostles alone should have this power. *No, Christ intended that this power should be exercised also by their successors, the bishops of the Church.*

Besides giving them the power to teach and govern, Christ had also ordained His Apostles priests with the right to offer the sacrifice of the Mass. ". . . do this in remembrance of me" (1 Cor. 11:24).

The Apostles went to all the nations as Christ commanded them. As the number of Christians increased, the Apostles chose men who were outstanding in virtue and ability, and made them bishops and appointed them as rulers of the new

Christian communities. These new bishops also had power to ordain and appoint others. The bishops are the successors of the Apostles and, as such, they have the full power to teach, govern, and sanctify. The priests do not have the fullness of these powers. The deacons have less power than the priests. Today, *the priests, especially parish priests, assist the bishops in the care of souls.*

## 7. St. Peter Was the First Visible Head of the Church

Christ had instructed His Apostles to carry on His work in all nations. He knew that as the Church grew and spread, problems would arise. In His visible society there would have to be a visible head who would solve the problems as they came up. Whom did Christ choose for this important task? *Christ gave special power in His Church to St. Peter by making him the head of the Apostles and the chief teacher and ruler of the entire Church.* St. Peter, therefore, had the final word in all matters of faith and good conduct.

Christ said to St. Peter, "And I will give thee the keys of the kingdom of heaven; and whatever thou shalt bind on earth shall be bound in heaven, and whatever thou shalt loose on earth shall be loosed in heaven" (Mt. 16:19). St. Peter, therefore, had the supreme right to rule God's Church. He had the right to forgive or not to forgive. If Peter forgives, God forgives. If Peter removes punishment due to sin, so also does God. Peter binds and looses in the name of God and by His power.

But Peter could not live on this earth forever. He lived for a short time at Antioch. Then he went to Rome, and from there ruled the Church. He was the first bishop of Rome, the vicar or representative of Christ on earth, and the visible head of the Church. Rome thus became the city of the pope. There Peter died the death of a martyr about the year 67.

Linus succeeded Peter as pope. Because he was the lawful successor of St. Peter he became the head of the Church. Cletus succeeded Linus. So it has continued to our own day. Pope has succeeded pope in an unbroken line to our present Holy Father. This happened because *Christ did not intend that the special power of chief teacher and ruler of the entire Church should be exercised by St. Peter alone, but intended that this power should be passed down to his successor, the pope, the bishop of Rome, who is the Vicar of Christ on earth and the visible head of the Church.*

## 8. We Are Members of the Church and Should Join in Catholic Action

The Church is made up not only of a pope, cardinals, archbishops, bishops, and priests, but of laity as well. *The laity of the Church are all its members who do not belong to the clerical or to the religious state.*

Ordained men belong to the clerical state, as bishops and priests. Priests, brothers, and sisters who have made the vows of religion belong to the religious state.

We, the laity of the Church, have a work to do in the Church. We must try to be good members of the Church, true Christians, other Christs.

The laity play an important part in the Church. Many saints were lay people as for example, St. Elizabeth of Hungary, St. Louis of France, St. Thomas More, and St. Dominic Savio.

The clergy cannot perform the great work of the Church alone, for as Christ says: "The harvest indeed is great, but the laborers are few" (Mt. 9:37). The clergy need the help of every member of the Church. But how can the laity help the Church in her care of souls? They can help by leading good lives that will show or reflect the holiness of the Church. ". . . let your light shine before men, in order that they may see your good works and give glory to your Father in heaven" (Mt. 5:16). The laity can engage in Catholic Action by being real apostles of Christ under the guidance of their bishops and priests. They can do this by helping the priest with parish activities, aiding the missions, performing spiritual and corporal works of mercy, attending parish functions, and in many other ways. Can you think of a few?

Briefly, *the laity can help the Church in her care of souls by leading lives that will reflect credit on the Church, and by co-operating with their bishops and priests, especially through Catholic Action.*

God's ministers in the priesthood, especially the Holy Father, have a heavy burden. We should pray earnestly and often for them.

*A Prayer for the Holy Father*

"Lord Jesus, shelter our Holy Father the Pope under the protection of Thy Sacred Heart. Be Thou his light, his strength and his consolation."

## REVIEW, VII–1

### WORD LIST

| | | | |
|---|---|---|---|
| consummation | laity | doctrine | congregation |
| regulations | authority | foundation | Sovereign Pontiff |
| prevail | | | excommunication |

### THINGS TO REMEMBER

1. God the Father and God the Son sent God the Holy Ghost to complete the instruction of the Apostles and to bring all men to salvation.

2. The Apostles prepared for the coming of the Holy Ghost by prayer.
3. Pentecost Sunday is often referred to as the "birthday" of the Church.
4. The Church needs the Holy Spirit to make it live and to keep it alive.
5. The Holy Spirit guides the Church in the way of holiness and truth.

## THINGS TO DISCUSS AND DO

1. Number one to five. Complete the sentences in Column Two by writing on your paper the letters in front of the phrases in Column One which complete them.

| *Column One* | *Column Two* |
|---|---|
| A. by the Holy Ghost | 1. The Holy Ghost proceeds |
| B. with the Church forever | 2. The Holy Spirit will abide |
| C. from the Father and the Son | 3. We should often pray to the Holy Ghost |
| D. for enlightenment | 4. The Church is sanctified |
| E. enables the Church to teach, sanctify, and rule | 5. The Holy Ghost |

2. On a separate sheet of paper, write the missing words.

Our bodies are ..(1).. of the Holy Ghost.

The Holy Spirit first comes to us when we receive ..(2)...

The ..(3).. and the ..(4).. sent the Holy Ghost upon the Apostles.

The Holy Ghost is equal to the ..(5).. and the ..(6)...

The Holy Ghost came upon the Apostles in the form of ..(7)...

Jesus Christ ..(8).. the Church to bring all men to salvation.

The Church is enabled to lead all men to salvation by the indwelling of the Holy Ghost, who gives it ..(9)...

The laity can help the Church in her care of souls by leading lives that will reflect credit on the ..(10)...

3. Why should we have great respect for every priest?
4. Give some examples of how the laity can help the Church today.
5. Why should we love the Catholic Church?
6. Write a paragraph on the present pope, on your bishop, and on your pastor.
7. Make a visit every day and pray for God's blessing on each of the authorities in the Church. Ask some special blessing for each of them.

Study Catechism Lesson 11, *The Catholic Church*, Questions 136–151, pp. 245–247.

# Part 2.  The Catholic Church Has Certain Marks and Attributes

Has anyone ever asked you why you believed that the Catholic Church is the true Church? Were you able to convince the person who asked you that *the one true Church established by Christ is the Catholic Church?* Were you also able to explain that *we know that the Catholic Church is the one true Church established by Christ because it alone has the marks of the true Church?*

## 1. The Marks of the Church

In an earlier grade we learned that the marks of the Church are like signposts. They point out the Catholic Church as the only true Church. Now that we are a bit older let us

# The Church is...

One

Holy

Catholic

Apostolic

see how this Church can be the only true Church by considering its special characteristics, that is, its signs or marks.

Our catechism says: *By the marks of the Church we mean certain clear signs by which all men can recognize it as the true Church founded by Jesus Christ.* Each person has his own individual features by which he can be recognized. In the same way the marks of the Church set it off as the one true Church, and not as any other organization. No other Church has all these marks or signs, by which it can be recognized as the true Church. *The chief marks of the Church are four: It is one, holy, catholic or universal, and apostolic.*

### The Church Is One

To understand how the Church is one we must recall that when Christ promised to make St. Peter the head of the

Church He said, ". . . upon this rock (Peter means "rock") I will build my Church" (Mt. 16:18). He clearly said "Church" not "Churches."

Since this one true Church was founded by Jesus Christ, all its members are united in three ways: first, in doctrine, that is, in truths taught and believed. No matter where we go, we will find the essential teachings of the Church are the same. This is what we mean when we say the Church is one in doctrine, or united in faith.

Second, the Church is united in worship. Everywhere in the world the Church offers the same sacrifice and administers the same seven sacraments. A Chinese baby is baptized with the same words as a child in Australia or America. The absolution of a priest takes away the sins of Catholics in any part of the world. Bread and wine are changed into the body and blood of Christ by all Catholic priests regardless of color, race, nationality, or rite.

Third, the Church is one in government. When Jesus promised to build the Catholic Church on one rock and gave special powers to St. Peter, He wanted only one chief ruler or head. He intended that Peter pass on his authority, or right to rule, to the popes who would come after him. Always and everywhere the Pope is the visible head of the Church as successor of St. Peter.

Now we understand that *the Catholic Church is one because all its members, according to the will of Christ, profess the same faith, have the same sacrifice and sacraments, and are united under one and the same visible head, the pope.*

## The Church Is Holy

*The Catholic Church is holy because it was founded by Jesus Christ, who is all-holy, and because it teaches, accord-*

*ing to the will of Christ, holy doctrines, and provides the means of leading a holy life, thereby giving holy members to every age.*

Christ founded the Church. He is Holiness itself. His Church    ches the holy doctrines which Christ taught. It offers everyone the means to lead a holy life. In this way the Church gives holy members to every age. This we can understand if we think of the saints who, at all times and places, followed Christ and became holy. Name some saints of various countries and different times. How much do you know about them?

Besides people whom the Church has declared to be saints, there are many other holy people in the Church. They use the means to become holy: the Mass, the sacraments, and good works. These are the same means the saints used. These are the means that we, too, must use to become holy.

## The Church Is Catholic

Does it seem strange that one of the marks of the Catholic Church is that it is "catholic"? Not if you know that the word "catholic" means "universal." Christ Himself explained it when He said, "Go, therefore, and make disciples of all nations . . ." (Mt. 28:19); ". . . behold, I am with you all days" (Mt. 28:20). The word "catholic," therefore, means *all* truths, to *all* nations, for *all* times.

Whenever we want to explain "catholic" we must remember three words: "time," "place," and "teaching." "Time" stands for all ages. "Place" means all nations. "Teaching" means all truths that Christ taught. It is not hard, therefore, to explain that *the Catholic Church is catholic or universal because, destined to last for all time, it never fails to fulfill the divine commandment to teach all nations all the truths revealed by God.*

**230**

## The Church Is Apostolic

The fourth mark of the Church is that it is apostolic. We say *the Catholic Church is apostolic because it was founded by Christ on the Apostles and, according to His divine will, has always been governed by their lawful successors.* From His disciples or followers, Christ chose twelve men to whom He gave more instructions than to the others who followed Him. He commanded these twelve to teach all nations. An apostle is one who is sent. This is why we call the twelve chosen disciples of Christ who received the command to teach everywhere the twelve Apostles. Christ gave to Peter, one of the twelve, outstanding power.

All people to the very end of time were to hear Christ's teachings, so the Apostles had to appoint others to succeed them. Today the bishops of the Catholic Church are the lawful successors of the Apostles, and the Holy Father is the lawful successor of St. Peter. They teach the same doctrine which the Apostles taught. They administer the same sacraments.

It is important that we know and understand the marks of the Church in these days when people think one religion is as good as another. We must study our religion to be able to explain that *we know that no other church but the Catholic Church is the true Church of Christ because no other church has these four marks.*

## 2. The Attributes of the Church

The four marks of the Church are like the rays of a lighthouse which give guidance to all those who are seeking the one true Church. Besides these marks, the Church also has three other great qualities, or attributes, which also point her out as the one true Church. *The chief attributes of the*

Catholic Church are authority, infallibility, and indefectibility. They are called attributes because they are qualities perfecting the nature of the Church.

## The Church Has the Attribute of Authority

To understand how authority perfects the nature of the Church, let us think of the way our homes are run. If there is to be happiness and order in the home, someone must have authority, or the power to tell others what to do. This place of authority is held by the father, because God wants it so. However, since the father cannot spend all his time at home, the mother of a family shares this authority and helps to make decisions. She also trains the children in all good habits so that they may grow in Christian living.

Just as the father, who cannot be at home at all times, shares his authority with the mother, so also does Christ share His with the Church. He did not intend to remain visibly on earth forever, and so He gave His authority to St. Peter, the head of His Church, who passed it on to the succeeding popes and bishops.

Thus we see that *by the authority of the Catholic Church is meant that the pope and the bishops, as the lawful successors of the Apostles, have power from Christ Himself to teach, to sanctify, and to govern the faithful in spiritual matters.*

## The Church Has the Attribute of Infallibility

When God created each one of us He planted deep down in our hearts a desire for the truth. When our older brothers and sisters or friends tell us something we find hard to believe, we immediately turn to our parents and say, "Is that true, Dad?" or "That's not right, is it, Mother?"

As we go to our natural parents to learn the truth, so we should also always go to our Mother the Church for divine truth. Sometimes our parents are not able to answer our questions or explain things clearly, but the Church never fails in her duty to guide us along the right path. She has divine help.

When Christ sent the Holy Spirit to guide the Apostles in their preaching of the truth, He promised that this Spirit of Truth would remain with the Church always. This special help of the Holy Spirit remains in the Church today through the gift of infallibility. This word means "freedom from error."

Let us name some ways in which the Church is free from error. The Holy Spirit guides the Church in all her teachings of faith and morals. In these matters the Church can never make a mistake. Faith means believing. Morals means the right or wrong in human conduct. Therefore, when the Church tells us what we are to believe or how we are to act, she is infallible.

Another way of saying this is that: *By the infallibility of the Catholic Church is meant that the Church, by the special assistance of the Holy Ghost, cannot err when it teaches or believes a doctrine of faith or morals.*

Christ gave this infallibility to St. Peter and the other Apostles. It is found today in the Pope, the successor of St. Peter, and in the bishops, who are the successors of the other Apostles. The pope, as Vicar of Christ and successor to Peter, is infallible when, as head of the Church, he teaches matters of faith or morals. The bishops, when united under the pope and called together in a General Council, or even when dispersed throughout the world are also infallible when they teach faith or morals.

We can be certain of what the pope and bishops teach us on matters pertaining to faith or morals. We can be certain because we know that Christ promised to remain with His Church forever (Mt. 28:20). He also sent the Holy Spirit, the Spirit of Truth, to guide His Church and to keep it from error. Knowing this, it is easy for Catholics to accept the teachings of the pope and bishops.

Sometimes false teachings spring up, and then the pope may call together a General Council, or meeting of the bishops, in order to make clear what is true in regard to these teachings. We firmly believe that when the pope announces to the Catholic world what he and the bishops united in Council have decided, their teaching is infallible. Sometimes the pope alone, as pastor and teacher of the entire world, explains what we are to believe and to do in order to be saved. Good Catholics accept these teachings without question.

We can summarize these thoughts in the following statement. *The Church teaches infallibly when it defines, through the pope alone, as the teacher of all Christians, or through the pope and the bishops, a doctrine of faith or morals to be held by all the faithful.*

## The Church Has the Attribute of Indefectibility

Christ is God, eternal and unchangeable. He founded the Church and said that the gates of hell will not prevail against it. This means that nothing will ever be able to destroy the Church. The Church is, therefore, indefectible. *By the indefectibility of the Catholic Church is meant that the Church, as Christ founded it, will last until the end of time.*

Is not that a consoling thought? Do not all these things make us grateful to God, especially for giving us the grace to be Catholics and members of His one true Church? Should we not resolve to help as many people as possible to find Christ's true Church?

## REVIEW, VII–2

### WORD LIST

| | | | |
|---|---|---|---|
| characteristics | apostolic | catholic | err |
| infallibility | administers | qualities | defines |
| indefectibility | attributes | morals | General Council |

### THINGS TO REMEMBER

1. The Catholic Church is the one true Church established by Christ.
2. The Church is united in doctrine, in worship, and in government.
3. The Church is catholic or universal in regard to time, place, and teaching.
4. The Church has given holy members to every age.
5. The Church was founded on the Apostles.
6. The pope cannot make a mistake when as head of the Church he teaches a doctrine of faith or morals.

### THINGS TO DISCUSS AND DO

1. Look up and discuss the parables of the Mustard Seed, the Marriage Feast, and the Leaven. Show how these parables of Christ foretold the spread of the Church in the whole world.
2. Reread the story of the descent of the Holy Ghost upon the Apostles. Be able to explain how Peter began the work of teaching all nations.
3. Prove that the Lutheran Church is not apostolic.
4. Prepare a discussion of the subject, "Can the pope make a mistake?"
5. Prepare a group discussion on the following problems. Elect a spokesman to give the findings of each group. Were they correct?

*a*) How can you be sure you have the same teachings the Apostles had?

*b*) The Sovereign of the British Empire is the head of the Church of England. Why isn't this the true Church?

*c*) Why don't Catholics eat meat on Friday? Explain the existence of days of fast and abstinence as a means of sanctifying the members of the Church.

*d*) Explain the existence of convents and monasteries as a sign of the holiness of the Church.

*e*) How do the many persecutions suffered by the members of the Catholic Church through the ages prove its indefectibility?

6. In what three ways is the Church one?
7. Where are the chief doctrines of the Church to be found?
8. What is meant by the power to teach, to govern, and to sanctify?
9. Under what conditions does the pope teach infallibly?
10. Why is the Church able to teach infallibly?
11. Choose the letter in front of the word below which is explained in the following statements.

A. One        E. Authority
B. Holy        F. Infallibility
C. Catholic     G. Indefectibility
D. Apostolic

1) The Church is destined to last until the end of time.
2) All the members profess the same faith.
3) The Church cannot err in teaching a doctrine of faith or morals.
4) The Church gives holy members to every age.
5) All the members of the Church are united.
6) The Church will never change its doctrines.
7) The Church is governed by the lawful successors of the Apostles.
8) The Church teaches all truths to all nations.
9) The power to teach, to govern, to sanctify came from Christ.
10) All members may receive the same sacraments.

Study Catechism Lesson 12, *The Marks and Attributes of the Church*, Questions 152–165, pp. 248–250.

I AM THE Vine AND

yOU ARE THE BRANCHES

## Part 3.   Other Things To Know About the Church

### 1. All Must Belong to the Church to Be Saved

Now that we have studied the marks and attributes of the Church we realize that *all are obliged to belong to the Catholic Church in order to be saved.*

The Ark of Noah is a symbol of our Church. Just as only those who remained in the Ark were saved, so also, only those who belong to the Catholic Church will be saved. This means that all who are saved are saved because they are united to the Church whether they know it or not. *When we say, "Outside the Church there is no salvation," we mean that those who through their own grave fault do not know that the Catholic Church is the true Church or, knowing it, refuse to join it, cannot be saved.*

The Holy Father, Pope Pius XII, and the Cardinals of the Sacred Congregation of the Holy Office explained the phrase "Outside the Church there is no salvation" in an official letter in 1949. They wrote, ". . . it is not always required (that one may obtain eternal salvation) that he be incorporated into the Church actually as a member, but it is necessary that at least he be united to her by desire and longing." This desire is defined as a "good disposition of soul whereby a person wishes" to do God's will. Those who live as the voice of conscience tells them to live certainly have this "good disposition."

Cardinal Newman is an outstanding convert to the Catholic Faith. He came into the Church as a result of his own study. Because he was not able to trace the Church of England back to the time of Christ, he joined the Catholic Church. Newman was famous as a speaker and writer about religion, so his conversion brought many of his followers into the Catholic Church. One of the poems he wrote when he was trying to make up his mind to join the Church is "Lead Kindly Light." Are you familiar with the words of this poem that have also been put to music?

God bestowed a great grace on Cardinal Newman, showing him where to find the truth and giving him the grace to embrace that truth. Many people, however, are not as fortunate as he. They love God and make use of the graces He has given them, but are not members of the true Church. They are deprived of the precious gifts and helps from heaven which one can enjoy only in the Catholic Church. We

**238**

should, therefore, do all that we can to encourage them to join the Catholic Church. At the same time we must not forget that *they who remain outside the Catholic Church through no grave fault of their own and do not know it is the true Church, can be saved by making use of the graces which God gives them.*

Pray this invocation for the conversion of non-Catholics: "That Thou wouldst vouchsafe to bring back into the unity of the Church all that stray, and to lead all unbelievers to the light of the Gospel, we beseech Thee to hear us, O Lord."

## 2. The Church Is the Mystical Body of Christ

A famous convert who lived many years ago called the Catholic Church the wonderful body of the living Christ. This description of the Church is another way of saying what the great St. Paul said, ". . . He (Christ) is the head of his body, the Church" (Col. 1:18). The human body has many members — arms, legs, eyes, ears, etc. — each distinct and different from the others, yet closely united. Like the body, the Church has many members in its faithful, in all parts of the world, united through baptism with Christ as their Head. As the head guides the human body, so Christ directs the entire Church.

This union between Christ and the members of the Church, and among the members themselves, is much closer than the union between the head and members of the human body, for it is a supernatural union. This explanation helps us to understand that *the Catholic Church is called the Mystical Body of Christ because its members are united by supernatural bonds with one another and with Christ, their Head, thus resembling the members and head of the living human body.*

**239**

### 3. We Should Be Worthy Members of the Church

In any club or organization, we are not considered active members if we just belong. We must work hard in every undertaking, be loyal to the leaders, and especially when wearing the uniform try not to do anything to disgrace the club. In this way we are benefiting ourselves and giving a good name to the organization. As good Catholics we, too, must be active workers for the Church. We must take part in the works of the Church and pray for its leaders. Above all, we should thank God for having called us to the Church, and promise to remain faithful always.

The Apostles received the gift of tongues on the first Pentecost. All the people listening to Peter's sermon, although not familiar with his language, understood him as though he were speaking in their own individual language. This miracle showed that the Catholic Church is for all men and nations.

As members of the Church charity places on us the great responsibility of trying to bring others into the Church. By our prayers to the Holy Spirit, our encouragement to non-Catholics, our clear explanation of what the Church teaches, and our own good example, we can help bring souls into the one true fold.

### 4. The Communion of Saints

Toward the end of the Apostles' Creed we use the term "communion of saints." Here the word "communion" means a union or group or society. This expression means that the supernatural bonds of sanctifying grace and charity unite us with Christ and many other souls.

### The Faithful on Earth Are Active Members of God's Family

The souls united in the communion of saints are, first of all, the faithful on earth. They make up the Church Militant. The word "militant" means fighting. This name is given them because all the members are still taking part in a war against the temptations of the world, the flesh, and the devil. We must gain heaven. We, here on earth, belong to the Church Militant. In order to strengthen ourselves, we perform the spiritual and corporal works of mercy, pray for one another, pray for the suffering members of Christ's family, and ask the help of those favored ones who have already reached heaven.

### The Souls in Purgatory Are Suffering Members of God's Family

The second group of souls in the communion of saints are the souls in purgatory, those who have died in the state of grace, but who have to atone for unforgiven venial sins or the punishment due to sin. These souls are unable to help themselves. They depend on the prayers of their friends both on earth and in heaven for release from the pains of purgatory. Their sufferings and trials should be a warning to us and should keep us watchful that we do all in our power to secure heaven for ourselves.

### The Souls in Heaven Are Victorious Members of God's Family

The communion of saints includes also the blessed in heaven. These members have already won heaven, and see God face to face. They pray for the faithful on earth and the souls in purgatory.

Now that we know about the saints in heaven, on earth, and in purgatory we know that: *By "the communion of saints" is meant the union of the faithful on earth, the blessed in heaven, and the souls in purgatory, with Christ as their Head.*

### 5. The Members of the Church Can Help One Another Through the Communion of Saints.

Since the spiritual bond of sanctifying grace and divine charity unites the members of the communion of saints, they are able to help one another, particularly in their spiritual needs. Many people whom we have never met pray for us every day. In the offertory of each Mass there is a prayer for all the faithful, living and dead. The saints in heaven, particularly those to whom we pray, help us with their prayers. *Through the communion of saints, the blessed in heaven can help the souls in purgatory and the faithful on earth by praying for them.*

Since the blessed have already won their reward, they are best able to help us. They deserve our gratitude and affection, as well as our imitation. We should celebrate their feast days and practice the virtues they exercised while on earth. We should especially love and imitate our patron saints. *The faithful on earth, through the communion of saints, should honor the blessed in heaven and pray to them, because they are worthy of honor and as friends of God will help the faithful on earth.*

When one of our brothers or sisters is ill or in trouble, Mother does all she can to help. Sometimes we may be tempted to complain that the sick or suffering member gets all the attention. Our Holy Mother Church cares for her suffering members in purgatory in just the same way. She shows us how our prayers and good works, which we could offer for ourselves, will also aid her suffering members.

The very best way to help these suffering souls is to have Masses offered for them. In doing this we offer an infinite sacrifice in and through Jesus Christ Himself. In addition, we may also say short indulgenced prayers for the poor souls. Briefly then, *the faithful on earth, through the communion of saints, can relieve the sufferings of the souls in purgatory by prayer, fasting, and other good works, by indulgences, and by having Masses offered for them.*

"Merciful Lord Jesus, grant them everlasting rest."

We must show the same charity to the faithful on earth that we have for the souls in purgatory and the blessed in heaven. Our Lord said to His Apostles, "Love one another." We must not be satisfied with just praying for our fellow men. We must also help them in other ways whenever they need it. We must help not only whose whom we like, but all of God's children, remembering that what we do for them we do for Christ. In other words, *the faithful on earth, as members of the Mystical Body of Christ, can help one another by practicing supernatural charity and, especially, by performing the spiritual and corporal works of mercy.*

The communion of saints encourages us to depend on the prayers and good works of the entire Church besides our own prayers and good works. It teaches us how, as healthy, holy members of the Church, we can help other members of Christ's Mystical Body.

## REVIEW, VII–3

**WORD LIST**

| deprived | spiritual needs | supernatural bonds |
| indulgences | gift of tongues | supernatural charity |
| Mystical Body | communion of saints | |

## THINGS TO REMEMBER

1. There is but one true religion, the Catholic religion.
2. Everyone must belong to the Catholic Church, at least in desire, in order to be saved.
3. We should thank God each day for the privilege of being members of His Church, and should encourage others who do not share our privilege of studying the teachings of the Catholic Church.
4. Those who are outside the Catholic Church through no fault of their own are not deserving of blame.
5. People who use all the means they know to save their souls, and who make use of the graces God has given them, have the desire to become members of the Church even though they are not actually members of it.
6. The term "Mystical Body" refers to the spiritual union which exists between Christ and the members of His Church and the members among themselves.

## THINGS TO DISCUSS AND DO

1. Prepare a talk on the communion of saints, showing why it can be called a Royal Family.
2. Explain how we members of the Church Militant are not fighting our battles alone.
3. Make a chart showing the members of the communion of saints in heaven, on earth, and in purgatory.
4. Why is it wrong to say one religion is as good as another?

Study Catechism Lesson 12, *The Marks and Attributes of the Church* (Con't.), and Lesson 13, *The Communion of Saints,* Questions 166–174, pp. 250–252.

# End-of-Unit Review — Unit VII

## PART 1

# CATECHISM

### LESSON 11

#### The Catholic Church

**136. What is the Church?**

The Church is the congregation of all baptized persons united in the same true faith, the same sacrifice, and the same sacraments, under the authority of the Sovereign Pontiff and the bishops in communion with him.

**137. Who founded the Church?**

Jesus Christ founded the Church.

**138. Why did Jesus Christ found the Church?**

Jesus Christ founded the Church to bring all men to eternal salvation.

**139. How is the Church enabled to lead men to salvation?**

The Church is enabled to lead men to salvation by the indwelling of the Holy Ghost, who gives it life.

**140. When was the dwelling of the Holy Ghost in the Church first visibly manifested?**

The dwelling of the Holy Ghost in the Church was first visibly manifested on Pentecost Sunday, when He came down upon the Apostles in the form of tongues of fire.

**141. How long will the Holy Ghost dwell in the Church?**

The Holy Ghost will dwell in the Church until the end of time.

**142. Who sent the Holy Ghost to dwell in the Church?**

God the Father and God the Son sent the Holy Ghost to dwell in the Church.

143. **What does the indwelling of the Holy Ghost enable the Church to do?**

The indwelling of the Holy Ghost enables the Church to teach, to sanctify, and to rule the faithful in the name of Christ.

144. **What is meant by teaching, sanctifying, and ruling in the name of Christ?**

By teaching, sanctifying, and ruling in the name of Christ is meant that the Church always does the will of its divine Founder, who remains forever its invisible Head.

145. **To whom did Christ give the power to teach, to sanctify, and to rule the members of His Church?**

Christ gave the power to teach, to sanctify, and to rule the members of His Church to the Apostles, the first bishops of the Church.

146. **Did Christ intend that this power should be exercised by the Apostles alone?**

No, Christ intended that this power should be exercised also by their successors, the bishops of the Church.

147. **Did Christ give special power in His Church to any one of the Apostles?**

Christ gave special power in His Church to St. Peter by making him the head of the Apostles and the chief teacher and ruler of the entire Church.

148. **Did Christ intend that the special power of chief teacher and ruler of the entire Church should be exercised by St. Peter alone?**

Christ did not intend that the special power of chief teacher and ruler of the entire Church should be exercised by St. Peter alone, but intended that this power should be passed down to his successor, the pope, the bishop of Rome, who is the Vicar of Christ on earth and the visible head of the Church.

**149. Who assist the bishops in the care of souls?**

The priests, especially parish priests, assist the bishops in the care of souls.

**150. Who are the laity of the Church?**

The laity of the Church are all its members who do not belong to the clerical or to the religious state.

**151. How can the laity help the Church in her care of souls?**

The laity can help the Church in her care of souls by leading lives that will reflect credit on the Church, and by co-operating with their bishops and priests, especially through Catholic Action.

## OTHER QUESTIONS AND EXERCISES

1. Why should we be grateful for belonging to the Catholic Church?
2. What must a person do in order to belong to this society?
3. How did Christ try to make the people He preached to understand what the Church is?
4. Why did Jesus Christ go to so much trouble to found the Church?
5. How does the Church bring us to salvation?
6. To which Person of the Blessed Trinity do we ascribe the work of sanctifying the members of the Church?
7. Who has the place of St. Peter in the Church today?
8. Why are the laity important members of the Church?
9. Mention several particular ways in which the laity can help the Church.
10. Why should we pray for priests and bishops?
11. How can girls and boys your age help the parish priest?
12. How did the Holy Ghost appear to the Apostles on Pentecost?

# CATECHISM

## LESSON 12

### The Marks and Attributes of the Church

**152. Which is the one true Church established by Christ?**

The one true Church established by Christ is the Catholic Church.

**153. How do we know that the Catholic Church is the one true Church established by Christ?**

We know that the Catholic Church is the one true Church established by Christ because it alone has the marks of the true Church.

**154. What do we mean by the marks of the Church?**

By the marks of the Church we mean certain clear signs by which all men can recognize it as the true Church founded by Jesus Christ.

**155. What are the chief marks of the Church?**

The chief marks of the Church are four: It is one, holy, catholic or universal, and apostolic.

**156. Why is the Catholic Church one?**

The Catholic Church is one because all its members, according to the will of Christ, profess the same faith, have the same sacrifice and sacraments, and are united under one and the same visible head, the pope.

**157. Why is the Catholic Church holy?**

The Catholic Church is holy because it was founded by Jesus Christ, who is all-holy, and because it teaches, according to the will of Christ, holy doctrines, and provides the means of leading a holy life, thereby giving holy members to every age.

**158. Why is the Catholic Church catholic or universal?**

The Catholic Church is catholic or universal because, destined to last for all time, it never fails to fulfill the divine commandment to teach all nations all the truths revealed by God.

**159. Why is the Catholic Church apostolic?**

The Catholic Church is apostolic because it was founded by Christ on the Apostles and, according to His divine will, has always been governed by their lawful successors.

**160. How do we know that no other church but the Catholic Church is the true Church of Christ?**

We know that no other church but the Catholic Church is the true Church of Christ because no other church has these four marks.

**161. What are the chief attributes of the Catholic Church?**

The chief attributes of the Catholic Church are authority, infallibility, and indefectibility. They are called attributes because they are qualities perfecting the nature of the Church.

**162. What is meant by the authority of the Catholic Church?**

By the authority of the Catholic Church is meant that the pope and the bishops, as the lawful successors of the Apostles, have power from Christ Himself to teach, to sanctify, and to govern the faithful in spiritual matters.

**163. What is meant by the infallibility of the Catholic Church?**

By the infallibility of the Catholic Church is meant that the Church, by the special assistance of the Holy Ghost, cannot err when it teaches or believes a doctrine of faith or morals.

**164. When does the Church teach infallibly?**

The Church teaches infallibly when it defines, through the pope alone, as the teacher of all Christians, or through the pope and the bishops, a doctrine of faith or morals to be held by all the faithful.

165. **What is meant by the indefectibility of the Catholic Church?**

By the indefectibility of the Catholic Church is meant that the Church, as Christ founded it, will last until the end of time.

## OTHER QUESTIONS AND EXERCISES

1. Explain how the Church is one.
2. Why cannot the Lutheran Church be the one true Church?
3. In what three ways are the members of the one true Church united?
4. Who is the visible head of the Church?
5. What three means of becoming holy, mentioned in this lesson, should we use?
6. Why is "Catholic" an appropriate name for our Church?
7. What would you say to convince a friend that one religion is not as good as another?
8. Who gave St. Peter the authority to be the first head of the Church?
9. Who is it that keeps the Church from making a mistake?
10. In what matters does the Holy Spirit guide the Church?
11. Can the Catholic Church be destroyed?
12. What can you do to make yourself a more holy member of the Church?
13. What is a General Council?

**PART 3**

## CATECHISM

### LESSON 12 (Cont.)

166. **Are all obliged to belong to the Catholic Church in order to be saved?**

All are obliged to belong to the Catholic Church in order to be saved.

167. What do we mean when we say, "Outside the Church there is no salvation"?

When we say, "Outside the Church there is no salvation," we mean that those who through their own grave fault do not know that the Catholic Church is the true Church or, knowing it, refuse to join it, cannot be saved.

168. Can they be saved who remain outside the Catholic Church because they do not know it is the true Church?

They who remain outside the Catholic Church through no grave fault of their own and do not know it is the true Church, can be saved by making use of the graces which God gives them.

169. Why is the Catholic Church called the Mystical Body of Christ?

The Catholic Church is called the Mystical Body of Christ because its members are united by supernatural bonds with one another and with Christ, their Head, thus resembling the members and head of the living human body.

## LESSON 13

### The Communion of Saints and the Forgiveness of Sins

170. What is meant by the "communion of saints" in the Apostles' Creed?

By "the communion of saints" is meant the union of the faithful on earth, the blessed in heaven, and the souls in purgatory, with Christ as their Head.

171. Through the communion of saints, what can the blessed in heaven do for the souls in purgatory and the faithful on earth?

Through the communion of saints, the blessed in heaven can help the souls in purgatory and the faithful on earth by praying for them.

172. **Should the faithful on earth, through the communion of saints, honor the blessed in heaven and pray to them?**

The faithful on earth, through the communion of saints, should honor the blessed in heaven and pray to them, because they are worthy of honor and as friends of God will help the faithful on earth.

173. **Can the faithful on earth, through the communion of saints, relieve the sufferings of the souls in purgatory?**

The faithful on earth, through the communion of saints, can relieve the sufferings of the souls in purgatory by prayer, fasting, and other good works, by indulgences, and by having Masses offered for them.

174. **Can the faithful on earth help one another?**

The faithful on earth, as members of the Mystical Body of Christ, can help one another by practicing supernatural charity and, especially, by performing the spiritual and corporal works of mercy.

## OTHER QUESTIONS AND EXERCISES

1. How did Cardinal Newman discover that the Catholic Church is the one true Church?
2. How are the members of the Church united?
3. Should we take part in the activities of the Church? Why?
4. In what ways can we bring others into the Church?
5. What do we call the union that exists among the members of the Church in heaven, on earth, and in purgatory?
6. How can you be a militant Catholic?
7. What can you do to shorten the time spent in purgatory by yourself, or others dear to you?
8. Do people whom we do not know pray for us? When and how?
9. Why is the Mass the best way of helping the souls in Purgatory?
10. What is meant by belonging to the Catholic Church in desire?

**252**

# Unit VIII.  The Forgiveness of Sins and Life Everlasting

# Part 1.  The Forgiveness of Sins

### 1. Christ Gave His Church the Power to Forgive Sins

One day while Jesus was traveling through Galilee healing the sick and afflicted, four men brought to Him a paralyzed man lying on a cot. But there was such a large crowd around the house where Jesus was, that the men could not get in through the door. So they made a hole in the flat roof and, let the cot down through it. When Jesus saw how much faith the people had He said to the sick man, "Son, thy sins are forgiven thee" (Mk. 2:5). Some of the Scribes accused Jesus of blasphemy for they knew only God could forgive sins.

Then to prove that He had the power to forgive sins, Christ restored the power of walking to the paralytic.

This took place before Christ instituted the sacrament of penance. From earlier lessons we remember that on the evening of His resurrection, Christ said to His Apostles: "Receive the Holy Spirit; whose sins you shall forgive, they are forgiven them; and whose sins you shall retain, they are retained" (Jn. 20:23). Through these words of Christ, penance became a sacrament, and the Apostles were given the power to forgive sins.

## 2. The Church Administers the Sacrament of Penance

A story from the life of Abraham Lincoln reminds us of the goodness of God in pardoning our sins. One day this great president wanted to pardon a soldier when the cabinet officials thought the soldier should be punished. Lincoln's excuse in signing the pardon was, "You do not know how hard it is to let a human being die when you feel that a stroke of the pen will save him." God also is merciful — infinitely merciful. He is the only One who can forgive sins, and He never loses an opportunity to do so if the sinner is truly sorry. He wanted so much to save us from hell that, besides dying on the cross, He instituted the sacrament of penance.

The power of forgiving sins was not to be used only while our divine Lord was on earth. He knew that man would sin and sin again. He gave the power to the Apostles, and they in turn ordained priests to help them. In this way they passed on the power that Christ had given to them. Through all the years since then, the Church has continued to ordain men to the priesthood, so that they might restore grace to souls that had lost it.

**255**

By "the forgiveness of sins" in the Apostles' Creed is meant that God has given to the Church, through Jesus Christ, the power to forgive sins, no matter how great or how many they are, if sinners truly repent.

Through the sacrament of holy orders the priests have the power, as ministers of God, to forgive sins in God's name. And we ought to ask God to help us remember always, that our sins can be forgiven, no matter how serious they are. This thought should be a great comfort to us. It should make us thank God for the sacrament of penance. One way of showing gratitude is by receiving the sacrament often. For we must not forget that Christ instituted the sacrament of penance not only to forgive sins, but also to provide the means of leading a holier life.

When we go to confession, we should prepare ourselves fully for this great sacrament. Do you recall the five things we must do to make a good confession? Every Catholic should know them by heart. They are: first, examine our conscience; second, be sorry for our sins; third, have the firm purpose of not sinning again; fourth, confess our sins to the priest; fifth, be willing to perform the penance the priest gives us.

## REVIEW, VIII–1

### WORD LIST

paralytic        minister of God        requisites        blasphemy

### THINGS TO REMEMBER

1. Christ gave the Apostles the power to forgive sins on the first Easter Sunday night.
2. The best way to thank God for the sacrament of penance is to make use of it often.

3. We should make a careful preparation for the reception of this sacrament.
4. No matter how often or how seriously we sin, our sins may be forgiven if we are sorry for them.

### THINGS TO DISCUSS AND DO

1. Make a chart showing the most important words connected with the sacrament of penance. Be able to explain the terms.
2. Write a letter to a non-Catholic friend explaining why we go to confession.
3. Find a copy of the words of Our Lady of Fatima in regard to the forgiveness of sins. Memorize it.
4. Write an act of thanksgiving for the gift of the sacrament of penance.
5. How would you explain the saying, "Despise sin, but not the sinner"?
6. What five things are necessary for the worthy reception of the sacrament of penance?

Study Catechism Lesson 13, *The Communion of Saints and the Forgiveness of Sins* (Con't.), Question 175, p. 267.

# Part 2. The Resurrection of the Body and Life Everlasting

## 1. The Catholic Church Teaches the Meaning of Death

One day Jairus, an important man of Capharnaum, begged Jesus to lay His hands upon his very sick little daughter. While Jesus was on the way to the home, messengers came to tell Jairus that his daughter had died. When our Lord arrived at the home of Jairus there was a great clamor. Jesus went into the house and said, "Why do you make this din, and weep?" Then sending the people outside, He brought the lovely twelve-year-old girl back to life. Imagine how happy and grateful her father was!

Although this event does not tell us what death is, it does give an idea of the sadness a death causes in a family. For this reason very few people like to think about death. When they do, they usually picture it as something very far away. Perhaps it is far away for some of us, but no matter how far off, death is one thing we cannot escape. St. Paul says, ". . . it is appointed unto men to die once" (Hebr. 9:27).

At the moment of death we know the soul leaves the body. All the earthly pleasures which our bodies have enjoyed are ended. Our eyes are no longer able to see the beauties which God has created. Our feet no longer are able to carry us. Our hands are not able to feel. Our bodies return to the earth to await resurrection day.

## 2. Death, Though a Punishment for Sin, Is a Blessing

It is true that death is a punishment for sin, but death is also a blessing. If we have been faithful, death is the gateway to heaven. It means going home to God. Just when or how we will pass through this gateway none of us knows. Only one thing is certain; there will be no escaping it.

## 3. We Must Always Be Prepared for Death

We must keep ourselves ready for the coming of the Master as did the wise virgins in the Gospel. Then we will not fear the sentence that will be passed at death. Holy Mother Church reminds us frequently of death in her favorite prayer to our Lady: "Pray for us sinners, now and at the hour of our death. Amen."

## 4. All Men Will Rise From the Dead

One of the beautiful scenes in the life of our Lord is the restoring of His friend Lazarus to life. The first message to our Lord when Lazarus was dying was, "He whom Thou lovest is sick." Instead of hurrying to Bethany as we would imagine our kind and loving Lord would do, He waited a few days.

When Christ and His disciples finally reached Bethany, they learned that Lazarus was already dead. According to the custom at that time, he had been buried the day he died. Our Lord was sad when He saw the grief of His two friends, Mary and Martha, the sisters of Lazarus. We know that He actually wept. He went to the entrance of the tomb and in a loud voice called, "Lazarus, come forth!" Picture the body beginning to move, sitting up, and finally standing up. Lazarus had been brought back to life. How surprised the people were! How grateful Mary and Martha felt!

One day our bodies, too, will rise from the dead. St. Matthew describes the scene in the Gospel when he says that God "will send forth his angels with a trumpet and a great sound, and they will gather his elect from the four winds, and from one end of the heavens to the other" (Mt. 24:31).

At this summons the resurrection of the body will take place. *By "the resurrection of the body" is meant that at the end of the world the bodies of all men will rise from the earth and be united again to their souls, nevermore to be separated.* The very same body which was ours during life will be restored to us for eternity.

In his epistle St. Paul says, ". . . we shall all indeed rise, but we shall not all be changed" (1 Cor. 15:51). *The bodies of the just will rise to share forever in the glory of their souls.* This means the body, which during life took part in many actions which were worthy of reward, will share the reward with the soul for all eternity. The body will not feel pain or suffering, and all the blessed will experience great joy and will share perfect peace and love. All the things our hearts desire will be found in heaven. The greatest joy of all will be found in seeing God face to face in heaven and possessing Him as our very own. This happiness will last forever.

*The bodies of the damned will also rise to share in the eternal punishment of their souls.* As the bodies of the just shared in their good works during life, so also did the bodies of the wicked share in their evil pleasure. In death the wicked will be able to feel every form of pain. Even in the midst of dreadful torments, they will live forever.

The resurrection of the body applies to all human beings who have died. It will not apply to the Blessed Mother. At the end of her life on earth *by the special privilege of her*

*Assumption, the body of the Blessed Virgin Mary, united to her immaculate soul, was glorified and taken into heaven.* In the year 1950, Pope Pius XII defined this teaching of the Church and declared it an article of faith. He said that at the end of her life on earth Mary was assumed into heaven, body and soul. This means that all Catholics must believe that our Blessed Lady's body and soul, free from any stain of sin or decay, was taken into heaven.

## 5. The Particular Judgment Will Take Place Immediately After Death

What will happen to us after we die? The time immediately after death will be very important for us because our everlasting home will then be decided upon. As soon as the soul leaves the body, God judges us. Every thought, word, and act of our life will flash in review before God and ourselves. Then God will pass upon us an eternal sentence. He will never change it. *The judgment which will be passed on each one of us immediately after death is called the particular judgment.*

Whatever reward or punishment we receive at this particular judgment will be the result of our behavior while on earth. There will be no time to beg for mercy. The sentence of the Judge will be carried out at once. There are three possibilities. *The rewards or punishments appointed for men after the particular judgment are heaven, purgatory, or hell.*

### Purgatory

It is possible that few people will go straight to heaven when they die. Nothing soiled can enter heaven, so it is seldom that even a person whom we consider good escapes purgatory.

When Lucia, one of the children of Fatima, was talking

to our Lady, she asked her if two little girls from their village who had recently died, had gone to heaven. Our Lady replied that one of them was in heaven, but that the other little girl would be in purgatory until the end of the world. This private revelation agrees with the teaching of the Church that: *Those are punished for a time in purgatory who die in the state of grace but are guilty of venial sin, or have not fully satisfied for the temporal punishment due to their sins.*

Our wills are so weak that often we do not fight off temptations of the world, the flesh, and the devil. We sometimes wrongly tell ourselves, "Oh, it's only a venial sin," or "I know it is a sin, but I can confess it and be forgiven." Our souls will need to be purified from these sins when we die. The place where they are purified is purgatory.

Sometimes we do not do enough penance for the sins we have committed, especially the more serious sins. We know that the eternal punishment due to these sins is taken away through the sacrament of penance. The penance which we do after confession remits some of the temporal punishment. But it does not always fully make up; there still remains some temporal punishment. In purgatory this punishment is made up.

## Hell

One of the things we often hear people speak of as a great evil is a sudden and unprovided death. Perhaps we have never thought too much about this. If we did, we would realize how dreadful it is to die in mortal sin. For, *those are punished in hell who die in mortal sin; they are deprived of the vision of God and suffer dreadful torments, especially that of fire, for all eternity.*

**262**

The first part of this answer needs no explanation. On this earth we cannot understand the beauties of the vision of God. We must accept the words of the saints who have tried to describe them for us. St. Paul tells us that "eye has not seen, nor ear heard, nor has it entered into the heart of man, what things God has prepared for those who love him" (1 Cor. 2:9). St. Stephen, the first martyr of the Church, saw the heavens opened and was encouraged by this wonderful sight. St. John Chrysostom said he would pass through hell-fire to possess God in heaven.

If, however, we have not repented and confessed our mortal sins, we cannot enjoy heaven. Our greatest sorrow will be that through our own dreadful fault we have deserved the awful tortures of hell. We hardly have an idea what the punishment will be like. None of our earthly sufferings are like it. We do know that there is a fire in hell from these words of our Lord: "It is better for thee to enter into life everlasting lame, than, having two feet, to be cast into the hell of unquenchable fire" (Mk. 9:44). If we think of our last end we will not sin. "Holy Mary, deliver us from the pains of hell."

## Heaven

If the thought of hell makes us sad, let us turn to a happier thought, heaven. It is a place of perfect and everlasting joy. It will continue for all eternity, and we will never fear losing it.

*Those are rewarded in heaven who have died in the state of grace and have been purified in purgatory, if necessary, from all venial sin and all debt of temporal punishment; they see God face to face and share forever in His glory and happiness.*

All those who have been faithful in this life will have a

home there with God, with our Lady, the angels, the Apostles, and all the saints. Our own dear ones, who have died in grace, will be there with us, too, and we will have none of the cares and worries of life to annoy us.

The degree of glory we will have in heaven depends on the amount of sanctifying grace we have at the time of our death. Let us always keep our souls in the state of grace and increase our merit by good works, prayer, and the reception of the sacraments.

### 6. The General Judgment Will Take Place Immediately After the General Resurrection

No one knows, except God, where we will be on the last day. Wherever we are, we know that after all the bodies and souls are reunited, there will be another judgment. *The judgment which will be passed on all men immediately after the general resurrection is called the general judgment.* This will be the same sentence that was passed at the particular judgment.

This general judgment may not seem to be necessary to us, since each human being is judged at once after death. But if we recall the lesson of the Providence of God, perhaps we may understand His reason for a general judgment. In this life, good people often suffer great evils while the wicked seem to be well off. At the general judgment God will show to all men His infinite justice, His infinite goodness, His wise management of all things in each individual's life. So *although everyone is judged immediately after death, it is fitting that there be a general judgment in order that the justice, wisdom, and mercy of God may be glorified in the presence of all.*

After death there will be no time for repentance. It is,

therefore, good for us to think of death, heaven, and hell. Let us often pray, "From a sudden and unprovided death, deliver us, O Lord."

## 7. The Apostles' Creed Ends With the Word "Amen"

"Amen" is a Hebrew word. Placed at the end of the Apostles' Creed, it means that all those who make that profession of faith agree to all the truths contained in this prayer. If we say the word thoughtfully, it is the same as saying, "So be it." "This I believe." It also means that we are begging for the graces we need to help us live according to what we believe. *By the word "Amen," with which we end the Apostles' Creed, is meant "So it is," or "So be it"; the word expresses our firm belief in all the doctrines that the Creed contains.*

At death our life on earth ends, but if we have lived according to our faith, a greater, fuller life opens for us in heaven. Only then will we really appreciate the words of St. Augustine: "Thou hast made us for Yourself, O Lord, and our hearts are restless till they rest in You."

"Lord, I fear Your justice, I implore Your mercy, deliver me not to everlasting pains. Grant that I may possess You in the midst of everlasting joys."

### REVIEW, VIII–2

**WORD LIST**

| | | | |
|---|---|---|---|
| corruption | temporal | deprived | assent |
| Assumption | unprovided | unquenchable | |

### THINGS TO REMEMBER

1. I am certain that I will die.
2. I do not know when or how I will die.

3. I will be judged immediately after death.
4. I will be in heaven or in hell for all eternity. I will not be given another chance.
5. On the last day my body will rise and be united again to my soul.
6. I will be eternally rewarded or eternally punished.

## THINGS TO DISCUSS AND DO

1. Discuss some of the following:
    Why do Catholics honor the dead?
    Why do some people remain faithful to God despite great hardships?
    How do things appear at the moment of death?
    How will people feel when they come together for the general judgment?
    Why did Christ describe death as a thief in the night?
    Why does the Holy Scripture say we will not sin if we remember our last end?
2. Locate and write the important fact which is described in each of the following scriptural quotations: (*a*) Hebr. 9:27, (*b*) Apoc. 22:5, (*c*) 1 Cor. 2:9, (*d*) 2 Thess. 1:9, (*e*) Jn. 5:28–29.
3. Number one to twelve on your paper. After each number write the appropriate letter from the second column.

| | |
|---|---|
| 1) Virtue of goodness, pity, or kindness | A. just |
| 2) Decay, return to dust | B. mercy |
| 3) Those who have kept God's laws | C. vision |
| 4) Arising to life | D. resurrection |
| 5) Truths, teachings | E. Assumption |
| 6) Having been taken up | F. privilege |
| 7) Right or proper | G. corruption |
| 8) Sight | H. temporal |
| 9) Only for a time | I. doctrines |
| 10) Kept from having | J. deprived |
| 11) Exception, away from common rule | K. preserved |
| 12) Saved | L. fitting |

Study Catechism Lesson 14, *The Resurrection and Life Everlasting*, Questions 176–187, pp. 268–269.

**PART 1**

## CATECHISM

### LESSON 13 (Cont.)

#### The Communion of Saints and the Forgiveness of Sins

175. What is meant in the Apostles' Creed by "the forgiveness of sins"?

By "the forgiveness of sins" in the Apostles' Creed is meant that God has given to the Church, through Jesus Christ, the power to forgive sins, no matter how great or how many they are, if sinners truly repent.

## OTHER QUESTIONS AND EXERCISES

1. Did Christ institute the sacrament of penance?
2. Did Christ give the Apostles the power to forgive sins?
3. Is any sin too great to be forgiven?
4. Is sorrow for sin a necessary condition for forgiveness?
5. Does the sacrament of holy orders give priests the power to forgive sins?
6. Does penance give grace to those already in the state of grace?
7. Should we be afraid to confess any sin to the priest?
8. Does a daily examination of conscience help us in preparing for confession?
9. Does the penance we say remit all the temporal punishment due to our sins?
10. Should we try to make up in some way for the wrong we do, even though it is not seriously sinful?

# CATECHISM

### LESSON 14

#### The Resurrection and Life Everlasting

**176. What is meant by "the resurrection of the body"?**

By "the resurrection of the body" is meant that at the end of the world the bodies of all men will rise from the earth and be united again to their souls, nevermore to be separated.

**177. Why will the bodies of the just rise?**

The bodies of the just will rise to share forever in the glory of their souls.

**178. Has the body of any human person ever been raised from the dead and taken into heaven?**

By the special privilege of her Assumption, the body of the Blessed Virgin Mary, united to her immaculate soul, was glorified and taken into heaven.

**179. Why will the bodies of the damned also rise?**

The bodies of the damned will also rise to share in the eternal punishment of their souls.

**180. What is the judgment called which will be passed on all men immediately after the general resurrection?**

The judgment which will be passed on all men immediately after the general resurrection is called the general judgment.

**181. What is the judgment called which will be passed on each one of us immediately after death?**

The judgment which will be passed on each one of us immediately after death is called the particular judgment.

182. **If everyone is judged immediately after death, why will there be a general judgment?**

Although everyone is judged immediately after death, it is fitting that there be a general judgment in order that the justice, wisdom, and mercy of God may be glorified in the presence of all.

183. **What are the rewards or punishments appointed for men after the particular judgment?**

The rewards or punishments appointed for men after the particular judgment are heaven, purgatory, or hell.

184. **Who are punished in purgatory?**

Those are punished for a time in purgatory who die in the state of grace but are guilty of venial sin, or have not fully satisfied for the temporal punishment due to their sins.

185. **Who are punished in hell?**

Those are punished in hell who die in mortal sin; they are deprived of the vision of God and suffer dreadful torments, especially that of fire, for all eternity.

186. **Who are rewarded in heaven?**

Those are rewarded in heaven who have died in the state of grace and have been purified in purgatory, if necessary, from all venial sin and all debt of temporal punishment; they see God face to face and share forever in His glory and happiness.

187. **What is meant by the word "Amen," with which we end the Apostles' Creed?**

By the word "Amen," with which we end the Apostles' Creed, is meant "So it is," or "So be it"; the word expresses our firm belief in all the doctrines that the Creed contains.

## OTHER QUESTIONS AND EXERCISES

1. Why must we die?
2. Can anyone escape death?

3. What can we do to be prepared to meet death at all times?
4. Will our bodies and souls be separated at death?
5. When will the particular judgment take place?
6. When will the general judgment take place?
7. Does death mean the beginning of life for everyone?
8. Why do we visit the graves of the dead?
9. What will happen to our bodies and souls on the day of judgment?
10. What faculty that God has given us is going to determine whether we will merit heaven or hell?

## Section Review

Now we should take a general review of SECTION III
*The Holy Ghost and the Church*
using the End of Unit Tests as a guide to locate the most important points. Cf. pp. 207 sqq.; 245 sqq.; 267 sqq.

# Our Duties To God

"I the Lord, am your God, who brought you out of the land of Egypt, that place of slavery. You shall not have other gods besides me. You shall not carve idols for yourselves in the shape of anything in the sky above or on the earth below or in the waters beneath the earth; you shall not bow down before them or worship them. For I, the Lord, your God, am a jealous God, inflicting punishment for their fathers' wickedness on the children of those who hate me, down to the third and fourth generation; but bestowing mercy down to the thousandth generation, on the children of those who love me and keep my commandments.

"You shall not take the name of the Lord, your God, in vain. For the Lord will not leave unpunished him who takes his name in vain.

"Remember to keep holy the Sabbath day. Six days you may labor and do all your work, but the seventh day is the Sabbath of the Lord, your God. No work may be done then either by you, or your son or daughter, or your male or female slave, or your beast, or by the alien who lives with you. In six days the Lord made the heavens and the earth, the sea and all that is in them; but on the seventh day he rested. That is why the Lord has blessed the Sabbath day and made it holy" (Exod. 20:2–11).

## Overview

In Sections I to III we have learned much about God and the three Divine Persons. We have learned of God's great goodness to us.

Now, to prove to God that we are grateful, we must:

Live according to what we believe (Unit IX).

Adore God and Him only (Unit X, Parts 1 and 2).

Use His name with reverence (Unit X, Parts 3 and 4).

Worship Him as the Church directs (Unit X, Parts 5 and 6).

# Unit IX.  Living According To
## What We Believe

## Laws in General

We have learned the part which the Holy Ghost plays in the drama of Redemption. We have seen how the third Person of the Blessed Trinity works in the Church and in each soul. We have gained greater knowledge of the divine origin of the Church, of its mission on earth, and of the marks and attributes which point to the Church as the one true Church of Christ. We learned to appreciate our membership in the Church and in the Communion of Saints, and to understand better the doctrines of the resurrection of the body and life everlasting. We also gained a deeper knowledge of actual and sanctifying grace.

Now we shall see how we can co-operate with these graces by avoiding sin and doing good; how we can lead a Christian life on earth in preparation for the happiness of heaven; how God's laws will guide us to this goal.

## Part 1. Laws Help Us Live as We Believe

Have you ever stopped to think how very necessary laws, as well as rules and directions are in our daily lives? We could not possibly play games without rules. How could you make a birdhouse, an airplane, or a flower garden without directions? What would your home, school, or community life be like without rules? Imagine, if you can, a busy highway where no one obeyed traffic regulations, or a ball game where everyone made up rules as the game was being played. Laws bring order and peace; laws faithfully observed bring greater security, better regulated lives, and therefore actually more freedom.

As you know, there are certain laws of nature which help the plants and animals to carry out God's plan for them. Flowers and plants grow and provide food and beauty for man; ice and snow melt and become a means of irrigation for crops; soil absorbs moisture and nourishment necessary for the growth of vegetation; the sun and stars shine and furnish light and heat. If any one of these lower creatures were to stop following the laws of nature, confusion would result. We must, therefore, observe the laws of nature in our treatment of these lower creatures in order to help carry out God's plan for them. So also must we observe the laws of nature which govern our bodies. Most of all we must obey the laws which govern our minds and wills and especially the Commandments of God and His Church, in order that we may reach our eternal destiny.

## 1. The Laws of God — A Means of Salvation

Since the very beginning of time, long before anyone had ever heard of the ten commandments, God deeply imprinted on the souls of men the laws which govern human nature. This natural inborn knowledge of right and wrong taught that the highest honor is due to God; that man could not willfully injure himself; that man must do to others as he would have them do unto him. Conscience, or the voice of reason within each of God's human creatures, helped man in choosing good and avoiding evil.

You remember that man's mind became darkened and his will weakened as a result of original sin. So God made His law known to man in words that could not be mistaken. Read the story of the ten commandments in the twentieth Chapter of Exodus, the second Book of the Old Testament. The powerful words used by God in giving these commandments to Moses prove to us that *besides believing what God has revealed, we must keep His law.* Faith alone, therefore, is not enough for salvation. Man must indeed use his intellect to know and believe what God has revealed, but he must also use his will to keep God's law.

God did not mean these commandments merely for the small group of Israelites. He intended that all men should use them as guides to help them live peacefully on earth in such a way as to prepare for union with Him in heaven. We cannot reach this destination safely unless we follow the spiritual road signs, or commandments, which God and His Church have placed along the way. And we cannot keep God's law without His help. This he will give us if we ask Him.

God's first and foremost law commands us to love God above all things, and to please Him each moment of the day by doing the things He wants us to do. You have often heard the expression, "Offer it up." Do you understand the meaning of these words? Do you really make each daily action, whether pleasant or not, an act of love of God?

God demands that we love Him with our whole heart, as He deserves. Loving Him means at least obeying Him. God and His divine will must come first in our affections. We may not love ourselves or any creature more than we love God. True love of God prompts us to wish Him all honor and glory and every good; and to do all in our power to obtain it for Him. Again, true love of God shows itself in action, for our Lord said, "He who has my commandments and keeps them, he it is who loves me" (Jn. 14:21).

Besides loving God, we must love our neighbor as ourselves. This means that we should wish those things for our neighbor that we would like to have for ourselves — happiness and holiness in this life and glory in the next. It means

**275**

we must help our neighbor if he is in need, in body or in soul. We must treat everyone in the world as Christ would, for all men are our brothers.

## 2. God Reduced His Commandments to Two — Love of God and Love of Neighbor

To have happiness and holiness in this life and glory in eternity we must keep the whole law of God. If we are to do this we must let the advice of our Lord guide us. One day a doctor of the law asked Him which was the greatest commandment of the law. Our Lord answered that it was to love God completely and then to love our neighbor. *The two great commandments that contain the whole law of God are: first, Thou shalt love the Lord thy God with thy whole heart, and with thy whole soul, and with thy whole mind, and with thy whole strength; second, Thou shalt love thy neighbor as thyself.*

God loves us with an infinite love. In return, He demands that we love Him, and that we show this love by obeying His law.

The whole law of God binds us to love of God, of self, and of neighbor. True love of God, of self, and of neighbor, means among other things: adoration of God; respect for His holy name; observance of Sundays and holydays; obedience; respect for life; purity in thought, word, and deed; justice and truth; observance of Church laws on marriage; and helping our neighbor. We therefore realize that *to love God, our neighbor, and ourselves we must keep the commandments of God and of the Church, and perform the spiritual and corporal works of mercy.*

# REVIEW, IX-1

## WORD LIST

divine origin      Israelites
security      binding
eternal destiny      abstinence
unmistakable

## THINGS TO REMEMBER

1. Laws are intended to produce order and peace which will bring about freedom and happiness.
2. God's first law is that we love Him above all things; and show our love by obeying His laws.
3. Laws guide us to our heavenly goal.

## THINGS TO DISCUSS AND DO

1. The text says that our most important duty in obedience is fulfilled when we obey the laws which govern our minds and wills. Explain what these laws are, why this statement is true and how it applies to us.
2. Which faculty do you use especially in obeying God's laws?
3. How do little acts of mortification enable us to obey God's laws?
4. Draw up a list of commandments which apply to your daily life. Examine your conscience on them each evening.
5. What kind of neighborhood do you live in? Do you give an example of obedience to God's law to your neighbors rather than try to impress them with your beautiful home?
6. Say a special prayer each day to our Lady asking her to help you to be faithful to God's laws. Since she fulfilled the laws not meant for her, ask her to help you obey the laws which were made for you.

Study Catechism Lesson 15, *The Two Great Commandments,* Questions 188–190, pp. 289–290.

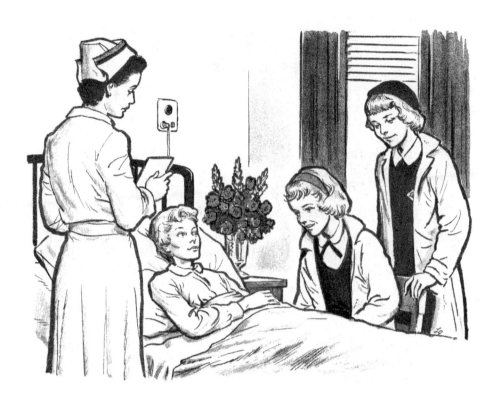

# Part 2.  The Works of Mercy; The Commandments; The Counsels

The laws of God include our performing the works of mercy. In fact on the last day we will be judged on whether we have performed them or not (Mt. 25:31–46).

### 1. The Corporal Works of Mercy

We know that our Lord was kind to everyone in word and deed. He especially sympathized with the poor and suffering, and even performed miracles to relieve their miseries. In this way He clearly showed His love of neighbor through the corporal works of mercy which He performed — that is through the good deeds done for men's bodies. Remember His words: "Amen I say to you, as long as you did it for one of these, the least of my brethren, you did it for me" (Mt. 25:40).

Since the corporal works of mercy will help us gain merit for heaven, it is important that we know them. *The chief corporal works of mercy are seven: (1) to feed the hungry; (2) to give drink to the thirsty; (3) to clothe the naked; (4) to visit the imprisoned; (5) to shelter the homeless; (6) to visit the sick; (7) to bury the dead.*

Very often we are able to help our neighbor spiritually through the corporal works of mercy. Because of our kindness, he may open his heart to us and eventually to God.

*To Feed the Hungry:* This is the first want to be attended to, for without food we die. We can fulfill this first work of mercy by giving food to those who are in need; by giving money to purchase food for the needy; by contributing to societies for funds for this purpose, for example the St. Vincent de Paul Society, the Bishops' Relief Program, and the like.

Examples:  Joseph feeding the Egyptians (Gen. 41:56).
Our Lord and the Multitude (Mk. 8:2).
St. Elizabeth of Portugal whose alms turned to roses. Feast — July 8.

*To Give Drink to the Thirsty:* Thirst, like hunger, is a very painful experience. Our Lord promises a reward for even a cup of water given in His name. "For whoever gives you a cup of water to drink in my name, because you are Christ's, amen I say to you, he shall not lose his reward" (Mk. 9:40).

Examples:  The woman at the well (Jn. 4:1–42).
Rebecca to the servant (Gen. 24:18).
Christ on the cross: "I thirst" (Jn. 19:28).

*To Clothe the Naked:* This is a necessary work if the needy or destitute are to preserve modesty and protect themselves from the cold. We perform this work by giving clothing to the poor, to refugees, and to those stripped of their belongings by floods, hurricanes, or fire; by making garments for those in need; by contributing the means with which to purchase these articles, for instance, the Christ Child Society.

Examples:   Tabitha at Joppa made garments for destitute
widows (Acts 9:36).
St. Martin shared his cloak with a beggar.
Feast — November 11.
St. Catherine of Siena. Feast — April 30.

These first three corporal works of mercy can be classed as *almsgiving*.

Almsgiving obtains for us remission for venial sins, brings the blessing of God upon us, makes atonement for the temporal punishment due to our sins, and assures eternal merit hereafter. By almsgiving we make friends with the poor; they in turn pray for us, and their prayers have great power with God.

*To Visit the Imprisoned:*   It is a charity to visit the imprisoned in order to encourage and comfort them. St. Paul tells us to: "Remember those who are in bonds as if you were bound with them" (Hebr. 13:3).

Examples:   The Christians visited St. Paul at Jerusalem and
Damascus (2 Cor. 11:32–35).
St. Peter Claver visited the slaves.
Feast — September 9.
St. Francis Xavier. Feast — December 3.

*To Shelter the Homeless:*  Hospitality is a duty recommended to us by St. Paul when he says: "Let brotherly love abide in you, and do not forget to entertain strangers; for thereby some have entertained angels unawares" (Hebr. 13:1–2). We have many opportunities to shelter the homeless in our care of orphans and displaced persons. Even when

**280**

we are not actually giving these latter a home, we can treat them in such a way that they will be made to feel at home in our country, where even the language is strange.

Examples: Martha and Mary received our Lord into their home as a guest (Lk. 10:38).
The disciples at Emmaus (Lk. 24:29).
The Great St. Bernard in the Alps.

*To Visit the Sick:* The object of the visit to the sick or injured in home, hospital, on the battlefield, or elsewhere is to bring spiritual or temporal relief to the sufferer. We can perform this work of mercy by sympathizing with the sick, by helping them to be patient and resigned; by bringing them food, delicacies, and little comforts; by procuring doctor, nurse, medicine; and by calling the priest to attend them. These charitable deeds are done very well by the Legion of Mary and by such other organizations as the St. Vincent de Paul and the Christ Child Societies.

Examples: Jesus at the pool (Jn. 5:6).
Damien and the Lepers.
St. Vincent de Paul, patron of charities.
Feast — July 19.
The priest visiting the sick.

*To Bury the Dead:* It is a particularly meritorious work of mercy to provide the dead with decent burial, and to attend funerals or to drop in to pay our respects at the wakes of those with whom we may have associated. St. Augustine says: "We ought to show respect to the bodies of Christian people, because they have been the instruments employed by the soul."

Examples: The people of Naim (Lk. 7:12).
Joseph of Arimathea and Nicodemus (Mk. 15:46).

Have you ever read the poem, "How the Great Guest

Came" by Edwin Markham, or the story, "Where Love Is There God Is Also," by Leo Tolstoy? Both of these writings help us to see the corporal works of mercy in action.

Daily, God gives us the opportunity to perform some one or more of the corporal works of mercy. Recall how many times your companions forgot their lunches, and you shared your sandwiches and milk with them; how often you contributed to collections requested by the bishop in order to help bear the expense of the clothing, food, and medical needs of the orphans and the homeless; how the mission bank jingled with your pennies and dimes as you helped to fill it for the spread of the kingdom of Christ on earth; how often you wrote a letter to, or visited a sick classmate personally. Or perhaps your class might even have adopted a mission baby.

## 2. The Spiritual Works of Mercy

The corporal works of mercy, which care for the wants of the body, are very good and necessary. But the spiritual works of mercy, which concern the soul, are even more important. Jesus did not merely cure the sick and feed the hungry. He also made every effort to relieve the spiritual needs of the people. He performed the greatest work of mercy when He redeemed man by His suffering and death on the cross. Again He is our Model.

Next to concern for our own salvation, is the need to help our neighbor attain his eternal happiness. When we realize that the chief likeness to God is not in the body but in the soul which is spiritual, and free, and immortal, it makes it easier for us to carry out the command of God to help our neighbor save his soul. In what better way can we do this than through the spiritual works of mercy? Do you know them? *The chief spiritual works of mercy are seven: (1) To admonish the sinner; (2) To instruct the ignorant; (3) To counsel the doubtful; (4) To comfort the sorrowful; (5) To bear wrongs patiently; (6) To forgive all injuries; (7) To pray for the living and the dead.* Let us explain each one.

*To Admonish the Sinner:* We can understand the value of this great work of mercy if we recall the words of St. James: "He ought to know that he who causes a sinner to be brought back from his misguided way, will save his soul from death, and will cover a multitude of sins" (James 5:20). We perform this work of mercy by kind but firm words, by good example, by wise zeal, and by prayer.

Examples: The thief on our Lord's right hand (Lk. 23:42).
St. Paul at Athens (Acts 17:22).
Elias and the false prophets (3 Kings 18:21–39).

*To Instruct the Ignorant:* Ignorance is often the source of such evils as missing Mass, neglecting the sacraments, or doing things to excess. We can be helpful by answering doubts and difficulties, by directing persons to hear sermons and catechism instructions, by lending or recommending good books, and by wise and charitable correction. Later we might help in the Confraternity of Christian Doctrine.

Examples: Our Lord in the parables — New Testament.
St. Peter, after Pentecost (Acts 2:14).

*To Counsel the Doubtful:* This work of mercy calls for gentleness and kindness. We can often lighten the mental strain of our neighbor by giving advice to him in his temporal or spiritual trials and difficulties. Sometimes a kind word or gentle act is all that is needed to help those who are in doubt to see what God expects of them. Sometimes we can bring or direct a person to a priest.

Examples:   Christ to the rich young man (Mt. 19:21).
            Gamaliel to the Council (Acts 5:35).

*To Comfort the Sorrowful:*   Our own experience shows us how great a charity is this work of mercy. We may practice it toward others by showing sympathy to them in their trials, encouragement in their difficulties, and by kindness in time of trouble and sorrow.

Examples:   Our Lord and Magdalen (Lk. 7:48).
            Joseph and his fellow prisoners (Gen. 40:7).
            The widow's son (Lk. 7:13).

*To Bear Wrongs Patiently:*   By this work of mercy we help both our neighbor and ourselves. Our good example of cheerfulness and patience when unjustly accused or treated or when things are difficult encourages our neighbor, and at the same time merits a reward for ourselves.

Examples:   Our Lord in His Passion (Lk. 23:34).
            David, being stoned (2 Kings 16).
            St. Joseph on the flight into Egypt (Mt. 2:13).

*To Forgive all Injuries:*   This is the lesson taught by our Lord on Calvary. Christ prayed to His heavenly Father to forgive His executioners. "Father, forgive them, for they do not know what they are doing" (Lk. 23:34). The true Christian loves all men, even those who reproach and persecute him. We too, because of our love of God, should forgive all injuries; not once but as many times as necessary, as our Lord told St. Peter (Mt. 18:21-22).

Examples:   Our Lord on the Cross (Lk. 23:34).
            Joseph and his brothers (Gen. 45:5).
            St. Stephen (Acts 7:60).

*To Pray for the Living and the Dead:*   The conversion of a soul may at some time or other depend on our prayers. We must pray for the pope and the Church, for our parents, relatives and friends, for bishops and the clergy, for civil leaders, and for the holy souls in purgatory. To be able to help our deceased relatives by prayer should be a comfort and a consolation to us. The Raccolta has many indulgenced prayers for such purposes; for instance, All Souls' Day, the Portiuncula (August 2).

Examples:  Our Lord for His disciples and the entire Church (Jn. 17:9-23).
Moses for his people (Exod. 32:11).
St. Augustine for his mother.

*Everyone is obliged to perform the works of mercy, according to his own ability and the need of his neighbor.* This does not mean that we neglect our own salvation in order to aid our neighbor. The phrase "according to his own ability" tells us that each must do what he is able to do. "According to the needs of his neighbor" indicates that one need not always evenly distribute his charity, but should regulate it according to the condition of the neighbor in question. The help or good example we give to our companion in school, at play, or otherwise, may make a difference in the conduct of some boy or girl, not only now, but also in later life.

But then we must not think of helping our neighbor only so far as these seven corporal and seven spiritual works of mercy are concerned. *All the ordinary deeds done every day to relieve the corporal or spiritual needs of others are true works of mercy, if done in the name of Christ,* that is, to please Christ, or to show our love for Him. Let us use every opportunity to practice the beautiful virtue of charity. Often repeat the ejaculation:

"All for Thee, Most Sacred Heart of Jesus," especially when performing a good deed.

## 3. The Ten Commandments

You will remember that our Lord said there are two great

commandments: (1) to love God; (2) to love our neighbor as ourself. The Ten Commandments are included in these two commandments. Three of the ten commandments tell us of our duties to God directly. The other seven commandments tell us of the duties we owe directly to our neighbor and to ourselves.

**The commandments of God are these ten:**

1. I am the Lord thy God; thou shalt not have strange gods before Me.
2. Thou shalt not take the name of the Lord thy God in vain.
3. Remember thou keep holy the Lord's day.
4. Honor thy father and thy mother.
5. Thou shalt not kill.
6. Thou shalt not commit adultery.
7. Thou shalt not steal.
8. Thou shalt not bear false witness against thy neighbor.
9. Thou shalt not covet thy neighbor's wife.
10. Thou shalt not covet thy neighbor's goods.

Did you notice the repetition of one particular word in each of the first three commandments? What is that word? It is the word "Lord." In the first, the Lord; in the second, the Lord's name; in the third, the Lord's day. The word "Lord" does not appear in any of the remaining commandments. The repetition of this word not only directs our thoughts to God but also shows us that the work commanded by these three commandments tends directly toward the honor and glory of God. These first three commandments are an explanation of the first great commandment; the last seven commandments are an explanation of the second great commandment.

God in His infinite goodness and love has given us these ten commandments to guide the actions of our whole life; every minute of every day. There is nothing that He, our Creator and our Redeemer, has not done for us to help us to gain heaven. Truly, He is our dear Father and closest Friend. Knowing this, *we should not be satisfied merely to keep the commandments of God, but should always be ready to do good deeds, even when they are not commanded.* Generous lovers of God do not measure their generosity. They give themselves wholeheartedly to a life of good deeds.

### 4. "If Thou Wilt Be Perfect"

The young man who had asked Christ what he must do to gain eternal life was told by our Lord to keep the commandments. When he replied that he had kept the commandments since youth, Christ answered: "If thou wilt be perfect, go, sell what thou hast, and give to the poor, and thou shalt have treasure in heaven and come, follow me" (Mt. 19:21). By these words, Christ invited this rich man to a life of perfection. Do you know what that means? Christ was asking this young man to spend his life for God in a manner far more perfect than that required by the commandments.

In order to follow such a high calling, or vocation, *our Saviour especially recommends the observance of the evangelical counsels — voluntary poverty, perpetual chastity, and perfect obedience.* These three evangelical, that is gospel counsels are like words of advice. To follow this advice and take the three vows of poverty, chastity, and obedience is especially pleasing to our Lord, and will help us to serve Him in a more perfect manner.

Voluntary poverty means giving up earthly possessions.

**287**

Perpetual chastity means giving up the right to marriage and promising to remain pure in soul and body.

Perfect obedience means fulfilling the commands of appointed superiors as making known the will of God to us.

To you also, our Lord says: "Keep the commandments if you wish to serve Me and to save your soul." Perhaps He is also saying: "Come, follow Me, through the practice of the three vows." Pray every day that you may know the will of God in regard to what He wants you to do. Memorize the ten commandments not only for the sake of reciting them, but for the sake of living them. Often say the prayer: "Jesus, teach me what You want me to be."

## REVIEW, IX–2

### WORD LIST

| | | |
|---|---|---|
| corporal | perpetual | chastity |
| brethren | refugees | evangelical |
| destitute | temporal | meritorious |
| remission | spiritual | works of mercy |
| admonish | atonement | counsel |
| excess | instruct | doubtful |
| conversion | ignorant | voluntary |
| poverty | perfection | obedience |

### THINGS TO REMEMBER

1. The Ten Commandments are our guides on the way to heaven.
2. The Ten Commandments of God are summarized in the law of charity.
3. The Ten Commandments express God's will for us.
4. The two great Commandments are: (1) love of God; (2) love of our neighbor.
5. The first three Commandments are an explanation of the first great Commandment of God.

6. The spiritual and corporal works of mercy help us gain merit for heaven.
7. The lives of Christ and the saints give us examples of the practice of the spiritual and corporal works of mercy.

## THINGS TO DISCUSS AND DO

1. Draw two tables of stone. On the first print: *God*, I–III. On the second print: *Self and Neighbor*, IV–X. Under each list what belongs there.
2. Look up the story of the Ten Commandments in the Bible. Plan a short talk to the class, telling what book of the Bible the Commandments are contained in, and why they are there, and how they were given.
3. Make a chart of the corporal works of mercy. Show how Christ exemplified each one — and how you can practice each one.
4. Explain what is meant by performing the spiritual and corporal works of mercy with the right motive.
5. St. Vincent de Paul had an organization named in his honor. How could you become a worthy member of this society?
6. How can the help you give to others throughout the day earn a heavenly reward?

Study Catechism Lesson 15, *The Two Great Commandments*, Questions 191–197, pp. 292–293.

# End-of-Unit Review — Unit IX

## PART 1

# CATECHISM

### LESSON 15

#### The Two Great Commandments

188. **Besides believing what God has revealed, what else must we do to be saved?**

Besides believing what God has revealed, we must keep His law.

189. Which are the two great commandments that contain the whole law of God?

The two great commandments that contain the whole law of God are:

*first,* Thou shalt love the Lord thy God with thy whole heart, and with thy whole soul, and with thy whole mind, and with thy whole strength;

*second,* Thou shalt love thy neighbor as thyself.

190. What must we do to love God, our neighbor, and ourselves?

To love God, our neighbor, and ourselves we must keep the commandments of God and of the Church, and perform the spiritual and corporal works of mercy.

## OTHER QUESTIONS AND EXERCISES

1. Are laws necessary in our daily life?
2. Are laws necessary in our spiritual life?
3. Do God's laws govern our minds and wills?
4. Does conscience sometimes regulate our actions?
5. Is the story of the Ten Commandments told in the book of Genesis?
6. Did God compose the Ten Commandments only for the Israelites?
7. Should we try to please God every minute of the day?
8. May we love any creature more than we love God?
9. Is the whole law of God contained in the first three commandments?
10. Do we have any opportunities to prove our love of God?

**PART 2**

1. Match the following spiritual and corporal works of mercy, on your own paper.

| | |
|---|---|
| 1. To feed the hungry | A. Sending clothing to needy families |
| 2. Give drink to the thirsty | B. Reminding our friends of the wrong they may be doing |
| 3. Shelter the homeless | C. Not excusing ourselves when we are accused of doing something we did not do |
| 4. Clothe the naked | |
| 5. Visit the imprisoned | D. Getting a glass of water for a hard-working man |
| 6. Visit the sick | E. Paying a visit to a classmate who was in an accident |
| 7. Bury the dead | F. Giving advice to someone not well instructed in our religion |
| 8. Admonish the sinner | G. Sending food to children whose father is unemployed |
| 9. Instruct the ignorant | H. Paying a visit to someone who is in jail |
| 10. Counsel the doubtful | I. Explaining the teachings of our Church to those who do not know them |
| 11. Comfort the sorrowing | J. Offering a Mass for a deceased relative or friend |
| 12. Bear wrongs patiently | K. Attending a funeral |
| | L. Giving a home to refugees from other countries |
| 13. Forgive all injuries | M. Consoling those who are in trouble |
| 14. Pray for living and dead | N. Excusing those who have hurt our feelings |

# CATECHISM

### The Two Great Commandments

191. Which are the chief corporal works of mercy?

The chief corporal works of mercy are seven:
1. To feed the hungry.
2. To give drink to the thirsty.
3. To clothe the naked.
4. To visit the imprisoned.
5. To shelter the homeless.
6. To visit the sick.
7. To bury the dead.

192. Which are the chief spiritual works of mercy?

The chief spiritual works of mercy are seven:
1. To admonish the sinner.
2. To instruct the ignorant.
3. To counsel the doubtful.
4. To comfort the sorrowful.
5. To bear wrongs patiently.
6. To forgive all injuries.
7. To pray for the living and the dead.

193. Is everyone obliged to perform the works of mercy?

Everyone is obliged to perform the works of mercy, according to his own ability and the need of his neighbor.

194. Are all the ordinary deeds done every day to relieve the corporal or spiritual needs of others true works of mercy?

All the ordinary deeds done every day to relieve the corporal or spiritual needs of others are true works of mercy, if done in the name of Christ.

**195. Which are the commandments of God?**

The commandments of God are these ten:

1. I am the Lord thy God; thou shalt not have strange gods before Me.
2. Thou shalt not take the name of the Lord thy God in vain.
3. Remember thou keep holy the Lord's day.
4. Honor thy father and thy mother.
5. Thou shalt not kill.
6. Thou shalt not commit adultery.
7. Thou shalt not steal.
8. Thou shalt not bear false witness against thy neighbor.
9. Thou shalt not covet thy neighbor's wife.
10. Thou shalt not covet thy neighbor's goods.

**196. Should we be satisfied merely to keep the commandments of God?**

We should not be satisfied merely to keep the commandments of God, but should always be ready to do good deeds, even when they are not commanded.

**197. What does our Saviour especially recommend that is not strictly commanded by the law of God?**

Our Saviour especially recommends the observance of the evangelical counsels — voluntary poverty, perpetual chastity, and perfect obedience.

## OTHER QUESTIONS AND EXERCISES

1. What motive should we have for all our good deeds?
2. How are we to observe the commandments?
3. How did Christ perform the spiritual and corporal works of mercy?
4. Why should we visit the sick? The imprisoned?
5. What was Jesus' greatest work of mercy?
6. What is almsgiving? What does it do for us?
7. Give some examples of Christ's spirit of forgiveness.
8. In what ways did Christ practice obedience to God's laws?

# Unit X.  The First Three Commandments:
## Love of God

# Part 1. The First Commandment: We Must Worship God

Thus far this year we have studied about God, Father, Son, and Holy Ghost. Now we shall study in detail each of the first three commandments of God. They tell us our duties to God. The first commandment is: *I am the Lord thy God; thou shalt not have strange gods before Me.*

## 1. What the First Commandment Commands

Did a friend of yours ever try to call you away while you were playing a good game of baseball? What did you do? Suppose that instead of a friend, your father came all the way over to the ball field and told you to come home at once. Why would you stop playing at once when your father called? Your father has authority over you; he has the right to punish you, and you know for your own good that you had better obey.

Our Father in heaven wanted His family on earth to live in peace and good order. He, therefore, gave man the Ten Commandments. God knows that it is hard to obey laws, but He also knows that it is much harder to live in a world where there are no laws.

To show how necessary it is for us to observe His laws God introduced the very first commandment by reminding us who He is. "I am the Lord thy God." What thoughts come to your mind as you think over these words? The little word "I" tells us that there is only one God. The word "Lord" means more than "master." It means the one from whom all have existence.

God, we learned, is the Supreme Being, infinitely perfect, who made all things and keeps them in existence. Therefore,

**295**

the very first words of the first commandment remind us
that He who gives us the laws is our Creator and Preserver.
They help us to realize how important it is to obey God's
laws. They remind us that we must not only acknowledge
God as our Lord and Creator but that we must worship and
honor Him in a special way.

The second part of the first commandment says: ". . . thou
shalt not have strange gods before Me." What is meant by
strange gods? What pictures have you seen of strange gods
in geography books or movies? Buddha? A mummified animal? Strange gods, we may say, are false gods, or any
creature adored in the place of the one true God. The pagans
worship the sun, moon, stars, and animals. This is idolatry
and is sinful. These things have no power to help us. God

alone can answer our prayers. He alone has a right to supreme worship as the Creator and Preserver of all things. The catechism explains it this way: *By the first commandment we are commanded to offer to God alone the supreme worship that is due Him.*

## 2. How We Worship God

In order to understand how to give God supreme worship, let us think about our parents. How do we honor and please them? Our fathers and mothers are pleased and happy when we listen to them and believe what they tell us. Moreover, they are glad when we come to them with our troubles. Why? We show that we trust them. We show our love for our fathers and mothers by respect and obedience, and by making little sacrifices to do things for them. So too *we worship God by acts of faith, hope, and charity, and by adoring Him and praying to Him.*

### Faith

Faith helps us to observe the first commandment. We give God supreme worship by believing Him because He is infinite truth. We believe as unchangeably true all that He has revealed and we believe it on His own word. Christ worked great miracles for those who had faith in Him and He also praised them highly. "And wherever He went, into village or farm or town, they laid the sick in the market places, and entreated him to let them touch but the tassel of his cloak; and as many as touched him were saved" (Mk. 6:56). We too can show our faith in God by doing the things which faith demands of us; by making acts of faith often; and by professing our faith whenever God's honor demands it.

In order to have this belief we must do certain things. *Faith obliges us, first, to make efforts to find out what God has revealed.* We can do this by studying our religion and finding out as much as we can about it. *Second, faith obliges us to believe firmly what God has revealed.* As soon as we know the truth we must believe it. It is good for us to say the prayer recorded in St. Mark 9:23: "I do believe; help my unbelief." *Third, faith obliges us to profess our faith openly whenever necessary.*

All of us have shown our faith openly many times. We have done so when we prayed reverently in school, in church, or at home; when we went to church on Sunday; when we bowed our heads on hearing the name of Jesus. Christ has promised to claim us as His own before His Father in heaven for our open profession of faith. The Church grants an indulgence of 300 days even for so small a profession of faith as tipping your hat, or bowing your head when you pass a Catholic church.

There are times when it is absolutely necessary that we profess our faith openly. These are the occasions when God's honor requires it, or the good of our neighbor demands it. Can you think of such instances? The lives of the early martyrs or modern martyrs have many examples.

Since a Catholic must worship God by faith he must guard it carefully. How? The introduction of this book discusses this matter. We can, however, summarize it here. *A Catholic can best safeguard his faith by making frequent acts of faith, by praying for a strong faith, by studying his religion very earnestly, by living a good life, by good reading, by refusing to associate with the enemies of the Church, and by not reading books and papers opposed to the Church and her teaching.* You might discuss each point.

## Sins Against Faith

The first commandment forbids sins against faith. Few Catholics after being instructed in their religion go so far as to doubt or deny any of the Church's teachings. Even those unfortunate persons who leave the Catholic Church, usually do not do so because of difficulties concerning their faith. A bad marriage, the desire for worldly success, or some other unworthy motive tempts them.

Joan is a sad example of a girl who was thus tempted. Educated in Catholic schools, a member of the parish study club, and active in the sodality, one would not expect Joan to do what she did. However, when the time came to break off company with a young man who spared no words in condemning the Church and its teachings. Joan was weak. She "loved" herself and the man more than she loved God. She unwisely renounced her faith. Joan committed the sin of apostasy — or complete rejection of the truths of the Catholic faith.

Unbelief or lack of faith is the sin of infidelity. Those people commit it who know the truths of faith and deliberately refuse to accept them.

An instructor in a Catholic college acted against faith in another way. He taught that all who are not members of the Catholic Church would go to hell. This is against that teaching of the Church which explains that: "They who remain outside the Catholic Church through no grave fault of their own and do not know it is the true Church, can be saved by making use of the graces which God gives them." The teacher, in this case, refused to give up his wrong belief even after the Church explained it to him; he was a heretic. His sin is called heresy. Heresy is willingly refusing to believe one or more truths of the Catholic faith.

*Indifferentism* is a common sin against faith. It is the sin of those who act or speak as if all religions were equally good, or who say that you can believe what you choose to believe. Parents can commit the sin of indifferentism if they do not take care that their children receive sufficient religious instruction, for instance, if they allow them to go to non-Catholic summer Bible schools or the like. Many times the priest warns people about indifferentism when he commands parents whose children are in public schools to send them to instruction classes.

Catholics who take part in non-Catholic services also sin against faith. *A Catholic sins against faith by taking part in non-Catholic worship because he thus professes belief in a religion he knows is false.* We may be present at a service such as at a marriage or a funeral of a non-Catholic for grave reasons, as long as we do not take part in the service. There is no sin unless we take part.

Briefly, then, answering the question how a Catholic sins against faith, we may say: *A Catholic sins against faith by apostasy, heresy, indifferentism, and by taking part in non-Catholic worship.*

## Hope

Hope helps us to observe the first commandment. We worship God by hope, that is, by expecting from Him eternal salvation and all the helps that are necessary to obtain it: pardon for our sins, and divine grace, the means of obtaining eternal life. *Hope obliges us,* therefore, *to trust firmly that God will give us eternal life and the means to obtain it.* We can strengthen our confidence in God by saying often: "Heart of Jesus, I put my trust in Thee."

**300**

Christ wants us to remember that when we hope we are placing our trust in God who is an all-powerful and all-good Father. Christ said if we ask the Father anything in His name He will give it to us. For what may we hope? Because we are made of soul and body, we may hope for everything we need for soul and body.

## Sins Against Hope

Just as there are sins against faith, so too, there are sins against hope. *The sins against hope are presumption and despair.*

We have learned that grace is necessary for salvation. Anyone, therefore, who thinks or acts as if he could be saved without the help of God commits the sin of presumption. A second way of sinning by presumption is by expecting to get to heaven without making proper use of the means God wants us to use. Some of the means we must use are prayer and the reception of the sacraments. Presumption, then, is one kind of sin against hope. *A person sins by presumption when he trusts that he can be saved by his own efforts without God's help, or by God's help, without his own efforts.*

When Judas hanged himself he committed a sin against hope. What was the sin he had committed? Despair. *A person sins by despair when he deliberately refuses to trust that God will give him the necessary help to save his soul.* Judas' sin of despair was the direct opposite of the sin of presumption. He did not have enough hope. Judas was completely discouraged. He abandoned all hope of forgiveness from Christ. He forgot that Christ had called him a friend even while he was sinning. He forgot that Magdalen had sinned and had been forgiven. No matter how bad things are or will become we must never give up hope. No matter how sinful we are, the merciful Christ wants us to hope in Him. Christ rewarded the thief who showed his trust to Him in almost his last breath on the cross (Lk. 23:43). Not to hope in God is a grave sin against so loving and forgiving a Father. God is nearest when the night is darkest. Remember Job!

## Charity

Charity helps us to observe the first commandment. Charity means love. When we speak of charity as a way of worshiping God, we do not mean feelings and words, but we mean essentially loving God with our heart and our will. We love God with our wills when we at least keep His commandments. A person who has not broken a commandment seriously and is free from mortal sin is worshiping God by charity, at least in the first and lowest degree. If he is keeping all the commandments then he also loves his neighbor. Why? Because he is not only observing the first three commandments which concern his duties to God directly, but also the last seven which pertain to his neighbor. *Charity obliges us to love God above all things because He is infinitely good, and to love our neighbor as ourselves for the love of God.*

The more we love God, the more carefully we fulfill His commands. Even small children have loved God so much that they performed all their actions out of love for God. This is perfect love of God. Name some children saints who even gave up their lives for God. Say often throughout the day: "My God, I love You."

## Sins Against Charity

There are many sins against charity. However, *the chief sins against charity are hatred of God and of our neighbor, envy, sloth, and scandal.*

**302**

Every sin is, in a way, an offense against charity because, by sinning, we choose some pleasure or created thing in place of God's wishes or commands. A mortal sin is a complete turning away from God. The worst mortal sin is hatred of God. Hate means to wish evil to, and to be happy at misfortune falling upon the one hated. Those who hate God wish or even try to cause evil to befall God and rejoice when grievous sins are committed. Hate is the sin that is found in hell just as charity is the virtue that is found in heaven.

*Hatred of one's neighbor* consists in wishing him harm and rejoicing at his ill fortune. If this involves deliberately wishing a serious evil, it is a mortal sin. If the misfortune wished upon another is not grave, the sin is venial.

Sometimes people, and even children, are jealous of the good things that others have. People might be jealous of their neighbor's car or home. Children are sometimes sad if others get better marks in school, or have toys which they do not have. Charity requires us to be happy with our neighbor over the good things he has. If we are jealous, we commit the sin of *envy.*

*Sloth* is another sin against charity. Sloth means laziness, especially in our duties to God and neighbor. A father who does not support his family through laziness is slothful. A person who neglects his prayers for a long time through laziness is also slothful. If we sometimes feel a dislike for the things of God, like prayer, the sacraments, or the study of religion, let us beg our Blessed Mother, who was the most diligent of God's creatures, to give us a love for them. A little prayer we can say to her is: "O Mary, make me to live in God, with God, and for God."

*Scandal* is another sin against charity. Scandal is any act, word, or criticism which causes another to sin or which weakens another's strength against sin. Our Lord said it were better that a person be drowned rather than give bad example or scandal to others. How do we sometimes, perhaps, scandalize our younger brothers and sisters? Our younger brothers and sisters are quick to imitate our behavior at home, at school, in church, or in public. They have a right to expect us to use decent language, to obey promptly, and in general, to live according to the commandments of God and of His Church. They look up to us and try to be like us. We must give them good example — always.

Thus we see that to keep the first commandment we must not only pray the acts of faith, hope, and charity, but must also grow in these virtues. By faith we believe in God; by hope we confidently trust that God will give us the help we need to save our souls; and by charity we love and reverence God and keep His commandments.

### Superstition and Sacrilege

The sins against the three theological virtues are not the only sins forbidden by the first commandment. *Besides the sins against faith, hope, and charity, the first commandment forbids also superstition and sacrilege.*

*Superstition* is a sin against the first commandment because through it either one gives God a worship that is not suited to Him as the Supreme Being or gives a creature the worship that belongs to God.

Some of us may have seen others giving creatures the worship due to God alone. For instance those who carry a rabbit's foot, or a four-leaf clover because they actually believe it will protect them, commit the sin of superstition. How about black cats and walking under ladders?

Others commit this sin by believing that certain words or actions have magical powers. They sin whether they say the words and do the actions themselves or whether they go to other persons who use them. They call these words or actions spells. Some foolishly superstitious people believe that human beings can fortell the future from the lines of a person's hand, tea leaves, constellations of stars, or playing cards.

Would Catholics who believed that certain prayers or the wearing of certain scapulars or medals would guarantee their eternal salvation even without a good and devout life be guilty of superstition?

To believe in dreams is also superstition. It is likewise superstitious to go to spiritists who falsely claim they can contact people who have died.

How, then, does a person sin by superstition? *A person sins by superstition when he attributes to a creature a power that belongs to God alone, as when he makes use of charms or spells, believes in dreams or fortunetelling, or goes to spiritists.*

*Sacrilege* is the next sin against the first commandment we shall study. *A person sins by sacrilege when he mistreats sacred persons, places, or things.*

In the Old Testament we read about King Baltassar, who at a banquet used sacred vessels stolen from the Temple in Jerusalem. God was so angry about the disrespect shown to these sacred vessels that the same night He permitted the king to be slain by an enemy and his nation conquered. The sin King Baltassar committed is called sacrilege.

You know some holy persons who are consecrated to God's service. It is a sacrilege to deliberately strike or ill-treat a bishop, priest, or other person dedicated to God. It was a great sacrilege for the communists when they tortured and imprisoned bishops, priests, and sisters in countries behind the Iron Curtain. Do you know of any such cases?

What are some holy places that you have seen? It is wrong

to break into or rob or improperly use churches, chapels, altars, and cemeteries. In Russia, communists have turned churches into club houses. They have destroyed statues and altars. Even in our own country at one time a group of people desecrated Catholic cemeteries by breaking the crosses and Christian monuments. To deliberately steal, break, or destroy important property belonging to the Church can be a sacrilege.

Adoration and prayer help us to observe the first commandment. We must adore God as our Creator. This means we must acknowledge both in our mind and in our conduct that we depend entirely upon Him. It means that we desire to do His will in all things because He is the Supreme Being and when we know His will we do it. This little prayer will serve as a reminder: "Teach me, O Lord, to do thy will, for thou art my God" (Ps. 142:10).

Perhaps the easiest way to worship God is by prayer, a loving raising of our minds and hearts to God. Our prayers and acts of worship reveal the love for God that is in our hearts. They keep us mindful that God is always with us and help us behave, as we should in His presence. They show that we realize that God is the Supreme Being and Creator of all things.

The greatest prayer and the highest form of worship that we can offer to God is the Holy Sacrifice of the Mass. We ought to learn all we can about the Mass, and to assist at it whenever we can. The blessings of the Mass will stay with us throughout the day.

Now we have learned what we mean when we say that *we worship God by acts of faith, hope, and charity, and by adoring Him and praying to Him.* This worship must be given both in mind and in behavior. An example might help us to understand better. A watch or clock has inside machinery and an outside face with hands which tell time. Can we tell time if we have only the inner works? Can we tell time if we have only the face and hands? No. In the same way worship of God must come from our hearts, and it must show in our words, our actions, and our entire conduct.

## REVIEW, X–1

### WORD LIST

| | | |
|---|---|---|
| atheist | acknowledge | elevation |
| apostasy | pagans | exposed |
| infidelity | preserver | condemning |
| heretic | unchangeable | sacrilege |
| presumption | superstition | indulgence |
| despair | entreated | |

### THINGS TO REMEMBER

1. We must worship God because He is the Supreme Being who made all things and keeps them in existence.
2. We worship God by faith, hope, charity, prayer, adoration.
3. The highest form of worship is the holy sacrifice of the Mass.
4. We are bound to profess our faith openly when God's honor or our neighbor's good requires it.
5. We cannot save our souls without God's help.
6. No matter how seriously we have sinned, God will forgive us if we are sorry.
7. The worst mortal sin is hatred of God.
8. To keep the first commandment we must not only pray the acts of faith, hope, and love, but we must also grow in these virtues.

### THINGS TO DISCUSS AND DO

1. Find places in the Old Testament where the worship of false gods is mentioned.
2. Compose original acts of faith, hope, and love. In them, tell God some special thing you will do to prove your faith, hope, love.

3. Explain why the sacrifice of the Mass is the highest form of worship.
4. Discuss the ways and means you have of worshiping God.
5. List the occasions during the day when you openly profess your faith.
6. How could you sin through presumption?
7. Explain indifferentism.
8. What examples from the life of Christ will comfort us if we feel our sins are too great to be forgiven?
9. Give some examples of how we can show our love of God in our everyday actions.
10. How can we show our love for our neighbor at school? at play?

Study Catechism Lesson 16, *The First Commandment of God*, pp. 341–343.

# Part 2. The First Commandment Permits Us To Honor the Saints

We have learned what it means to worship God. Now we are ready to learn more about the respect due to some very special friends of God — the saints.

## 1. Honor Given Saints Differs From Honor Given God

Let us first pay a visit to the home of a boy we shall call Terry. If Terry really loves his dad, how will he act toward him? He will always be very respectful and obedient. Now suppose that Terry's dad invites a relative or a dear friend of his to spend some time in his home. How would Terry's dad want him to act toward that person? Would he expect

Terry to show the same love for his friend as he did toward his father? Why not? He knows Terry feels closer to him because he is his father. The same is true when we consider the respect we owe the saints. *The first commandment does not forbid us to honor the saints in heaven, provided we do not give them the honor that belongs to God alone.*

Now let us suppose Terry's dad invites his friend, Mr. Smith, to live at his home for a long time. Terry spends more and more time with Mr. Smith because he has shown great interest in Terry. Gradually, Terry begins to realize how kind the man is. Terry also notices that his dad is pleased with the liking he shows for Mr. Smith. It is one way of approving his dad's choice of friends. In like manner, *we honor the saints in heaven because they practiced great virtue when they were on earth, and because in honoring those who are the chosen friends of God we honor God Himself.*

Terry has been watching Mr. Smith very closely. He notices that he has many good qualities. Terry has often watched his actions and listened to his conversation. Before long Terry finds himself walking, talking, and thinking in the same way as Mr. Smith. What is Terry doing? He is paying Mr. Smith a compliment by imitating him. This is one way in which we, too, honor the saints. In fact, imitating their holy lives is the best way to honor them and to please God.

One day Terry got into a fist fight with one of his comrades. Although Terry did his best, he returned home with visible signs of what had happened. On entering the back door he came face to face with Mr. Smith. Terry offered a hurried explanation, followed by a petition to help him break the news gently to his father.

Often when we get into a bout with sin and come limping home with a spiritual "black eye," we make use of the saints in somewhat the same way Terry made use of Mr. Smith. *When we pray to the saints we ask them to offer their prayers to God for us.*

After Terry had explained to Mr. Smith what had happened, he left to attend to his "battle trophies" confident that his hero would be able to intercede for him. Why did he place such trust in his friend? He knew Mr. Smith was a good friend of his father. Furthermore, Mr. Smith had shown that he loved Terry and therefore, Terry felt sure he would not disappoint him. We place even greater confidence in the saints, and with good reason for *we know that the saints will pray for us because they are with God and have great love for us.*

## 2. How We Honor the Relics of Saints

The time finally came for Mr. Smith to leave Terry's home. Before leaving, he gave Terry a picture of himself, a fishing pole and line which he had used, and a football. Terry cherished these possessions very highly because they were a constant reminder of his good friend. He was also determined to keep them for a long time. We can call these objects relics because the word "relics" means things left from the past. Just as Terry respected the articles given him by Mr. Smith, but in a much more reverent way, *we honor relics because they are the bodies of the saints or objects connected with the saints or with our Lord.*

Let us pause now and review the three ways of honoring the saints. *We can honor the saints: first, by imitating their holy lives; second, by praying to them; third, by showing respect to their relics and images.*

Some non-Catholics object to our having statues and pictures of saints in our homes or churches. But *the first commandment forbids the making or the use of statues and pictures only when they promote false worship.*

In the city of Ephesus in Asia Minor, silversmiths made miniature temples — small likenesses of the wonderful Temple of Diana, the goddess of all Asia. Use of these souvenirs encouraged the worship of Diana, therefore, they promoted false worship which is forbidden by the first commandment. When some of the Ephesians became Christians through the preaching of St. Paul, the silversmiths began to lose their trade so they caused trouble for the saint.

**311**

Now let us get back to Terry to help us understand another point. Terry's father told him that Mr. Smith had met with a serious accident. Upon hearing this news, Terry went at once to his own room. When his father came up, he found a solemn-faced Terry gazing admiringly at a picture of Mr. Smith. He was showing his respect before a picture of a very dear friend. Terry is not the only one who shows respect, in this way, for a friend.

We do the very same thing in our religious life. For *it is right to show respect to the statues and pictures of Christ and of the saints, just as it is right to show respect to the images of those whom we honor or love on earth.* They often suffered hardships for the love of God and made many sacrifices in order to spread His kingdom.

That God Himself approves devotion to images and relics may be learned from the following incidents. First, the body in the prophet's tomb coming to life. "And Eliseus died, and they buried him. And the rovers (robbers) from Moab came into the land the same year. And some that were burying a man, saw the rovers, and cast the body into the sepulcher of Eliseus. And when it had touched the bones of Eliseus, the man came to life, and stood upon his feet" (Kings 13:20–21). In the Acts of the Apostles we find a story of how the handkerchiefs of St. Paul were taken to the sick and healed them (Acts 19:11–12).

These examples concern happenings of the Old and New Testaments. We can, however, find that even today God does wonderful things through objects which have been used by His special friends. These incidents prove that God Himself honors the bodies of His saints and regards even objects that have touched them, as holy.

We Catholics know that God alone works miracles and

wonders. And if a miracle is worked through some relic, we know it is God who worked it, not the relic itself. So it is not superstition when we keep and honor some piece of bone from a saint, something that has touched his body, or an article that has been used by him. We do not adore and serve these things. We only venerate them, that is, show special respect toward them. We adore God alone. *We honor Christ and the saints when we pray before the crucifix, relics, and sacred images because we honor the persons they represent; we adore Christ and venerate the saints.* The honor we give to God is different from and much greater than the honor we give to the saints.

Non-Catholics seem to have a hard time understanding our veneration of the saints and their relics and images. Suppose a non-Catholic friend of yours would accuse you of praying to a statue, a crucifix, or a picture. How would you answer him? You could say: *We do not pray to the crucifix or to the images and relics of the saints, but to the persons they represent.*

The images and pictures serve only as a help to keep our attention on what we are doing. We place them in our churches and classrooms, to remind us of our heavenly friends just as we keep heirlooms or place the pictures of living, or especially of dead parents on our desks or dressers at home. We love our parents and like to have them near us even if only in this way. The pictures help us to look up to our parents, to respect them, and to be like them  This is the reason why we say that we do not pray to a crucifix or an image or relic of a saint.

## Summary of the First Commandment

The first commandment is: "I am the Lord thy God; thou shalt not have strange gods before Me." This commandment obliges us to give to God alone the supreme worship that is due Him. We do this by acts of faith, hope, and charity, and by adoring Him and praying to Him. All thoughts, words, deeds, or omissions that are contrary to these acts by which we worship God, are forbidden by this commandment. The following fourteen sins are the chief sins against the first commandment: infidelity, apostasy, heresy, indifferentism, taking part in non-Catholic worship, presumption, despair, hatred of God, hatred of our neighbor, sloth, envy, scandal, superstition, and sacrilege. We adore God and venerate the saints. We do not pray to the images or relics of God or His saints, but rather do we pray to the persons that they represent.

## REVIEW, X–2

### WORD LIST

| | | | |
|---|---|---|---|
| intercede | confident | miniature | false worship |
| venerate | imitating | petition | |
| approving | cherished | relics | |

### THINGS TO REMEMBER

1. I can best honor the saints by imitating their holy lives and heroic virtues.
2. When I venerate, or honor, the saints in a special way, I honor God Himself.
3. Our devotion to the saints must not be as great as our devotion to God.
4. We do not *pray* to images; we pray to the persons they represent.
5. Religious pictures and objects remind us of Christ and the saints and should be evident in every home.

1. Make a list of the ways in which saints are honored in your parish church; in your home.
2. What are relics?
3. How can the saints help us?
4. Of what value is it to have crucifixes and religious pictures in our homes?
5. Plan a program in honor of one of the saints.
6. How can one violate the first commandment?
7. List the names of several saints and tell in what way or ways you would like to imitate them.
8. How would you explain to a non-Catholic friend the presence of a crucifix in your bedroom?
9. If you could choose several religious pictures or objects for your home, what would you choose? Why?
10. What does the first commandment forbid?

Study Catechism Lesson 17, *Honoring the Saints, Relics and Images,* pp. 344–346.

# Part 3.  The Second Commandment

*The second commandment of God is: Thou shalt not take the name of the Lord thy God in vain.*

Let us now expand our knowledge about the second commandment. What do you already know about the second commandment?

*By the second commandment we are commanded always to speak with reverence of God, of the saints, and of holy things, and* as we shall study later, we are also commanded *to be truthful in taking oaths and faithful to them and to our vows.*

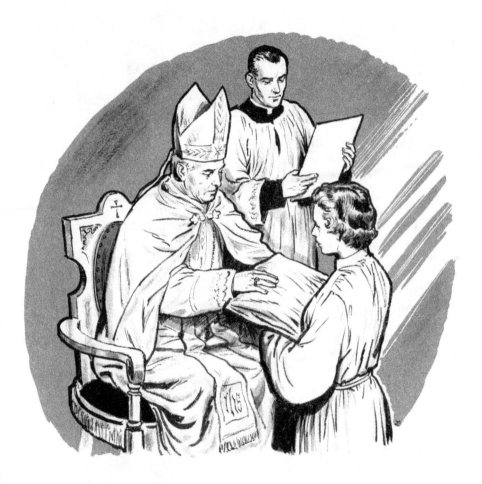

One of a person's most prized possessions is his name. His name tells who he is. To praise a man is to connect praise with his name. The names of two great Americans will never be forgotten. George Washington will always be remembered as he who was "First in war, first in peace, and first in the hearts of his countrymen." The name of Abraham Lincoln will never die as long as there are school children and lovers of freedom to appreciate him and to realize what he and his famous speech have meant to mankind: ". . . That this nation under God shall have a new birth of freedom; and that government of the people, by the people, and for the people shall not perish from the earth."

Again if a man is not upright or sincere, his name is not upheld or revered. Such are the names of Judas Iscariot — traitor to the divine Master — and that of Benedict Arnold — traitor to his country. You know the story of their wrong deeds and you also know how little regard men have for them.

If we consider the name of a man so precious, think of how we should respect and reverence the name of God and of holy persons or things.

## 1. Honor to God's Name

When a person is important to us, his name also becomes important. We honor our parents when we uphold and respect their names. We keep illustrious and alive our nation's heroes and leaders by writing songs and poems about them, and by erecting monuments and public buildings in their honor.

Think of the cities in our country named after saints and the schools and institutions honored by the names of famous or saintly people. What is the name of your school? You revere that name. You will always be respectful and loyal to it. You would not like to hear that name dishonored.

And yet we hear people using the sacred name of God or the Holy Name of Jesus Christ in an insulting manner. Even Christians do this sometimes, thoughtlessly of course, for the most part. Let us remember that the reverent use of God's name brings blessings. Jesus Himself said: ". . . if you ask the Father anything in my name, he will give it to you" (Jn. 16:23). In suffering, that name will be our consolation, and in death, our salvation.

## The Church and the Holy Name of Jesus

The Church grants us many favors and rich indulgences for reverently repeating our Redeemer's name. It would be well to learn some of the following ejaculations and say them often. "Blessed be the most holy name of Jesus without end." "Blessed be the name of the Lord." "Eternal Father, by the most precious blood of Jesus Christ, glorify His most holy name, according to the desires of His adorable Heart."

The Church bestows the sacraments and other blessings in and through the Holy Name: "I absolve thee, in the name of the Father, and of the Son, and of the Holy Ghost." The Bible tells us of miracles worked in His name. St. Peter cured the lame man at the temple gate saying: "In the name of Jesus Christ of Nazareth, arise and walk" (Acts 3:6). Holy Scripture reminds us that: "There is no other name under heaven given to men by which we must be saved" (Acts 4:12). The Bible again tells us that ". . . at the name of Jesus every knee should bend of those in heaven, on earth and under the earth" (Phil. 2:10).

Accordingly, let us show reverence for God's name by using it thoughtfully and respectfully in prayer, and by bowing our heads when we hear it mentioned. By honoring the holy name of God here on earth we merely do what the angels and saints will do for all eternity in heaven.

Have you heard of the good old lady who told the priest who had come to visit her that she was worried about what to say to God when she stood before Him in heaven. The priest advised her to bow her head and repeat the words she had so often spoken here on earth: "Praised be Jesus Christ!" He assured her that she would not have to wait long before the whole heavenly court would chime in with that glorious and thrilling answer to her words: "Forever and ever. Amen!" So it will be with us. If we honor His holy name here on earth, we have every reason to hope that God will call us to join in honoring His name in heaven.

Not only must we praise God and speak of Him with profound respect, but we must also speak with reverence of the Blessed Virgin, the angels, the saints, the Church and everything that pertains to her service, our Holy Father, the pope, our bishops and priests, and all members of religious orders and societies. As we have learned before, the saints are special friends of God, and we honor God when we honor them. We honor God also when we speak with reverence of any person or thing pertaining to God or consecrated or dedicated to His service. Never fail to tip your hat to a priest or religious wherever you meet them.

## 2. Proper Oaths

There are times when we may use God's name outside of prayer; as for instance when we take an oath. *An oath is the calling on God to witness to the truth of what we say.* "The Lord, your God, shall you fear; him shall you serve, and by his name shall you swear" (Deut. 6:13).

It is lawful at times to take an oath. In other words, swearing that a thing is true by asking God to confirm what we say can be permitted. An oath is a guarantee of truthfulness; it is useful in having our word accepted in important matters which concern the glory of God or the good of our neighbor or of ourselves. If, however, we take an oath for some small or unimportant thing we do wrong. And if we take an oath to do that which is wrong, or impossible, we likewise do wrong. However we are not obliged to keep such an oath; on the contrary we may never do something wrong even if we have taken an oath to do so. Such an oath is no good. It does not bind.

An oath reverently and properly taken is a meritorious act of divine worship; otherwise it is sinful.

The obligation to fulfill a promise made under oath is grave or light depending on the seriousness of that which is promised.

We must be careful not to treat an oath lightly. We cannot take an oath on a slight pretext. Sometimes we hear boys and girls say "Cross my heart," and even grownups say: "I'm telling the truth, so help me God!" This is seldom a true oath. We might call it a speech mannerism, that is, a way of talking which has become more or less a habit. As such it might be allowed. But it is not permitted to take an oath for a slight reason. *To make an oath lawful, three things are necessary: first, we must have a good reason for taking an oath; second, we must be convinced that what we say under oath is true; third, we must not swear, that is, take an oath, to do what is wrong.*

In our courts it is necessary at times to take oaths. Some day you may be a witness in a court of law and be required to raise your right hand and take an oath and say: "I swear to tell the truth, the whole truth, and nothing but the truth, so help me God." When a person is commanded by lawful authority to take an oath and he tells the truth, God is not offended. He is pleased because He is honored. Such oaths honor God because we call upon Him as all-knowing and all-truthful.

But suppose the witness tells a lie, for instance by saying that he saw what he knows he did not see, or by falsely naming some innocent person (perhaps someone he does not like) as the one guilty of the crime. In either case, this witness is asking God, who is Truth itself, to confirm his untruthfulness. Such false swearing is more than an ordinary lie. It is a mortal sin of perjury. Under oath, even a little lie is a serious matter. *A person who deliberately calls on God to bear witness to a lie commits the very grievous sin of perjury.*

To take an oath without sufficient reason, or to swear rashly, is ordinarily a venial sin but can be mortal if it is the occasion of scandal.

Very often the sin of perjury is the result of bribery. Someone bribes a witness (offers him a reward, usually money) to tell a lie. Perhaps the one who asks him to do this attempts to escape a jail sentence or to throw the blame on another — sometimes an innocent victim. It is a mortal sin for any man to bribe a witness to lie while under oath, no matter what the reward or benefit might be. Resolve never to take a false oath no matter what you might get for your action. Resolve never to lie under oath.

Government officials are often obliged to take oaths. An official calls on God to witness his promise to fulfill his office conscientiously. The president of the United States, the members of his cabinet, judges, senators, and representatives take such an oath by which they pledge themselves to be loyal to their country, its people, and to the duties entrusted to their care. We must always remember that taking an oath is no mere routine, matter-of-fact, everyday affair, but a serious religious act. It is something to be done prudently and carried out faithfully.

### 3. Lawful Vows

A vow is not the same as an oath. *A vow is a deliberate promise made to God by which a person binds himself under pain of sin to do something that is especially pleasing to God.* A vow is an act of divine worship by which we acknowledge God's supreme dominion. It is a promise voluntarily made to God alone, to perform some good action.

A vow renders the good action more acceptable to God. As a result we can make more progress in virtue. A vow is a promise made of our own free will; no one is bound or can be compelled to make one. "If thou wilt not promise, thou shalt be without sin" (Deut. 23:22). A vow made under force is not valid, that is, it does not bind.

What we promise by vow must be possible and morally good. The promise must be pleasing to God; not anything wrong, as Jephte's. Before going to battle he vowed to the Lord that if he were victorious, he would offer as a holocaust whoever should first come out of the doors of his house. His only daughter came to meet him, and she was sacrificed (Judges 11:30–40). Such a vow is not only foolish but also displeasing to God and should not be made or fulfilled. It is a sin to make such a vow. It is also a sin to keep such a vow.

Usually we promise something that we are not obliged to do — a pilgrimage, for instance; but we may also promise something which we are obliged to do anyway — for example, to observe the fasts of the Church, to keep the holydays, to be temperate in eating and drinking. In this case failure to keep one's promise is a twofold sin.

The owner of a factory, whose only child was dangerously ill, vowed before God that if she recovered, he would never have work done on Sundays and holydays. He was then doubly bound to observe the holydays. She got well and he kept his word.

There are different kinds of vows. Some are private vows made by individuals privately. Such vows are often made by a person when in trouble or affliction or as an act of thanksgiving. Often such vows are accompanied by a condition. The person makes a kind of bargain with God. Jacob promised to make an offering of part of his possessions to God provided He brought him back prosperously to his father's house (Gen. 28:20–22). We should never make a vow hastily or before seeking the advice of a priest or confessor, however. We must remember that a vow brings responsibility. We must do what we vow under pain of sin.

The processions on the Rogation days originated through a vow made about the year 500 by St. Mamertus, Bishop of Vienne, in time of famine; and about a century later, Pope Gregory the Great instituted the procession on St. Mark's Day as a result of a vow he made for the removal of a plague. The inhabitants of Oberammergau, Bavaria, pledged themselves to perform the Passion Play every ten years at the time of an epidemic in 1633. St. Louis of France promised, if he recovered from a severe illness, to undertake a crusade (1248).

In the present day many persons, in illness or affliction, promise to visit some place of pilgrimage, to make an offering to some church, to give a statue, to give an offering for a mission baby, or to fast on certain days, and the like. These can be simple promises or they can be vows, depending on the intention.

Some vows are public and officially accepted by the Church. Such are the vows of religion, or the vows taken by those especially who wish to dedicate themselves to the service of God. Poverty, chastity, and obedience are the three vows taken by religious. They are very useful, for by them an individual entirely gives up the world, in order to serve God better. These vows are most pleasing to God, for those who take them enter into the religious state and consecrate not only all they do, but their very selves to God. Such vows bring great blessings. They both bind and help a person to lead a life of perfection in Christ.

A vow is an act of religion and is something good like prayer. However, just as we are forbidden to take an oath about an unimportant thing, so also are we forbidden to make a vow about something unimportant.

We should keep a promise made to God; to do otherwise would be sinful. Whether it would be a mortal or a venial sin to break a vow would depend on the vow itself, and the intention a person had in making it.

Remember, one should never make a vow without consulting a confessor. A vow carries with it responsibilities. It must be made only after careful thought. We must fulfill the promise we make. "It is much better not to vow, than after a vow not to perform the things promised" (Eccles. 5:3–4).

## REVIEW, X–3

### WORD LIST

| | | | |
|---|---|---|---|
| upright | heavenly court | oath | meritorious |
| sacred | profound | witness | deliberate |
| perjury | rashly | bribery | Rogation Days |
| dominion | voluntarily | vow | consecrate |
| Oberammergau | crusade | affliction | |

### THINGS TO REMEMBER

1. The Holy Name of God is worthy of the highest respect.
2. Oaths and vows are serious matters; they should not be taken lightly.
3. To tell a lie while under oath is called perjury.
4. In making a vow we promise to do something especially pleasing to God.

1. Look up vows in the *Catholic Encyclopedia*. Prepare a talk to give to the class.
2. How is perjury committed? Give some examples.
3. Look up the regulations of the Holy Name Society. How do the members expressly obey the Second Commandment?
4. Gather information on the feast of the Holy Name. Report on it.
5. Compose a prayer in honor of the Holy Name. In it promise greater reverence and respect for this sacred name.
6. Listen to the conversation of others. If God's name is used irreverently, plan in some way to correct this evil.
7. If someone whom you could not correct spoke irreverently of God, what prayer might you say to help atone for it?
8. How could you decide how seriously you had sinned in breaking a vow?
9. How can we show respect for God's name by our actions?
10. Explain what is meant by a deliberate promise?

Study Catechism Lesson 18, *The Second and Third Commandments of God*, Questions 224–229, pp. 346–347.

# Part 4. What the Second Commandment Forbids

Besides improper oaths and vows, the second commandment also forbids blasphemy, profanity, and cursing.

*Blasphemy is insulting language which expresses contempt for God, either directly or through His saints and holy things.* It is said to be against God, but it may be indirect at times as when an utterance is made against the saints or sacred things. This is indirect blasphemy because of their close relationship with God.

Let us see how a person could be guilty of such an offense. People usually commit the sin of blasphemy because they are dissatisfied with something God has sent them — such as sickness, poverty, lack of talent, failure, and the like. As a result they complain against God, and actually hate Him, or are contemptuous (scornful) toward Him. We should never complain or murmur about what happens, but rather take everything, good as well as bad, as coming from the hand of God for our own or others' spiritual or bodily welfare. "Do all things without murmuring and without questioning" (Phil. 2:14). God knows what is best for us. Let us trust and thank Him for everything we have.

**326**

Loss of temper and lack of faith lead people to say things which they do not mean. At times they take the name of God in vain. *By taking God's name in vain is meant that the name of God or the holy name of Jesus Christ is used without reverence; for example, to express surprise or anger.* Surely you could give many examples of the use of profane language. Perhaps you have heard it used in an exciting baseball game, or by a boy who thinks it sounds big or smart.

Sometimes blasphemy is confused with taking God's name in vain, or as it is also called, *profanity.* They are different, however. Blasphemy shows willful hate or contempt for God, the saints, and holy things, while profanity is irreverent use of holy names. Profanity is committed by using the name of God without just cause, thoughtlessly, through habit, impatience, surprise, or merely to emphasize a point. The use of God's name is profane when it does not honor God, or help our neighbor or ourselves.

The sinfulness of profanity or using the name of God in vain, depends upon how deliberate it is, and the irreverence we intend toward God, or the scandal we might give by it. *It is a sin to take God's name in vain; ordinarily, it is a venial sin.* It can become serious and a mortal sin when there is deliberate and intentional contempt of God or His holy name.

*Cursing* is another sin against the second commandment. *Cursing is the calling down of some evil on a person, place, or thing.* The calling down of some evil can be good or bad. In certain cases it is lawful and sinless as when a judge sentences a criminal in court, or when God Himself decrees penalties against sinners. But then there are times when it is unlawful and sinful, for example: "Hope you break your leg!" or "Go to the devil!" Here we do not wish good but misfortune and harm to our neighbor. Such conduct is un-

**327**

charitable. Cursing is a venial sin when it is due to thoughtlessness, but it is a mortal sin when the evil wished is serious — when we really wish serious evil to some person, place, or thing.

Whenever we hear a person indulge in blasphemy, profanity, or cursing, let us quietly say a little prayer to Jesus to ask Him to forgive this person who has spoken so carelessly. Pray every day that you may not fall into these sins. God, to whom we owe everything and to whom we should utter only words of gratitude and praise, is insulted by them.

## Summary of the Second Commandment

The second commandment is: "Thou shalt not take the name of the Lord thy God in vain."

This commandment obliges us always to speak of God, of the saints, and of holy things with respect and reverence.

We honor God in a special way when the oath we take is lawful.

We honor God, also, when we keep the vow we make to God.

But we dishonor God: (1) by taking His name in vain; (2) by blasphemy, which is using insulting words about God, or the saints, or holy things; (3) by cursing, that is, wishing evil on any creature of God; (4) by taking an unlawful oath; and (5) by not keeping a vow we may make.

## REVIEW, X–4

### WORD LIST

| | | |
|---|---|---|
| blasphemy | contemptuous | willful |
| contempt | profanity | scandal |
| dedicated | irreverent | penalties |

## THINGS TO REMEMBER

1. Blasphemy and profanity are not the same things. Blasphemy shows willful hatred while profanity shows irreverence.
2. Prayer will help overcome the habit of blasphemy, profanity, or cursing.

## THINGS TO DISCUSS AND DO

1. What could you do or say if you heard one of your classmates or companions talking in a shocking way and often using the Holy Name without necessity?
2. Suppose you were heard to use the name of God thoughtlessly when your teammate failed to make second base. How would you make good the wrong you have done?
3. A pedestrian runs into the path of the taxi in which you are riding. The taxi driver utters a shocking and cursing remark. What could you say or do to repair this wrong?
4. Recite the Divine Praises as an act of reparation for the sins against the second commandment committed this day all over the world.
5. Can such expressions as "God never sends me anything good," "Why must it always happen to me?" "What good does it do to pray anyway?" be grievously sinful?
6. A certain boy, when engaged in excited play, constantly uses expressions which appear to be swearing, such as, "So help me," or "Honest to God I'm right." Would you say he expressed an oath?
7. A lady always says, "Oh my God." She promises her confessor that she will do better but her conduct has not improved. What have you to say about this?
8. If on your way home from school today you hear God's name used irreverently, what could you do?
9. Discuss the reverence the Church shows at Mass for the name of God, of our Lord, Mary, and the saints.

Study Catechism Lesson 18, *The Second and Third Commandments of God*, Questions 230–233, p. 348.

# Part 5. The Third Commandment

*The third commandment of God is: Remember thou keep holy the Lord's day.*

## 1. Worship of God

Every man's conscience tells him that he is obliged to worship God. He should, however, not only worship God by himself alone, but in public and with others. There never has been an age in which men have not publicly worshiped God. History records that men everywhere, even in pagan lands, have regularly set aside certain hours or days or seasons for public worship. You have no doubt read how the Mohammedans, at certain hours every day, turn toward Mecca, the birthplace of Mohammed, and pray. Are we as faithful in saying the Angelus?

All our time belongs to God, as the Psalmist says: "Yours is the day, and yours is the night" (Ps. 73:16). God gave us the seven days of the week but He asks us to return one of them to Him as a token of our gratitude. By special command the Lord appoints the portion of time He wants from us when He says: "Remember to keep holy the Sabbath day. Six days you may labor and do all your work, but the seventh day is the Sabbath of the Lord, your God" (Exod. 20:8–10).

The observance of this day of rest recalls God's rest after the work of creation, the rest of Christ in the tomb, and prefigures our rest with God in eternity. God meant it to teach consideration to those who hire others; and to remind us not only to take care of our own needs but to give particular attention to the worship we owe God. Perhaps that is why God started this commandment with the word "Remember." Men sometimes become so wrapped up in their own interests that they forget God. The Sabbath, therefore, gives man an opportunity to worship God, to rest from his labors, and to experience in a small measure, the unending rest and joy of heaven.

## 2. Observance of the Sabbath

The third commandment, as God gave it to the Jewish people, named the seventh day of the week, that is, the sabbath, as the special day of worship. God Himself laid down detailed rules as to the manner in which this day was to be observed (Exod. 20:8–11). Many Jews still keep Saturday holy to the Lord. We Christians, however, observe Sunday as the Lord's day.

Using the power given to her by her divine Founder,

**331**

the Catholic Church chose the first day of the week to replace the Sabbath of the Jews and determined just how Christians were to sanctify it to the Lord. The Church did not retain the various restrictions prescribed for the Sabbath among the ancient Jews; but all Catholics are obliged to attend Mass and to abstain from servile work.

The glorious events of Easter Sunday and Pentecost Sunday sanctified the first day of the week, so the Apostles spoke of it as the "Lord's Day" and kept it holy. We find in the Apocalypse that St. John the Apostle mentions the first day of the week as the "Lord's Day" (Apoc. 1:10). The Acts of the Apostles, which were written by St. Luke, and the First Epistle of St. Paul to the Corinthians speak especially of the "first day of the week" (Acts 20:7; 1 Cor. 16:2).

The Apostles, under the guidance of the Holy Spirit, made the change. The following are among the reasons: (1) the work of creation began on the first day of the week. (2) Our Lord rose from the dead on a Sunday. (3) The Holy Ghost came down upon the Apostles on Sunday. (4) The Apostles received the power to forgive sins on Sunday. (5) The Church was solemnly and gloriously launched on its work on a Sunday. Two of these reasons ought to be particularly remembered: *The Church commands us to keep Sunday as the Lord's day, because on Sunday Christ rose from the dead, and on Sunday the Holy Ghost descended upon the Apostles.*

We should give God the first day of the week. So we go to Mass, say our prayers, and do other good things on Sunday and know that we are doing right. Sunday observance brings down God's favor and blessings upon us. It gives us a special opportunity to thank God the Father who created us, God the Son who redeemed us, and God the Holy Ghost who sanctifies us.

**332**

There are many ways of worshiping God. When we are in the state of grace and have the intention of doing so we can make our every prayer, work, and play an act of worship. But, *by the third commandment we are commanded to worship God in a special manner on Sunday, the Lord's day.* The "special manner" consists in this that *the Church commands us to worship God on Sunday by assisting at the Holy Sacrifice of the Mass.*

## 3. Assistance at Mass

To take part in the Mass is the greatest act of religion we can offer to God. Certainly you know why. The Catholic Church teaches us that in the Mass the body, blood, soul, and divinity of Jesus Christ are offered as a sacrifice to the heavenly Father under the appearance of bread and wine. This act represents anew the offering of the Sacrifice of the Cross by Christ to God the Father.

When we assist at Mass we give God the best possible gift. We give Him the very gift by which Christ told us He wished to be remembered and which pleases His Father best. At the Last Supper when our Lord offered the first Mass, He took the bread, blessed it and gave it to His Apostles saying: "Take and eat; for this is my body." In like manner He took the wine and gave it to His Apostles saying: "All of you drink of this; for this is my blood of the new covenant, which is being shed for many unto the forgiveness of sins" (Mt. 26:26–28).

After this our Lord told His Apostles to do the same thing in remembrance of Him. In these words our Lord gave the Apostles and their successors the power to say Mass. In these words Jesus told us that the way He wanted to be remembered was by the Holy Sacrifice of the Mass.

To fulfill our obligation of assisting at Mass we must be actually present, inside the church if possible, so that we can see or hear the priest and follow the parts of the Mass. However, when attendance at Mass is heavy, presence in the vestibule or sacristy might be permitted. Even though we may not be able to enter a church because of its overcrowded condition, we can still hear Mass provided we are part of the congregation assisting at the Holy Sacrifice and are able to follow the Mass. A person who is separated by a considerable distance from the worshipers certainly is not present at Mass. Is a person whose body is present at Mass but whose mind and will are miles away really present?

Since attendance at Mass is the way God wishes us to honor Him, the duty to hear Mass on Sundays and holydays of obligation rests upon all Catholics who have reached the use of reason and are above seven years of age and who are not lawfully excused. Deliberately to miss Mass on a Sunday or holyday of obligation, without just cause, or to miss a considerable part of the Mass, is a mortal sin. To come a little late and not to make up for it in another Mass, is a venial sin. To come quite a bit late and to leave quite a bit early could be a grievous sin.

We must hear an entire Mass from beginning to end; that is, from the priest's entrance into the sanctuary till his departure into the sacristy. One is considered to have missed Mass if one is not present for all the three principal parts of the Mass: the Offertory, the Consecration, and the Communion.

Just being present at Mass is not enough. We must know what is going on. It will help to keep our attention from wandering if we remember that assisting at Mass is the same as if we stood at the foot of the cross when our Lord was crucified. We should not act like those who mocked

Christ and laughed at Him. Rather we will want to join with the Blessed Virgin to adore our Lord, to offer Him our love, to thank Him, to beg His forgiveness, to ask His grace, and to offer ourselves to God with our suffering Saviour.

### Reasons Excusing From Attending Mass

Because the obligation to assist at Mass is grave, no light reason, such as a slight headache, a short distance from church, or inability to be dressed in the newest or latest styles, is sufficient for staying away from Sunday Mass. Those who on every slight pretext excuse themselves from their obligation of hearing Mass on Sunday in addition to committing many serious sins will gradually slip into religious carelessless and indifference, perhaps even losing their faith.

A grave inconvenience to oneself or to another excuses one from the obligation. You have no doubt experienced or read about heavy snowfalls that crippled transportation or prevented the use of buses or other public vehicles. Perhaps in icy weather you have heard the warning over radio or television cautioning owners of private cars to remain off the highways. Very bad weather is certainly an excuse.

Other excusing causes may be illness, old age, or infirmity, a long distance from the church, unusual difficulties of transportation; a call of duty as in the case of a doctor, nurse, fireman, policeman, or other public welfare workers; or charity to a friend or neighbor. We should be sturdy Christians, nonetheless, and not let anything but really serious causes interfere with our hearing Mass on Sundays or days of obligation. One of the glories of our American Catholics is the fact that they take the Sunday obligation seriously. Might that be one of the reasons why God so richly blesses our beloved country, and the Church in America?

# REVIEW, X–5

## WORD LIST

public worship
restrictions
right intention
consideration

observance
prescribed
deliberately

## THINGS TO REMEMBER

1. It is not enough to just "go to Mass." We must also take part in it.
2. We must worship God both publicly and privately.
3. Holy Mass is the greatest act of worship man can offer God.
4. The three principal parts of the Mass are: Offertory, Consecration, and Communion.
5. We cannot fulfill our Sunday obligation by hearing Mass on radio or television.
6. Sunday is a day of rest, and provides us with the opportunity to give thanks to God for all His goodness to us.

## THINGS TO DISCUSS AND DO

1. Aunt Mary insists on your staying home from Sunday Mass. She is old and often feels quite ill. May you stay home if there is no other Mass? What reason can you give for your answer?
2. A boy who was out late Saturday night sleeps halfway through Sunday Mass. Has he fulfilled his obligation of hearing Mass? Why?
3. Mass is being shown on TV so you decide not to go to church this Sunday. Have you fulfilled your obligation?
4. Why do many Catholics look at the Host and whisper, "My Lord and my God" at the elevation of the Mass?
5. The third Commandment says, "Remember thou keep holy the Sabbath." How can you explain to your Jewish neighbor the Christian practice of observing Sunday rather than Saturday as the Sabbath.

6. The Mass is the most perfect act of worship man can offer God. Why? Are any other good works recommended to help us keep Sunday holy?
7. How do you help at home to make it easier for your mother to keep holy the Lord's day?
8. May a person be excused from hearing Mass on Sunday? For what reasons?
9. Read and discuss the prayers of the Canon of the Mass which follow the consecration.

Study Catechism Lesson 18, *The Second and Third Commandments of God,* Questions 234–237, p. 349.

# Part 6. The Third Commandment Forbids Unnecessary Servile Work on Sunday

The third commandment does not merely command us to attend Mass on Sunday. It commands more than that. *By the third commandment of God all unnecessary servile work on Sunday is forbidden.* But what is to be understood by this kind of work? *Servile work is that which requires labor of body rather than of mind.*

How clearly does the wisdom of God show forth in this commandment? He not only sets aside Sunday as a day of worship, but by so doing He gives man a chance to rest. Man lays down his usual tasks and is able to spend some time socially with his family and friends. Jesus said to the Pharisees: "The Sabbath was made for man, and not man for the Sabbath" (Mk. 2:27).

Servile work includes three types: first, tasks of farming, like plowing, planting, harvesting, mowing hay or mowing

the lawn; second, common labor, like digging, cutting trees, washing and ironing, and factory work; third, certain skilled labor, like that of a machinist, mason, carpenter, painter, tailor, or iron worker. The third commandment also forbids court work like that of a public trial, and business transactions such as buying and selling.

On Sunday a person should not landscape the yard, wash the clothes, paint the fence, or the like. Things like these call for heavy labor, and, if done without necessity, for a considerable length of time, may be mortal sins.

## When Servile Work Might Be Permitted

There are times, however, when Sunday labor is permitted. Necessity may be the reason. Have you heard the story of the man who was engaged in the trucking business? On Saturday afternoon a customer requested that he haul a cargo of fish which was expected late Saturday night. It would mean working Sunday morning. The Catholic truck driver did not want to take on the job saying that he had to attend Mass and did not accept or do Sunday work. When the fish dealer explained that his cargo would spoil if he waited until Monday, the trucker consented, saying: "I will not ask my men to work, my two sons and I will haul the fish." Here we have a valid excuse for Sunday labor. If the fish had not been hauled, the customer would have suffered considerable loss.

The Church permits the performing of necessary work in order that the blessings of God may not be lost. She teaches, therefore, that it is lawful to cut and to gather in crops if they are in danger of being destroyed. Urgent work may also be permitted if life and property are endangered by floods, fires, storms, tornadoes, accidents, or the like. Railroad, bus, and air lines must be kept in operation. Policemen, firemen, nurses, hospital attendants, bakers, caretakers of ball parks, golf courses, and bathing beaches must be allowed to work.

Charity offers a second excuse for servile work. Caring for the sick or digging a grave would come under this head. Religion permits servile work which directly renders honor to God. Janitors who take care of church furnaces on Sunday and ring the bell for the various services, perform works of piety toward God. The honor of God will require the preparation of the altar and vestments for Mass. Church functions

**339**

held on Sunday always necessitate a certain amount of servile work.

Work for our own need is lawful and may be performed on Sunday when it cannot be performed conveniently on another day. Such work as caring for livestock, cooking, dishwashing, and the like are works of necessity, and may be performed on Sundays and holydays of obligation. *Servile work is allowed on Sunday when the honor of God, our own need, or that of our neighbor requires it.* ". . . it is lawful to do good on the Sabbath" (Mt. 12:12). Can you think of examples?

Sunday, for the child who loves God, is not only a day of rest; it is a day to rejoice, a day set aside and entirely different from the rest of the week. It is a day that helps us to turn to God, to see Him in all the joy and peace around us and to adore and thank Him as He deserves. It is a day to re-create ourselves in body and soul.

"Amen. Blessing and glory and wisdom and thanksgiving and honor and power and strength to our God forever and ever. Amen." (Apoc. 7:12).

## REVIEW, X–6

### WORD LIST

| | | |
|---|---|---|
| servile | urgent | re-create |
| physically | piety | obliged |
| mentally | functions | |

### THINGS TO REMEMBER

1. Sunday is a day of religion, rest, and rejoicing.
2. Necessity, charity, and religion are sufficient excuses for servile work on Sunday.

## THINGS TO DISCUSS AND DO

1. The mother of a large family attends at the bedside of her sick husband all week. The laundry has piled up. May she do it on Sunday?
2. A farmer and his family were just ready to start for Mass on Sunday morning when they noticed that a heavy storm was threatening. In order to save his crops the farmer went out into the field and ordered his hired man to do the same. They all missed Mass. Were they justified in doing so? Give reasons for your answer.
3. Is it true that rest from servile work on Sunday benefits those who keep the Sabbath? Explain.
4. Make a chart showing the three types of servile work.
5. Should a storekeeper close his store on Sunday? Why?
6. Getting to Mass, and getting there on time.

Study Catechism Lesson 18, *The Second and Third Commandments of God,* Questions 238–240, p. 350.

# End-of-Unit Review — Unit X

## PART 1

## CATECHISM

### LESSON 16

#### The First Commandment of God

198. **What is the first commandment of God?**

The first commandment of God is: I am the Lord thy God; thou shalt not have strange gods before Me.

199. **What are we commanded by the first commandment?**

By the first commandment we are commanded to offer to God alone the supreme worship that is due Him.

### 200. How do we worship God?

We worship God by acts of faith, hope, and charity, and by adoring Him and praying to Him.

### 201. What does faith oblige us to do?

Faith obliges us:
*first,* to make efforts to find out what God has revealed;
*second,* to believe firmly what God has revealed;
*third,* to profess our faith openly whenever necessary.

### 202. What does hope oblige us to do?

Hope obliges us to trust firmly that God will give us eternal life and the means to obtain it.

### 203. What does charity oblige us to do?

Charity obliges us to love God above all things because He is infinitely good, and to love our neighbor as ourselves for the love of God.

### 204. How can a Catholic best safeguard his faith?

A Catholic can best safeguard his faith by making frequent acts of faith, by praying for a strong faith, by studying his religion very earnestly, by living a good life, by good reading, by refusing to associate with the enemies of the Church, and by not reading books and papers opposed to the Church and her teaching.

### 205. How does a Catholic sin against faith?

A Catholic sins against faith by apostasy, heresy, indifferentism, and by taking part in non-Catholic worship.

### 206. Why does a Catholic sin against faith by taking part in non-Catholic worship?

A Catholic sins against faith by taking part in non-Catholic worship because he thus professes belief in a religion he knows is false.

### 207. What are the sins against hope?

The sins against hope are presumption and despair.

**208. When does a person sin by presumption?**

A person sins by presumption when he trusts that he can be saved by his own efforts without God's help, or by God's help without his own efforts.

**209. When does a person sin by despair?**

A person sins by despair when he deliberately refuses to trust that God will give him the necessary help to save his soul.

**210. What are the chief sins against charity?**

The chief sins against charity are hatred of God and of our neighbor, envy, sloth, and scandal.

**211. Besides the sins against faith, hope, and charity, what other sins does the first commandment forbid?**

Besides the sins against faith, hope, and charity, the first commandment forbids also superstition and sacrilege.

**212. When does a person sin by superstition?**

A person sins by superstition when he attributes to a creature a power that belongs to God alone, as when he makes use of charms or spells, believes in dreams or fortunetelling, or goes to spiritists.

**213. When does a person sin by sacrilege?**

A person sins by sacrilege when he mistreats sacred persons, places, or things.

# OTHER QUESTIONS AND EXERCISES

Write 1 to 15 on a paper and after each number write the letter of the sentence which fits it best.

| | |
|---|---|
| 1. atheist | A. One who abandons his belief in the Church |
| 2. apostate | B. The greatest of the theological virtues |
| 3. heretic | |
| 4. pagan | C. Belief in dreams |
| | D. Admit openly |
| 5. faith | E. Expecting to be saved without God's help |
| 6. hope | |
| 7. love | F. Belief in the truths God has revealed |
| 8. infidelity | G. Laziness |
| 9. indifferentism | H. One who does not believe in God |
| | I. Trust in God's promises |
| 10. presumption | J. Loss of hope in God's mercy |
| 11. despair | K. One who refuses to believe some of the truths God has revealed |
| 12. superstition | |
| 13. sacrilege | L. Lack of faith |
| | M. One who worships false gods |
| 14. sloth | N. The belief that all religions are equally good |
| 15. profess | O. Mistreatment of a blessed object |

## PART 2

## CATECHISM

### LESSON 17

❖

#### Honoring the Saints, Relics, and Images

214. Does the first commandment forbid us to honor the saints in heaven?

The first commandment does not forbid us to honor the saints in heaven, provided we do not give them the honor that belongs to God alone.

**215. Why do we honor the saints in heaven?**

We honor the saints in heaven because they practiced great virtue when they were on earth, and because in honoring those who are the chosen friends of God we honor God Himself.

**216. How can we honor the saints?**

We can honor the saints:
*first*, by imitating their holy lives;
*second*, by praying to them;
*third*, by showing respect to their relics and images.

**217. When we pray to the saints what do we ask them to do?**

When we pray to the saints we ask them to offer their prayers to God for us.

**218. How do we know that the saints will pray for us?**

We know that the saints will pray for us because they are with God and have great love for us.

**219. Why do we honor relics?**

We honor relics because they are the bodies of the saints or objects connected with the saints or with our Lord.

**220. When does the first commandment forbid the making or the use of statues and pictures?**

The first commandment forbids the making or the use of statues and pictures only when they promote false worship.

**221. Is it right to show respect to the statues and pictures of Christ and of the saints?**

It is right to show respect to the statues and pictures of Christ and of the saints, just as it is right to show respect to the images of those whom we honor or love on earth.

**222. Do we honor Christ and the saints when we pray before the crucifix, relics, and sacred images?**

We honor Christ and the saints when we pray before the

crucifix, relics, and sacred images because we honor the persons they represent; we adore Christ and venerate the saints.

223. **Do we pray to the crucifix or to the images and relics of the saints?**

We do not pray to the crucifix or to the images and relics of the saints, but to the persons they represent.

## OTHER QUESTIONS AND EXERCISES

1. Does the first commandment forbid us to honor the saints?
2. May we give the saints greater honor than we give God?
3. Do we honor God in honoring the saints?
4. Are we forbidden to pray to the saints?
5. Do the saints love us?
6. Do we adore Mary and the saints?
7. Do we pray to the crucifix?
8. Can we ask the saints to obtain favors from God for us?
9. Should we have religious pictures in our homes?
10. Are parts of the bodies of saints called relics?

**PART 3**

## CATECHISM

### LESSON 18

#### The Second and Third Commandments of God

224. **What is the second commandment of God?**
The second commandment of God is: Thou shalt not take the name of the Lord thy God in vain.

225. **What are we commanded by the second commandment?**

By the second commandment we are commanded always to speak with reverence of God, of the saints, and of holy things, and to be truthful in taking oaths and faithful to them and to our vows.

**226. What is an oath?**

An oath is the calling on God to witness to the truth of what we say.

**227. What things are necessary to make an oath lawful?**

To make an oath lawful, three things are necessary:

*first,* we must have a good reason for taking an oath;

*second,* we must be convinced that what we say under oath is true;

*third,* we must not swear, that is, take an oath, to do what is wrong.

**228. What great sin does a person commit who deliberately calls on God to bear witness to a lie?**

A person who deliberately calls on God to bear witness to a lie commits the very grievous sin of perjury.

**229. What is a vow?**

A vow is a deliberate promise made to God by which a person binds himself under pain of sin to do something that is especially pleasing to God.

## OTHER QUESTIONS AND EXERCISES

1. How does the Church use the Holy Name?
2. What should we do when the Holy Name is mentioned?
3. Outside of prayer, when may we take God's name?
4. What do we do when we take an oath?
5. What are the conditions for making an oath lawful?
6. Can civil authorities demand that we take an oath?
7. Are we ever forced to make vows? Explain your answer.
8. What was wrong with Jephte's vow?
9. Give some examples of vows that have been made and kept.
10. What are the three vows taken by religious? What do they mean? What is their value?

## PART 4

# CATECHISM

### LESSON 18 (Cont.)

**230. What is meant by taking God's name in vain?**

By taking God's name in vain is meant that the name of God or the holy name of Jesus Christ is used without reverence; for example, to express surprise or anger.

**231. Is it a sin to take God's name in vain?**

It is a sin to take God's name in vain; ordinarily, it is a venial sin.

**232. What is cursing?**

Cursing is the calling down of some evil on a person, place, or thing.

**233. What is blasphemy?**

Blasphemy is insulting language which expresses contempt for God, either directly or through His saints and holy things.

## OTHER QUESTIONS AND EXERCISES

1. What do the words "in vain" mean?
2. Why should we try to control our tempers?
3. Is it a venial sin to take God's name in vain?
4. How can you help others overcome the habit of cursing?
5. Why is blasphemy such a serious offense against God?

**PART 5**

# CATECHISM

### LESSON 18 (Cont.)

**234. What is the third commandment of God?**

The third commandment of God is: Remember thou keep holy the Lord's day.

**235. Why does the Church command us to keep Sunday as the Lord's day?**

The Church commands us to keep Sunday as the Lord's day, because on Sunday Christ rose from the dead, and on Sunday the Holy Ghost descended upon the Apostles.

**236. What are we commanded by the third commandment?**

By the third commandment we are commanded to worship God in a special manner on Sunday, the Lord's day.

**237. How does the Church command us to worship God on Sunday?**

The Church commands us to worship God on Sunday by assisting at the Holy Sacrifice of the Mass.

## OTHER QUESTIONS AND EXERCISES

1. What great events have made Sunday an important day in the Catholic Church?
2. Why does God want us to observe Sunday as a day of rest?
3. Who changed the Sabbath from Saturday to Sunday? Why?
4. Why does the Church command us to worship God by hearing Mass?
5. Must we be present in the church to fulfill our Sunday obligation?
6. What reasons might exempt us from Sunday Mass?
7. With what words was the priesthood established?
8. In what other ways besides hearing Mass should we keep Sunday holy?

**349**

## PART 6

# CATECHISM

## LESSON 18 (Cont.)

**238. What is forbidden by the third commandment of God?**

By the third commandment of God all unnecessary servile work on Sunday is forbidden.

**239. What is servile work?**

Servile work is that which requires labor of body rather than of mind.

**240. When is servile work allowed on Sunday?**

Servile work is allowed on Sunday when the honor of God, our own need, or that of our neighbor requires it.

## OTHER QUESTIONS AND EXERCISES

1. What kind of servile work is forbidden on Sunday?
2. Name some occasions on which you might perform servile work.
3. Does servile work require labor of body or of mind?
4. Are holydays to be observed the same as Sunday?
5. Is mowing the lawn on Sunday a violation of the third Commandment?

## Section Review

Now we should take a general review of SECTION IV on
*Our Duties to God*
using the End of Unit Tests as a guide to locate the most important points. (Cf. pp. 290 sqq.; 341 sqq.)

After that take a quick look over the whole year and pull its main points together. The Table of Contents will help you.

CPSIA information can be obtained
at www.ICGtesting.com
Printed in the USA
FSHW011824181119
64225FS